PRAISE FOR MA ___ING FOR SOCIAL CHANGE

CW01497556

'This is a book for our time~...   ~ and possibil-
ity. Kian Bakhtiari is a determined young leaᴜᴄ   resh ideas and
new participatory models for citizens to actively shape the world and create
a more desirable future.'
**Mary Robinson, first female President of Ireland and former UN High
Commissioner for Human Rights**

'Represents a shift from consumer marketing to community building and
from top-down management to co-creation and collaboration. Essential
reading for progressive marketers.'
Ellie Norman, CMO, Formula E

'A groundbreaking guide that redefines the role of marketing in the 21st
century. Kian Bakhtiari brilliantly illustrates how businesses can prioritize
wellbeing and sustainability over mere profit. This book is a clarion call for
marketers to harness their power to promote social justice and advance
sustainability, offering practical tools and inspiring examples of companies
that lead with purpose. By applying his own skills in foresight and innovative thinking, Bakhtiari provides a roadmap for creating a more equitable
and sustainable future.'
Youssef Nassef, Director of Adaptation, UN Climate Change (UNFCCC)

'A new vision for system change that shows how companies can be more
successful by focusing on solving the world's problems, not creating them.
This is something I've experienced first-hand, developing both the UN
Sustainable Development Goals and Unilever Sustainable Living Plan. Kian
Bakhtiari is a bright thinker who brings humanity back to business. Its time
has come.'
Paul Polman, business leader, campaigner and former CEO of Unilever

'A powerful roadmap for building stronger brands and changing the world.
It centres on a number of big ideas that I have seen play out in practice
across Unilever's portfolio: business that is better for society or the planet is

better business; it must start with authentic products and actions; big change requires collaboration to change the system. This is a rattling good read with lots of great examples and practical steps to put the principles into action.'
Alan Jope, former CEO, Unilever

'Marketing isn't just about selling people things they want but don't need; it can also sell people things they need but don't yet want. In fact, without mass persuasion, every major societal innovation, from the smallpox vaccine to seatbelts to same-sex marriage, would be met with mass hostility. Only after we have changed our minds do we forget the work that went into changing them. This is what makes this book both so enjoyable and so necessary.'
Rory Sutherland, Vice Chairman, Ogilvy

'A fascinating and enlightening guide to how to make a difference. Compelling and powerful, this a rare book that makes you think and tells you how to bring about change.'
Tom Goodwin, innovation leader and author of *Digital Darwinism*

'Kian Bakhtiari is an ideas man! *Marketing for Social Change* is an extremely well-written book grappling with the most important issues of our times in completely new ways.'
Carole Stone CBE, UK's Queen of Networking

'This book on new collaborative business models stresses my statement that "you cannot be successful in a society that fails". *Marketing for Social Change* is a useful manual on how to use the power of marketing and communications to deliver business impact, and ecological and social improvements. It's important for leaders to change and adapt their companies to make them future proof.'
Feike Sijbesma, former CEO, Royal DSM

'The world has a new generation of young leaders, and we need them – people like Kian Bakhtiari. *Marketing for Social Change* is an important resource if you're looking to challenge the status quo and transform business and society for the better. This is a compelling call to action for changemakers.'
Kate Robertson, Co-founder, One Young World

'Kian Bakhtiari has redefined the highest use of marketing and communication skills – to help turn business from creating unconscious desire for things we don't need to celebrating the products and services we do need to restore human community and regenerate the natural world. With *Marketing for Social Change*, he redefines the future of the entire profession in a way that honours our human agency and brings pride to our practice.'
Vincent Stanley, Director of Philosophy, Patagonia

'This book fills an almost-empty niche in our cultural imagination: how can we redirect the powerful tools of persuasion honed over decades to influence people's buying decisions, to help change our thinking and actions as fast as we must in order to cope with the mounting challenges of our time? Bakhtiari provides answers and suggestions with admirable clarity and precision. It's a transformative set of concepts, and after reading them you can go into the world and put them to use, which is crucial.'
Kim Stanley Robinson, *New York Times* bestseller and author of *The Ministry for the Future*

'Trying to get your head around how you can use your skills, influence and opportunities to bring about positive social change – either at the micro or macro level – is hard. In reality, and without a practical guide to help organize your thoughts, keep your perspective and reinforce your purpose, it's so daunting you might never start. So reading this essential guide to getting started – on our collective journey towards social change, triggered and fuelled by responsible marketing and collaborative commerce – is a great first step towards using marketing to drive social change. Written with charisma, in plain English, and with naked honesty, it's an easy read and satisfyingly nourishing.'
Jem Lloyd-Williams, CEO, Mindshare UK

'A new playbook for 21st-century marketing. It is a valuable resource for marketing agencies, brands and independents looking to have a bigger business and social impact.'
Gemma Charles, Deputy Editor, *Campaign Magazine*

Marketing for Social Change

How to turn purpose into
business and social impact

Kian Bakhtiari

First published in Great Britain and the United States in 2025 by Kogan Page Limited

2nd Floor, 45 Gee Street
London
EC1V 3RS
United Kingdom
www.koganpage.com

8 W 38th Street, Suite 902
New York, NY 10018
USA

Kogan Page books are printed on paper from sustainable forests.

ISBNs
Hardback   978 1 3986 1686 8
Paperback   978 1 3986 1684 4
Ebook   978 1 3986 1685 1

British Library Cataloguing-in-Publication Data
A CIP record for this book is available from the British Library.

Library of Congress Cataloging-in-Publication Data
Names: Bakhtiari, Kian, author.
Title: Marketing for social change : how to turn purpose into business and social impact / Kian Bakhtiari.
Description: London ; New York, NY : Kogan Page Inc., 2024. | Includes bibliographical references and index.
Identifiers: LCCN 2024028674 (print) | LCCN 2024028675 (ebook) | ISBN 9781398616844 (paperback) | ISBN 9781398616868 (hardback) | ISBN 9781398616851 (ebook)
Subjects: LCSH: Social change. | Branding (Marketing)--Social aspects.
Classification: LCC HM831 .B337 2024 (print) | LCC HM831 (ebook) | DDC 303.4--dc23/eng/20240701]
LC record available at https://lccn.loc.gov/2024028674
LC ebook record available at https://lccn.loc.gov/2024028675

Typeset by Hong Kong FIVE Workshop, Hong Kong
Print production managed by Jellyfish
Printed and bound by CPI Group (UK) Ltd, Croydon CR0 4YY

For my parents.

CONTENTS

ACKNOWLEDGEMENTS

My acknowledgements for this book are many and varied. The process has made me reflect on the beauty of human connection and the power of community. This book has only been possible because people have believed in me and supported me throughout my journey.

I want to thank Maggie Mladenova for planting the seed of this book and encouraging me to write my first book. My Commissioning Editor Donna Goddard-Skinner for her vision and my Development Editor Jeylan Ramis for pushing the book further. My adviser Holly Roberts for your trust and support. My assistant Bracha Schnieder for her valuable contribution.

Thank you to my English teacher Ms Penny Johnson who believed in me. Thank you to Associate Professor Johanna Nalau for your perspective and feedback. And my publisher Kogan Page.

Thank you to the people who have taught me so much, opening doors and possibilities that I couldn't previously imagine. Thank you to Fayyadh Shamsuddin for sharing opportunities. Gareth Watt for seeing potential in me. Amy Watt for teaching me strategy. Matthew Hook for believing in my abilities. Tracy De Groose for showing me magic. Ben Cleaver for showing me that business can have a heart. Adam Freeman for teaching me how business works. Scott Thompson for helping me think differently. Maria Petnga-Wallace for championing me.

Thank you to Jem Lloyd-Williams for teaching me to stay true to myself. Mills for creating the space to experiment and play. Scott Sallée for your friendship and activism. A special thank you to all our partners who have believed in The People's mission. Without you, we wouldn't be able to make an impact.

I'm also grateful for people who have expanded my thinking. Thank you to Tom Goodwin for inspiring my first article. Gemma Charles for publishing my first article. Rory Sutherland for our conversations and perspective. George Lois for showing me the power of the big idea. Noam Chomsky for your honesty and activism.

Thank you to my parents for their unconditional love. My grandparents for sharing their world with me. My two aunties for being present. My friends and family.

I want to thank everyone who has ever encouraged, supported and taught me something. Thank you to everyone who has been on this journey with me. A special thank you to anyone who I have forgotten to mention.

Finally, I want to thank God because without God this book wouldn't exist.

Introduction

Off with their heads! Beheading by guillotine was first introduced in France in 1792. But the last person to be executed by the French government using the guillotine was Tunisian immigrant Hamida Djandoubi in 1977.

On 7 February 1971, women in Switzerland were finally granted the right to vote, 71 years after Afghanistan. The problem was, to change the constitution the majority of men in Switzerland had to vote in favour of women participating.

In 1960, a six-year-old child called Ruby Bridges got dressed and went to elementary school. Unlike other school children, Ruby was escorted by federal marshals to protect her from the angry crowds. Ruby was the first Black child to desegregate a white-only elementary school in New Orleans. Ruby is still alive to tell the tale.

The world moves forward but many social practices remain unchanged. The world of marketing is experiencing a similar challenge. Modern marketing was born from the ashes of the Industrial Revolution. The increased supply of consumer goods required mass marketing to generate demand, maintain economic growth and prevent excess supply. The Industrial Revolution has ended but marketing practices remain unchanged. What is the role of marketing in the 21st century? What if the same tools used to sell more products and services could be harnessed to accelerate social change?

Consumerism is the dominant ideology and main engine of economic growth. We are stuck in a system that measures progress using the total products and services created within the economy. But what if we valued community, wellbeing and humanity?

We are not passive subjects but active agents of change. We are not powerless. We are powerful. The world isn't fixed, motionless or unbending. We have the power to shape the world around us. We can create social change.

Marketing for Social Change is a practical book on how to use the power of marketing and communications to positively impact business and society. A playbook on how to challenge the status quo, find your community and accelerate social change. It represents a fundamental shift from competition to collaboration, extractivism to regeneration and from scarcity to abundance. There are enough opportunities and resources for everyone to thrive. Unlike the business models of the Industrial Revolution, progress doesn't have to come at the expense of others.

Business is not separate from society. We are standing on the precipice of more collaborative, inclusive and participatory business models where employees, communities and citizens are involved in the decision-making process.

Marketing for Social Change is a call to adventure. What if we used the power of marketing to accelerate social change? If we can imagine it, we can create it. Because imagination creates reality.

1

Can I really create change?

When I randomly stumbled into the world of media, marketing and advertising in the summer of 2016, I had no idea what the industry did. Soon enough, I realized that the purpose of marketing was to sell more products and services to more people. Millions of smart and creative people, spending billions of hours and dollars to generate consumer demand. The question I asked was what if we used the same tools to accelerate social change? For the last eight years, I've dedicated my life to answering this very question. I have worked with some of the world's biggest advertising agencies, Fortune 500 companies, FTSE100 companies, national governments, international organizations and charities. Many of these lessons come from launching a mission-led start-up (The People) challenging the conventions of the marketing industry. This is not a theoretical thesis, but a book born from lived experience and perpetual struggle. Marketing for social change is a call to adventure. What if we used the power of marketing for good?

Anyone can create change!

When I mention social change, you probably think of Mahatma Gandhi, Nelson Mandela or Greta Thunberg. But all of us have the power to create change – in big and small ways. Whether you're a global brand, scrappy start-up or independent freelancer, this book will give you the tools to accelerate social change.

The primary ingredient for creating change is imagination. If we can't imagine a more desirable future, we certainly won't be able to create it. Imagination is the foundation of creation. Imagination is a unique human capacity. Humans are the only species that can voluntarily conjure up things that don't yet exist. Using imagination, our ancestors discovered fire, built mega cities and placed a man on the moon. Everything in the human-made world has been imagined into reality. But we somehow view the world as fixed, constant and unbending. What if we viewed the world like play-dough? Flexible, fluid and malleable. Kids have an abundance of imagination – continuously questioning social norms – but this curiosity is beaten out of us as we get older. Adulthood is marked by conformity and acceptance of convention. We learn the rules but lose our sense of wonder and imagination.

Creating social change feels like a Herculean challenge. You're probably thinking: I'm only one person, what can I do? I have good news for you – there are another eight billion people who are thinking the exact same thing. This book is about starting small and encouraging collective action. Change doesn't have to be stressful or scary, it can even be fun. It can be as simple as smiling at a stranger, leaving a positive review for a small business and letting your friends know how much you appreciate them. Small acts of kindness can create a virtuous ripple effect.

Marketing can change the world

Marketers are in the business of shaping collective minds and behaviours. Historically, the main purpose of marketing communications and advertising has been to sell more stuff to more people. However, the same tools used to sell products and services can be harnessed to accelerate social change.

In the 1920s, mass production (supply) required mass consumption (demand) to maintain economic growth and prevent excess supply. Using advertising and public relations (PR), corporations manufactured consumer demand. More than a century later, consumerism is still the dominant narrative and main engine of economic growth. But we can no longer continue the current trajectory. Environmental destruction and global inequality demand a new way of seeing and doing things.

How can we harness the power of communications to tackle the climate crisis? How can we promote gender and racial justice? How can we build a more equitable society? These are all questions that marketing can answer! We simply need to direct our time, money and talents towards the right projects. This is a practical book on how to use the power of marketing and communications to positively impact business and society.

Good for business

Using marketing to accelerate social change isn't about charity. Business as usual is not an option anymore. The average age of an S&P 500 company is under 20 years, down from 60 years in the 1950s.[1] Only 26 of the original 100 companies remain listed on the FTSE 100.[2] More than 50 per cent of the world's population is under 30, but the average age of a board director is almost 60. This is about futureproofing business and society. If the rate of change in society surpasses the rate of change in business, then the end is near.

Generation Z is the largest and most diverse generation globally with the fastest-growing income of any generation. The traditional marketing play-book is delivering diminishing returns. Young people expect brands to go beyond selling products and maximizing shareholder profits. The modern marketer needs to navigate new social and environmental dimensions. All other things being equal, consumers are buying brands that share their values and beliefs. A new generation of active citizens expect companies to be a vehicle for social change. At a time when business is viewed as more competent and ethical than government young people want to work for a company which is trying to positively impact the world. A company's commitment to social justice will not only attract consumers but employees, too. The companies that build sustainability and inclusion into the heart of their business practices will become the most valuable brands of the 21st century.

Change is hard, but why?

Change is hard. If it were easy, everyone would do it. Throughout your jour-ney you're likely to face numerous obstacles, but nothing worth doing is easy. Before we explore how to create social change, it's worth exploring why change can be challenging. After all, understanding the problem is half the solution.

Most people aren't lazy, stupid or self-serving. Resistance to change has been an effective mechanism for human progress and survival. As humans, we desire safety and security. Much of our history has been volatile and unpredictable. Through evolution, we have developed heuristics: rules of thumb to facilitate faster decision-making. Heuristics help us make quick decisions and reduce cognitive overload when dealing with uncertainty. Humans have developed codes, norms and values to make everyday life more certain. In contrast, change triggers feelings of anxiety and fear of the unknown. Unlike our ancestors, modern humans are the most dominant species on Earth. In general, we live in the most peaceful, healthy and settled period in human history. Most people no longer need to worry about cave bears or lions chasing them. And yet we still maintain the same level of anxiety and fear when responding to uncertainty. Whether it's our workplace switching to a new software, our favourite restaurant updating the menu or our partner rocking a new hairstyle, our internal alarms start ringing as soon as the familiar becomes unfamiliar. This could explain why we have had 25 James Bond films, 11 Fast and Furious releases and 10 Batman movies. The unknown is as scary as when our ancestors battled with other carnivores for survival. Thus, we are hardwired to overestimate risks and underestimate our ability to handle them. It is our brain's way of protecting us from existential and imaginary risk, an evolutionary consequence of early humans being chased by predators, fighting against deadly diseases and avoiding starvation or dehydration.

Research shows that humans would rather be unhappy than uncertain.[3] During an experiment, 45 volunteers played a game in which they had to turn over virtual rocks. They were then asked to guess whether the rock had a snake underneath. When a snake was discovered, participants received an electric shock. The study found that the uncertainty of receiving a shock caused significantly more stress than knowing that you would 100 per cent be shocked. We would rather be unhappy than uncertain. We resist change because it goes against our very nature. The establishment of permanent human settlements in Mesopotamia, the Nile delta and the Indus Valley was a triumph of order over uncertainty. Similarly, the invention of written scripts which enabled the creation of laws, stories and learning. These were attempts to control our destiny, minimize uncertainty and maximize wellbeing.

Status quo bias

Once social norms and values are developed, it can be hard to override them. This is known as the status quo bias: an emotional preference for the current situation. Examples of status quo bias are abundant in everyday life. Like when you go to the same restaurant because you know exactly what you're going to get. On special days, you might be tempted to try a new dish but default back to your usual choice because of that voice in your head. It can also explain why we choose boring hotel chains; we already know what the bed, breakfast and overall experience feel like. In all examples, we're simply reducing variance and uncertainty.

The status quo bias is why subscription services auto-renew unless you cancel them. Tech companies know we are less likely to cancel a subscription once registered. In the UK, £300 million is spent on unused subscriptions.[4] It's the same reason why opt-out organ donorship systems have higher donation rates. In other words, the default becomes the standard. And once the norm has taken shape, it becomes challenging to dislodge. Change requires more energy than the continuation of the status quo.

As seen in Daniel Kahneman's book *Thinking, Fast and Slow*,[5] System 1 thinking happens automatically, intuitively and with minimal effort. When was the last time you thought about how you walk? Though we have no control over System 1 it is suggested that we use System 1 thinking for approximately 98 per cent of our decisions, whereas System 2 is analytical, deliberate and effortful. As wonderful as System 2 sounds, if we made every single decision using slow thinking our brains would crash. The human brain has a limit on how much information it can process at once.[6] This is not too dissimilar to a computer with too many tabs open at the same time. The computer begins to slow down. Carefully examining every minor detail would lead to cognitive overload and mental fatigue. If we allocate too much attention to minor activities, less brain energy would be available for more important tasks. We need both systems to function, but System 2 thinking can facilitate the invention of new norms and behaviours. With enough practice, System 2 can turn into System 1 – think about when you first started driving, playing the piano or learning a new language. In other words, change is possible.

Status quo bias minimizes the risks associated with change, but it can also prevent us from exploring more beneficial options. Loss aversion partly explains why people opt for the status quo. The pain of losing is twice as powerful as the pleasure of gaining. Put simply, we would be twice as sad losing $100 than we would be gaining the same amount. We stick to what we know not because it's the optimum option but because of the risk associated with change. This is why marketing campaigns for tech services include a trial period. Companies know people are more likely to continue with the service once it's ingrained into their existing routine. A whopping 44 per cent of Americans have never switched mobile networks.[7] And we're more likely to head into Nando's despite the opportunity to discover the greatest chicken of our life at the new Mozambiquan restaurant next door.

Identity and familiarity

There are other less obvious reasons for opposing change. When something changes – regardless of whether positive or negative – it distorts our sense of identity. We lose a connection with the familiar and with it any perceived notion of control. Change is the loss of the familiar for the new. We hold on to our favourite jumper, even though it doesn't fit us anymore and won't be wearing it again. There's something strangely comforting about the familiar. When things change, we're forced to reorient ourselves and establish our position and identity within the new ecosystem. Cognitive dissonance is the uncomfortable feeling that comes when our beliefs and social identity don't align with our behaviour. We know junk food is bad for our health, but we still eat them. We are aware smoking increases the risk of lung cancer, but we still smoke. We accept climate change is happening, but we still buy from fast fashion brands. Humans seek comfort and consistent mental models. Avoiding psychological discomfort when our beliefs are inconsistent with our actions. It can be easier to justify our behaviours than to change them. Changing our behaviour threatens our social identity and sense of self. Cognitive dissonance is a coping mechanism to resolve such inconsistencies.

It could explain why prisoners struggle to adapt to civilian life. In a parallel marketing world, when our favourite brand changes its logo or recipe we don't grieve the change itself but rather the loss of meaning and shared social codes and identity. We no longer recognize ourselves in the new product. It means starting from scratch. It's back to the first day of school where we have to make friends again and establish our place in the pecking order. The UK tax on sugar in soft drinks caused a major headache for most beverage companies due to reformulation (although it has also prevented 5,000 cases of obesity per year).[8]

There's a sunk cost associated with our existing identity and way of life. I'm a Liverpool supporter – imagine telling my friends that I've suddenly changed allegiance to Manchester United after two decades. It would shatter everything I would know that's true about myself. They would think that I'd been abducted by aliens. Our identity is as much shaped by the external work and groups we're not part of as much as the ones we are. You're either iPhone or Android, BMW or Mercedes, Coke or Pepsi, Republican or Democrat. Changing your mind could be seen as disastrous for a political campaign – even though it might be the right thing to do. The same premise applies in the world of business. Familiarity and consistency create the illusion of confidence and certainty. We often feel compelled to maintain our beliefs because of external pressures, especially once they are in the public domain. Every human seeks to build and sustain an identity. We build an idea of who we are based on our values, attitudes and experiences. Interestingly, certain milestones like getting a new job, having kids or moving home can reorder how we view the world.

Mere exposure effect

We reject change because new norms don't fit with our existing mental models. Being confronted with unfamiliar ideas can feel at best awkward and at worst painful. The mere exposure effect posits that people show an increased preference for things because they are familiar with them. For example, we are more likely to buy products and services we have seen advertised regularly. The more we see someone, the more attractive we find them. Most married couples met at school, work or via friends before the creation of the internet. This is also how pop music works; we usually hate that song when we first hear it but once it's played everywhere we unknowingly begin singing the lyrics (don't pretend you don't). There's a simple explanation for all of this: we're programmed to be careful around new things because they could kill us. Many of our unconscious biases, including the mere exposure effect, are driven by the need to survive.

Some of us are more open to new experiences than others. Openness is one of the 'big five' personality traits. The trait is associated with creative imagination, curiosity and a hunger for discovery. People with high openness are more willing to try new experiences. We need explorers to experiment and innovate, helping us progress and discover beyond our existing pool of knowledge and capabilities. We all can think of someone who fits this description or maybe we are that someone. People who are open to new experiences are generally more comfortable with uncertainty and receptive to different cultures, ideas and lifestyles. While some people are naturally more open to new experiences than others we can all develop our openness to new experiences by creating a culture of creative exploration. There is no such thing as a stupid question. Often, and especially in business, established knowledge can prevent the emergence of new thoughts and approaches. If we want to reach new destinations, we need to create the conditions for exploration.

At the same time, it's important to note that not everything needs to change. There's a $860 million consulting industry predicated around selling change. There are more than 700,000 management consultants in the world.[9] I'm sure most of them are talented, intelligent and honest. But much of the industry is built on selling solutions to invented problems. In the consultancy world, change is the name of the game. Companies sell using the fear that things are changing faster than ever. I'm sure the statement has been true at every juncture in human history. In the last decade, we have experienced economic uncertainty, a global pandemic and the exponential rise of AI. However, despite the outside world changing dramatically the human brain has remained largely unchanged for 160,000 years.[10] Put simply, the hardware has changed but the software is the same. Therefore, understanding the human psyche – and resistance to change – is critical before attempting to create change, whether for business or society.

Being cautious of new things poses a considerable threat to creating a more desirable future. The problem is that our vision of the future is viewed through the lens of the past. Our obsession with the familiar might even explain why movements like diversity, equity and inclusion and climate justice struggle to enter the mainstream psyche. New actions no matter how admirable represent a threat to existing paradigms and self-identity. Our hunter-gatherer ancestors were right to be cautious of new ideas. Eating an unknown berry might kill you and walking in the wrong direction might mean starving to death. But today we have supermarkets and Google Maps. And still, we carry the same resistance to change.

Neophobia

Let's take a moment to read the following statements:

> 'This "telephone" has too many shortcomings to be seriously considered as a means of communication. The device is inherently of no value to us.' – Western Union internal memo, 1876.[11]

> 'Good enough for our Transatlantic friends... but unworthy of the attention of practical or scientific men.' – A British Parliament Committee into Thomas Edison's light bulb in 1878.

> 'I do not believe the introduction of motor-cars will ever affect the riding of horses.' – John Scott-Montagu MP, UK, 1903.[12]

> 'Airplanes are interesting scientific toys, but they are of no military value.' – Ferdinand Foch, French General and Allied Commander during World War I.

In 1995, *Newsweek* made a big and bold prediction titled: 'Why the internet will fail'.[13]

As you can see, many of the greatest breakthroughs of modern history were rejected. The Eiffel Tower was treated with great disdain when it was first constructed. Parisians originally hated the tower because it clashed with the architecture of the rest of the city. The Eiffel Tower is now considered the most valuable monument in Europe, worth £344 billion to the French economy.[14] On a more anecdotal note, dads hate the idea of getting a new family dog but when the puppy comes home, they end up loving them the most. Apartheid in South Africa was supported by most European countries. Racial segregation was the norm in the United States until 1964. What seems the norm today, can be viewed as unbelievable tomorrow. No doubt, many of our current norms will be viewed differently in the future.

Climate change

But when is change required? It's simpler than we make it. Change is required when the current system stops working. The very norms, laws and practices that were designed to serve our lifestyle, society or business become a hindrance. If your car breaks down, you either have to fix the problem or buy a new car. We cannot continue with the status quo. However, most transformations occur more incrementally. The famous quote goes: 'Rome wasn't built in a day' – but people were laying bricks every minute. I much prefer the Lenin quote: 'There are decades where nothing happens, and there are weeks where decades happen.' Change has a way of gaining speed and velocity. The absurd can become the norm within a matter of days. The rate of change accelerates when our current ways stop serving us. Fossil fuels are made from decomposing plants and animals: truly incredible when you think about it. The use of fossil fuels catapulted industrialization and standards of living globally. Oil, gas and coal have enabled electrical production, industrial manufacturing, economic growth and transportation. But in the 20th century, we learned that fossil fuels have negative externalities. Burning fossil fuels releases greenhouse gases like carbon dioxide into the atmosphere, contributing to climate change and planetary destruction. Fossil fuels are a macro example of how a process that benefited business and society has become a barrier to future progress and existence.

Governments, companies and individuals recognize the need to change. Yet, for the reasons highlighted in previous sections, we are resistant to change. Even when the change is necessary – and our species' livelihood depends on it – the fear of the unknown supersedes the promise of a more prosperous future. There's a perfectly reasonable explanation: we're unsure of what the future looks like and more specifically our role within it. Another factor strengthening the resistance to change is a vested interest in the status quo. Many wealthy individuals, companies and shareholders benefit immensely from the fossil fuel economy. Moving from fossil fuels to renewables would deliver a tangible threat to their influence and income, at least in the interim. But still, many companies are unwilling to make short-term investments for long-term sustainability since shareholders demand quarterly profits. More interesting is how the majority of global citizens, who aren't invested in the capital markets, are neutral, simply because the current situation is more predictable than the uncertainty of a more sustainable future.

Business change

In the business world, a company grows when it develops a new product, sells more products, creates new markets or improves existing processes. Nokia started life as a paper mill operation. The company was still producing rubber boots until 1990. In the 1960s, Nokia expanded into electronics and telecommunications, thanks to exports from Finland into the Soviet Union. But in the late 1980s the company nearly went out of business due to the collapse of the Soviet Union and overexpansion. What happened next was remarkable. The struggling company went all-in on 2G technology and in 1992 Nokia produced the world's first commercially available GSM digital mobile phone. By 1998, Nokia was the best-selling mobile phone brand in the world. Nokia's market share peaked in 2007 at a massive 48.7 per cent.[15] At the time, it was inconceivable that Nokia's dominance could be challenged. It seemed like the business and executive leadership could do nothing wrong. But complacency is the enemy of longevity. Excess comfort is a slow but sure descent into irrelevance. Change is necessary for business and life. You could argue that Nokia struggled to keep up with Apple, Google and Samsung. But why? Nokia failed to embrace change, therefore forfeiting its dominant position in the market. Sometimes the riskiest move is doing nothing, especially when you're the incumbent. Nokia overlooked changing consumer needs and underestimated the role of software in the mobile market. While Nokia was too focused on optimizing features, Apple reinvented the category with the launch of the iPhone. The iPhone changed the world by placing the internet – and the world's knowledge – in people's pockets. At the time of writing, Apple is the world's most valuable company. The key is to change before external factors force you to change. No matter how pioneering your company might be, after some time you will encounter diminishing returns. You can either make change happen or it will happen to you.

Personal change

On a more personal level, most of us have ambitions we want to achieve but never manage to actualize them. The gap between who we are and our ideal future self can be deeply frustrating. Humans are innately ambitious, driven by a persistent desire to grow and reach new heights. Every year, many of us make New Year's resolutions, whether to lose weight, quit alcohol or exercise more. In the US, at least 44 per cent of adults make a New Year's resolution – with 'more exercise' being the most popular. But we also know that almost a quarter quit in the first week.[16] And 80 per cent scrap their resolution by February.[17] There's an obvious disconnect between our goals and habits. Once again, change requires creating a new set of beliefs and behaviours. Often, this challenge is too great once the excitement and motivation of New Year's Eve dissipates. We expect too much, setting the bar so high that failure becomes inevitable. In contrast, some conditions enable personal change. For instance, we're more open to change when on holiday, starting a new job or after having a near-death experience. What's common in all these scenarios is that our identity and sense of self become more fluid. And this creates the conditions to re-evaluate our values and beliefs. For long-lasting change to happen, we need enough buffer between our past and future selves. I'm sure we've all experienced an inspirational conference whose influence quickly melts away as we leave the event and re-assume our business-as-usual identities and responsibilities. The same is true when we feel relaxed after coming back from summer holidays, before returning to the office. We might still have some sunshine vibes in the first couple of weeks but soon enough it's back to business. Long-lasting change requires new conditions. It demands a break from the past – there's no point in breaking up with your partner and deciding to start a new life only to continue living under the same roof. That's not to say motivation isn't important. Humans have achieved great feats using motivation, but when combined with the right conditions, that's when magic happens.

The comfort zone

There's great comfort in the status quo. Change requires expanding our comfort zone and seeking uncharted waters. Growth is only possible outside the comfort zone. Think back to some of the most challenging tasks you've undertaken. It might be when you were studying for an exam at school, managing a work project with a tight deadline or became a first-time parent. In 2018, I was asked by the *Independent* to write an opinion piece for them in two hours. This might be normal for journalists working in newsrooms, but I was a twenty-something strategist who would usually take anywhere between one and six months to write an article because I had no external deadline. However, I said yes, downed four shots of espresso and somehow managed to deliver on time. And, to date, I've never felt more accomplished than walking home while listening to David Bowie's *Heroes*. We're capable of extraordinary things if we push ourselves beyond the familiar and into the unknown.

Discomfort is a catalyst for personal, professional and societal growth. On the contrary, we should be more worried when things become too easy. Being a big fish in a little pond can be extremely rewarding for our self-esteem. But it prevents us from swimming in the ocean. When a flower outgrows its home, it requires a bigger pot. To quote John A Shedd: 'A ship in a harbour is safe but that is not what ships are built for.' We humans are no different. Unless you've attained mastery, comfort is the enemy of progress. If you're not stretching, you're in decline. We're either climbing up mountains or rolling down the hill. While it's okay to stop and smell the flowers along the way, we shouldn't dwell too long. The only way comfort zones are expanded is through exposure to discomfort. However, contrary to all the popular self-development books and gurus, there are some tangible benefits to remaining within our comfort zones. First and foremost, we get to draw on our existing domain experience. In many scenarios, including work, it would be unwise not to use the experience we've accumulated over many years, if not decades. Second, being confident in our ability to perform, which has been proven in the big fish/little pond effect, where being a high performer in a smaller pool gives us the necessary confidence to work hard and maintain and improve abilities. This could also explain why billionaires never retire, despite not being able to physically spend all the money they've accumulated. Billionaires have a different frame of reference, perpetually competing with bigger fish, which creates the motivation and need to continue. It could also explain why we secretly take pleasure in other people's small misfortunes (schadenfreude). It makes us more confident and assured of our abilities and circumstances. The comfort zone can be an acceptable place to return to, like our real homes. But, just like our homes, if we don't leave then will never get to experience anything new.

The growth zone

Mindset plays an important role in determining personal, business and social outcomes. You're probably familiar with the terms 'fixed' and 'growth' mindset. People who believe their intelligence, talent and abilities are permanent have a fixed mindset. Think about when people say 'I'm terrible at maths.' Sure enough, you might not be the next Al-Khwarizmi, but you can improve your maths skills. Much worse is a schoolteacher stating that a student has no talent in language, art or music. The assumption is we are born with a certain ability, and it will determine our future. On the flip side, people who believe they can change have a growth mindset. Skills can be nurtured through continuous learning and hard work, according to people with growth mindsets. J K Rowling had a growth mindset, despite being rejected by countless publishers, while being jobless, depressed and on welfare. Fast forward to today and the books in her Harry Potter series have sold more than 600 million copies. Colonel Sanders had his recipe rejected more than 1,000 times by the time he was in his 50s. But he kept perfecting his recipe despite being penniless again in his 60s. At the ripe age of 65 and reliant on a $105 a month social security check, Sanders started KFC. There are now 25,000 KFC outlets across the world, from Central Asia to Oceania. Frederick Douglass had a growth mindset. Having been born into slavery and taught himself how to read and write. After several failed attempts, Douglass finally escaped the shackles of slavery and became a leading voice in the anti-slavery movement. His book, *Narrative of the Life of Frederick Douglass*,[18] received international acclaim and shifted public perception of slavery. Douglass's work created the foundations for the civil rights movement of the 1960s.

Scientists have shown that a growth mindset stimulates neuroplasticity. As we push beyond our comfort zone – exposed to new experiences – the brain forms new neural connections to accommodate the growth and learning processes. The brain is a pattern-seeking machine. As we experience and perform routine tasks the brain strengthens links between neurons. Novel experience, new challenges and focused attention can create new neural connections. Learning new words, playing video games or using your non-dominant hand can promote neuroplasticity. Until recently, neuroscientists believed that changes in the brain could only take place during infancy and adolescence. While the brain is more flexible in early life, our brains remain plastic throughout our lifetime. For instance, children acquire language through osmosis without any formal training. But the good news is humans can form new neural connections at any age. We can literally rewire our brains. A key determinant of growth is our attitude to new stimuli, challenges and general uncertainty. Though it sounds non-sensical, at least on the surface, our mindset shapes our outcomes. This is even more poignant when it comes to responding, creating or accelerating social change.

The placebo effect

For years, the placebo effect was viewed as a failure in the field of medicine. The placebo effect is when a drug improves physical or mental health without having any functional properties. Placebos are used in clinical trials to test the effectiveness of treatments. Group One gets the actual drug and Group Two receives the placebo. However, neither side knows who's getting which treatment. Placebos shouldn't work, but in reality, they do. The placebo effect is activated by individuals' belief in the benefit of the treatments and expectation of feeling better. We have scientific evidence that your mindset can shape your reality. According to empirical evidence, 30–40 per cent of people can have significant improvement in their symptoms even when taking a placebo (sugar) pill.[19] What if we applied the placebo effect to our everyday challenges? What if we redefined what we can achieve? Equally interesting is the nocebo effect, when negative expectations of treatment – even when given a sugar pill – produce adverse side effects based on what our mind expects. This is not limited to medicine, either. A study by Yale University reveals that people's state of mind may influence how physically satisfied they feel after a meal.[20] Two separate groups of participants were given a 380-calorie milkshake under the pretence that it was either a 620-calorie 'indulgent' shake or a 140 calorie 'sensible' shake. Those who thought they drank the 'indulgent' shake had a dramatically steeper decline in ghrelin, which is the hormone that makes you feel hungry. Our internal beliefs impact our external reality. If we view challenges as a threat, we're less likely to travel beyond our zone of comfort and familiarity. But if we view challenges as an opportunity to learn and grow, then we will learn something new and expand our frame of reference of what's possible. In the words of Rumi: 'What you seek, is seeking you.'

The growth mindset is not too dissimilar to the immigrant mindset. Unsurprisingly, immigration causes the rewiring of the brain. People who have moved to a new country or culture will be aware of this mindset shift. Immigrants need to grapple with a new language, cultural norms, environment and people. New norms need to be learned and existing norms unlearned. In the US, nearly 25 per cent of start-ups are founded by immigrants despite making up 13 per cent of the overall population. According to a *Harvard Business Review* study by William R Kerr and Sari Pekkala Kerr, immigrant-led companies grow at a faster rate and are more likely to survive long-term than native-led companies.[21] A growth mindset and neuroplasticity can explain the success of immigrant entrepreneurs against all odds. People who uproot their lives in the hope of a better future have a high level of tolerance for uncertainty. In many cases, immigrant parents have no other choice. And yet, being exposed to such high levels of uncertainty instils a belief in children of immigrants that humans can adapt and figure out pretty much any circumstance. Immigrants have minuscule – if existent at all – comfort zones, therefore they are more likely to explore the unknown, innovate and adapt to the changing landscape. The lack of inheritance means that immigrants have less to lose and more to gain when change happens. Conversely, people with legacy knowledge and assets view change as a threat to their existing paradigm. But we all know that adaptation is the key to survival. More than survival, the human ability to adapt makes life more beautiful, diverse and meaningful. How boring would life be if things never changed?

Professional growth

The ability to adapt to change is equally important for professional development. Navigating new and uncertain circumstances can improve your effectiveness and wellbeing at work. If we only performed jobs within our comfort zone, then there would be no space for growth.

Fear of the unknown prevents us from speaking out in the meeting, although we know the right answer. It stops us from applying for the new job, even though we're unhappy with our current position. And it blocks us from starting our own business or attempting a new approach at work. Don't forget, we would rather be mildly electrocuted than experience any form of uncertainty. Paradoxically, we live in an uncertain world and the only way to stay relevant is by being open to new experiences. In Zen Buddhism, this is known as *shoshin* which translates as 'beginner's mind'. It refers to a state of openness and exploration void of pre-conceptions, biases and habits accrued through knowledge and experience.

To arrive at a new destination, we must depart from our existing mental model. According to the World Economic Forum, 65 per cent of students will be employed in jobs that don't yet exist.[22] Our future careers are going to look different from what they are today. Unless we're able to grapple with the discomfort and adventures of uncertainty we'll get left behind. Some skills are timeless, like critical thinking, creativity and imagination – but even then, we'd need to apply them within a different context. Updating your career trajectory doesn't have to be a revolutionary act – unless you want it to be – it can be as simple as being curious about emerging trends within your business, category and profession. Enrolling in a new online course or simply reading about a topic you usually wouldn't boosts your neuroplasticity. Not taking calculated risks in our careers can end up being the riskiest decision of them all. The solution is to act and increase our uncertainty tolerance – adapting to change and being okay with not knowing what's next. A continuous dislike of uncertainty can cause anxiety and avoidance behaviours. Simply put, we end up doing nothing even though we know change is needed. Things don't change because the fear of the unknown is greater than our desire to change. Luckily, there's a formula for change!

The change formula

How is change created? What are the conditions for change? Luckily there's an easy and practical formula for change. The idea was first developed by David Gleicher and later refined by Richard Beckhard and Reuben S Harris.[23] The formula has mainly been applied to organizational change, but it can equally be used for social change:

$$C = D \times V \times F > R$$

Change = dissatisfaction × vision × first concrete steps > resistance to change

For example:

- The change (C) might be that you want to move from your current job.

- Dissatisfaction (D) – you are no longer gaining meaning from your job in project management in financial services and no longer feel like you're learning.

- Vision (V) – you are looking to become a product manager in financial inclusion in developing countries to help lift people out of poverty.

- First concrete steps (F) – you start volunteering at a charity working to advance financial inclusion for refugees.

- Resistance to change (R) – your resistance to change is reduced as you begin to see the impact you're making.

After three months of volunteering, you apply for a role in a financial tech company and are given the position. All because your dissatisfaction with your job, vision for a better future and first step of volunteering were stronger than the pain of transitioning from your current role. Unless we understand the resistance to change, then the status quo will remain intact. We won't achieve the desired change despite our good intentions.

Social norms

I have updated the formula to add social norms into the equation. After all, the book is about social change, not personal change – even though the two are strongly connected. We humans are social beings. From an evolutionary perspective, we have relied on cooperation to survive and thrive. When our ancient ancestors first roamed the African savannah, collaboration was the only way to gain access to food, shelter and protection from attacks. There-fore, social change happens at a collective, not individual, level. Whether we like it or not, social norms determine our behaviour. In social situations we follow rules because the benefits of adhering to them outweigh the conse-quences of breaking them. We tell the truth because we want others to do the same. We pay taxes because it benefits society. We wait in line since we don't want someone cutting in front of us. Social norms play a crucial role in maintaining a long-term cooperative relationship between members. They provide order and predictability – remember our fear of uncertainty. We develop social norms from an early age. Sociologists call the process inter-nalization. Most people are either rewarded or punished for showcasing acceptable or unacceptable social behaviours. This is a pattern reinforced by our parents, teachers, workplace and society at large. What begins as external social guidelines becomes an internal compass for decision-making. External expectations can reinforce compliance with social norms. For good reason, too; it would be hard to operate in a society without a shared set of invisible rules and standards that govern behaviour in groups. However, existing norms can also block, punish and slow down new social movements.

Social norms change

Social norms can and do change! Until the Covid-19 pandemic, people worked from the office. In most companies, it was inconceivable to work from home – not because the technology didn't exist but because it went against the social norm. Employees felt they would get punished or viewed less favourably if they didn't make an effort by commuting 200+ hours per year. It was a signal of intent and determination, like a corporate bird dance. But then lockdown happened, and everyone – except frontline workers – was forced to work from home. Suddenly, the norm was broken, and so-called knowledge workers realized that output was no longer correlated with geographic proximity.

Cigarette smoking was initially confined to early adopters. It started with wealthy men and became aspirational, prompting uptake across social categories. Before you knew it, smoking became a norm. In the 1920s, tobacco companies commissioned extensive research and marketing campaigns to make smoking mainstream. These included doctors endorsing and prescribing cigarettes and the proliferation of different brands and positionings within the market. Tobacco paraphernalia, lighters, ashtrays and free cigarettes were distributed in all the coolest bars. Smoking became cool and cigarette brands served as a badge of identity. The macro-environment also plays a critical role in the enabling or disabling of social norms. The onset of World War I turned smoking into an acceptable form of physical and mental relief. But perhaps the most interesting case study in making smoking a social norm is the work of Edward Bernays, the father of PR and propaganda. In the 1920s, the America Tobacco Company realized they could double their market for Lucky Strikes brands if smoking wasn't a social taboo for women. Bernays was recruited to attract women smokers and eliminate the social taboo of women smoking in public. He got advice from the Austrian psychoanalyst A A Brill who told him cigarettes were a symbol of oppression and male dominance. And Bernays came up with the infamous 'Torches of Freedom' campaign – framing cigarettes as an emblem of emancipation.[24] Next up, Bernays paid women to smoke their 'torches of freedom' at the Easter Sunday parade – hiring photographers to take pictures and publish them around the world. Today, smoking has lost its cachet as a social norm in most countries and cultures. Smoking rates have declined due to knowledge of the health effects and changes in laws where people can no longer smoke in public spaces. Norms can be both constructed and destructed.

How change happens

Change comes from the periphery. It begins on the margins of society before expanding into the mainstream. History is littered with outsiders who seemed foolish, eccentric and odd but ended up changing our social norms. The centre and periphery exist in a constant state of friction. Outsiders are often uninhibited by the rules of the establishment. In other words, they have nothing to lose. Conversely, those at the centre possess a wealth of resources and worry about losing their privileges. Life at the centre is highly regulated, managed and standardized. In general, people and groups join the centre if they obey and uphold existing social norms. The closer we are to the heart of power and decision-making, the less likely we are to challenge the status quo. Social change happens when a small minority change the norms of the majority. Fidel Castro overthrew the government of Cuba with 200 men.[25] The Stonewall uprisings in Greenwich Village, New York – again, roughly 500 people – paved the way for gay liberation movements and LGBTQ+ rights globally. Rosa Parks' resistance to segregation (Jim Crow laws) and arrest sparked the Montgomery Bus Boycott by 17,000 people: a catalyst for the civil rights movement.[26]

The work of Professor Erica Chenoweth reaffirms the power of a small number of committed people. After studying 323 violent and non-violent protests that occurred between 1900 and 2006 worldwide, Chenoweth posited the 3.5 per cent rule.[27] It takes 3.5 per cent of the population to actively participate in protests to create political change. On the surface, this seems like a small and insignificant percentage. Especially if 96.5 per cent of the population remains inactive. Like lighting a match in a dry forest, once there's a spark then the rest of the trees will catch fire too. Next, the work of Professor Damon Centola shows that as soon as a movement reaches

25 per cent of the population we reach a tipping point.[28] The norm crosses a certain threshold and rapidly changes the core. The periphery becomes the mainstream. Countries accepted slavery as a legitimate economic activity until the 19th century. Darwin's theory of natural selection was initially rejected. Most women were not allowed to vote until the 20th century. The list goes on! What seems improbable can become unstoppable.

Summary of actions

How can you create change? The first step is recognizing your ability to create change. Unless we can imagine and believe change is possible, the status quo will prevail. Now that we've established change is possible, here are some actionable steps you can take to begin your journey of creating social change.

1 **Start small**

   The biggest barrier to change is perfection. The pressure of getting things right and making sure everything is aligned can inhibit action. Perfection is the enemy of progress. In our well-intentioned attempt to create the perfect conditions, we empower inaction. Over-thinking and over-planning can result in things remaining the same. Instead, small steps can lead to big changes. In tech, start-ups adopt the minimum viable product (MVP) approach: a version of a product with just enough features to be usable by early customers who can then provide feedback for future product development. When it comes to change, what's your minimum viable change? What's something you can do today? The key is to start small, learn from the process and scale accordingly. You can begin today with things that are in your circle of influence.

2 **Escape your comfort zone**

   Change begins at the end of your comfort zone. Find interesting, fun and novel ways to expand our tolerance to discomfort. Nothing will change if we do the same things that we always have. We have to be open to new experiences and opportunities beyond our existing bank of knowledge and experience. This requires being okay with uncertainty. There's a whole new world outside our comfort zones but we won't experience it without venturing into uncharted waters. Adopt a beginner's mind by asking new questions. It's perfectly okay to not know all the answers. A good question is better than a great answer – we can promote neuroplasticity by embracing new experiences.

3 Experiment

Exploring and experimenting is part of the game. When activating change – and attempting to do something new – no one has all the answers. The status quo is a well-trodden path with neatly defined structures, processes and ways of working. We should view it as a call to adventure – exploration is a fundamental part of innovation. There's no such thing as failure, only feedback and lessons. However, make sure you're experimenting around the edges, not the core. Experiments are beneficial unless they're consequential. For example, don't bet your 90 per cent of the company's marketing budget on an untested idea.

Begin with small steps, explore ways to travel beyond your comfort zone and experiment on the edges. This is the start of your journey to becoming a champion of change!

ACTIVITY

1 Select one thing that you can change

This should be something within your circle of influence. Here are some examples to spark your imagination:

o Buy from an independent business.
o Join an interest group.
o Smile at strangers.

2 Do one thing differently from how you've always done it

The purpose of this exercise is to form new neural pathways. Here are some examples to spark your imagination:

o Brush your teeth with your non-dominant hand.
o Take a different route to work.
o Read a book outside your comfort zone.

3 Launch a social change experiment

We know what the status quo looks like, but change requires experimentation and new ways of working. There's no such thing as failure, only lessons. Here are some examples to spark your imagination:

o A/B test between your default action (A) and something radically different (B).
o Kickstart a new project or crowdsource new ideas.

o   Allocate 10 per cent of your time/budget to an experimental project with no expectations.

o   Explore a new consumer segment or untested hypothesis.

The intention is to uncover an MVC: the smallest possible action that creates social change. This process is designed to overcome the greatest internal barriers to social action: not getting started and overcomplicating things.

Notes

1 D Clark. Average company lifespan on Standard and Poor's 500 Index from 1965 to 2030, in years, Statista, 27 August 2021. www.statista.com/statistics/1259275/average-company-lifespan (archived at https://perma.cc/3GGV-9UWH)

2 R Mould. FTSE 100 readies for its fortieth birthday with twenty-six founder members still in the index, AJ Bell, 6 October 2023. www.ajbell.co.uk/articles/investmentarticles/266834/ftse-100-readies-its-fortieth-birthday-twenty-six-founder-members (archived at https://perma.cc/9JC2-SW42)

3 A O de Berker et al. Computations of uncertainty mediate acute stress responses in humans, *Nature Communications*, 2016, 7, 10996. www.nature.com/articles/ncomms10996 (archived at https://perma.cc/EJY7-JEKT)

4 Citizens Advice. Half a billion pounds spent on subscriptions that rolled over without people realising, Citizens Advice, 1 December 2022. www.citizensadvice.org.uk/about-us/about-us1/media/press-releases/half-a-billion-pounds-spent-on-subscriptions-that-rolled-over-without-people-realising-during-the-cost-of-living-crisis (archived at https://perma.cc/RHL3-YLGH)

5 D Kahneman (2011) *Thinking, Fast and Slow*, Penguin Books, London

6 M Bruckmaier et al. Attention and capacity limits in perception: A cellular metabolism account, *Journal of Neuroscience*, 26 August 2020, 40 (35), 6801–11. www.jneurosci.org/content/40/35/6801 (archived at https://perma.cc/NZ9H-5WS6)

7 A Moscaritolo. 44 percent of Americans have never switched mobile carriers, *PC Magazine*, 22 October 2019. uk.pcmag.com/news/123166/44-percent-of-americans-have-never-switched-mobile-carriers (archived at https://perma.cc/S3GL-QS5W)

8 N T Rogers et al. Associations between trajectories of obesity prevalence in English primary school children and the UK soft drinks industry levy: An interrupted time series analysis of surveillance data, *PLOS Medicine*, 2023, 20 (1): e1004160. doi.org/10.1371/journal.pmed.1004160 (archived at https://perma.cc/7A9Z-DM87)

9 IBISWorld. Global management consultants: Market size, industry analysis, trends and forecasts (2024–2029), March 2024. www.ibisworld.com/global/market-research-reports/global-management-consultants-industry (archived at https://perma.cc/KH7J-YAE5)

10 C P E Zollikofer et al. Endocranial ontogeny and evolution in early *Homo sapiens*: The evidence from Herto, Ethiopia, *Proceedings of the National Academy of Sciences of the United States of America*, 2022, 119 (32), e2123553119. doi.org/10.1073/pnas.2123553119 (archived at https://perma.cc/DW7R-QRF5)

11 R Watson. Timeline of failed predictions, Fast Company, 1 December 2010. www.fastcompany.com/1706712/timeline-failed-predictions-part-1 (archived at https://perma.cc/R36R-TEE9)

12 UK Parliament. Motor-cars bill Lords, Volume 126: Debated on Tuesday 4 August 1903. hansard.parliament.uk/Commons/1903-08-04/debates/b44a6b90-7d2a-4c37-86ea-9be70b55994f/Motor-CarsBillLords (archived at https://perma.cc/34AM-XA9F)

13 C Stoll. Why the Web won't be Nirvana, *Newsweek*, 26 February 1995. www.newsweek.com/clifford-stoll-why-web-wont-be-nirvana-185306 (archived at https://perma.cc/R9NP-NFNG)

14 H Samuel. Eiffel Tower worth £344 billion to French economy – or six Towers of London, *Telegraph*, 22 August 2012. www.telegraph.co.uk/news/worldnews/europe/france/9492500/Eiffel-Tower-worth-344-billion-to-French-economy-or-six-Towers-of-London.html (archived at https://perma.cc/D264-RSLK)

15 Statista. Global market share held by Nokia smartphones Q1 2007–Q2 2013, 25 July 2013. www.statista.com/statistics/263438/market-share-held-by-nokia-smartphones-since-2007 (archived at https://perma.cc/W97F-LR9J)

16 S Fielding. Are you making a New Year's resolution this year? Readers weigh in, Verywell Mind, 20 January 2023. www.verywellmind.com/reader-survey-new-years-resolutions-5093510 (archived at https://perma.cc/PU7M-7N5B)

17 S Ali. Why New Year's Resolutions Fail, Psychology Today, 5 December 2018. www.psychologytoday.com/gb/blog/modern-mentality/201812/why-new-years-resolutions-fail (archived at https://perma.cc/P6TV-K3E4)

18 F Douglass (2009) *Narrative of the life of Frederick Douglass*, Oxford World's Classics, Oxford

19 M Primeau and J Towery. Your powerful, changeable mindset, Stanford Report, 15 September 2021. news.stanford.edu/report/2021/09/15/mindsets-clearing-lens-life (archived at https://perma.cc/TGB9-XVFG)

20 A J Crum et al. Mind over milkshakes: Mindsets, not just nutrients, determine ghrelin response, *Health Psychology*, 2011, 30 (4), 424–29. doi.org/10.1037/a0023467 (archived at https://perma.cc/S2H5-UWTF)

21 S P Kerr and W R Kerr. Immigrant entrepreneurship, Harvard Business School Working Paper, No 17–011, July 2016

22 World Economic Forum. *The Future of Jobs: Employment, skills and workforce strategy for the Fourth Industrial Revolution – global challenge insight report, 2016*, 2016. www3.weforum.org/docs/WEF_Future_of_Jobs.pdf (archived at https://perma.cc/H4AQ-E2DG)

23 S H Cady et al. The Change Formula: Myth, legend, or lore? *OD Practitioner*, 2014, 46 (3)

24 E L Bernays (2005) *Propaganda*, Ig Publishing, New York

25 Office of The Historian. Telegram from the Embassy in Cuba to the Department of State, 7 July 1959. history.state.gov/historicaldocuments/frus1958-60v06/d330 (archived at https://perma.cc/H329-555X)

26 E Gringberg. How the Stonewall riots inspired today's Pride celebrations, CNN, 28 June 2019. edition.cnn.com/2019/06/28/us/1969-stonewall-riots-history (archived at https://perma.cc/PFE5-GYTE)

27 E Chenoweth. *Questions, Answers, and Some Cautionary Updates Regarding the 3.5 Percent Rule*, The Carr Center for Human Rights Policy, Harvard Kennedy School, 2019. www.hks.harvard.edu/sites/default/files/2024-05/Erica%20Chenoweth_2020-005.pdf (archived at https://perma.cc/ZBG4-93AW)

28 D Centola. Tipping point for large-scale social change? Just 25 percent, Penn Today, University of Pennsylvania, 7 June 2018. penntoday.upenn.edu/news/damon-centola-tipping-point-large-scale-social-change (archived at https://perma.cc/6NG9-YV98)

2

Challenge the status quo

In 1976 Anita Roddick started a little green shop in Brighton called The Body Shop. Anita wanted to challenge the status quo with her shop. Her products were never tested on animals. It might sound normal today but in the 1970s this broke all the standard protocols of the beauty industry. Not testing on animals wasn't enough – Anita wanted to change the industry. In 1989 The Body Shop started campaigning to end animal testing in cosmetics. An unusual move at a time when most companies were only preoccupied with economic activity. The company continued its advocacy work in collaboration with animal rights group Cruelty-Free International. In 1996 The Body Shop delivered a petition signed by four million people to the European Commission and in 1998 Britain introduced a ban on animal testing on cosmetic products and ingredients. Animal testing was the status quo and Anita made it her mission to challenge the cruel practices of the cosmetics industry. Today, 44 countries have banned cosmetic animal testing. This all started with a single demand. As Anita said, 'Business shapes the world. It is capable of changing society in almost any way you can imagine.'[1]

In the opening chapter we explored the internal and external barriers to change. The status quo is a comfortable place with embedded systems and structures. It can take considerable energy to uproot the existing way of seeing and doing things. Facilitating change can feel like an overwhelming undertaking. When there is so much to do where do you even start? How can you challenge the dominant narrative? How can you show people that the status quo is outdated, unjust and defunct? The answer might come from an unlikely place: epistemology – a fancy Greek word for theory of knowledge.

Thomas Kuhn and paradigm shifts

The term 'paradigm shift' is the epitome of marketing corporate speak. It falls in the same category as 'thinking outside the box', 'circling back' and 'moving the needle'. Yet behind the much used (and abused) term is a concept that will help us understand how new ideas can break old patterns of thinking. Paradigm shift comes from Thomas Kuhn's *The Structure of Scientific Revolutions*[2] – the most cited book in the social sciences. It argues that science develops in four stages: 1. pre-science, where no agreement has been reached; 2. normal science, when a paradigm is established and taken for granted; 3. model shift, when anomalies begin to challenge the existing paradigm; and 4. model crisis, when new theories and concepts are developed. There are two ways to solve a crisis: it can either be resolved with responses within the paradigm or lead to a scientific revolution. Kuhn believed that science alternates between normal and revolutionary. Importantly, we can't judge different paradigms using a common standard. Paradigms are incommensurable – they can't be judged using a common standard. This makes paradigms a psychological and sociological product. Progress is the result of fundamental change rather than the steady accumulation of new ideas. Kuhn believes that the people who have achieved fundamental innovations were either very young or beginners in the field. They were less invested in the previous game and more likely to invent new rules to replace them, highlighting the power of a beginner's mind.

Paradigm shifts can be applied to marketing and social change. Under normal conditions, existing ideas and norms are undisputed. There exists a well-functioning paradigm which we are all contributing towards. The existence of normal conditions is necessary because if we questioned everything all the time we would have no progress, only mayhem. It would be impossible to operate in a constant state of revolution. But paradigms change. Anomalies stress the 'disciplinary matrix' – the collection of values, beliefs and assumptions that form a shared worldview within normal conditions. Such anomalies can either be resolved through the existing paradigm or challenge the validity of the status quo. If the current paradigm is unable to solve the anomalies, we enter upon crisis, which Kuhn describes as 'a proliferation of compelling articulations, the willingness to try anything, the expression of explicit discontent, the recourse to philosophy and to debate over fundamentals'. The crisis is eventually resolved by a revolution and a paradigm shift. Disbelief in old models produces enough oxygen for the exploration of new answers. Examples of paradigm shifts are plenty throughout history. Normal today can be weird tomorrow. When the current system no longer serves us, we need to look for a new map. This is only possible if we can question the existing paradigm. In the words of the Iranian poet Sohrab Sepehri, 'Eyes should be washed, to see things in a different way.'[3]

Social constructs

What makes paradigm shifts relevant to social change is the notion that progress is not linear but revolutionary. We construct our knowledge and beliefs through social interaction. Knowledge is a social phenomenon, a collective view, not just pure objective facts. Our perception of reality is formed through social interactions and norms. Examples include beauty standards, nation states and religion which depend on a shared set of beliefs – and differ across cultures and contexts. The German philosopher Friedrich Nietzsche boldly stated: 'Facts do not exist, only interpretations.' We cannot discount the fundamental role of language and communication in constructing a shared worldview. Here are a few simple examples of social constructs that we rarely question. The idea of a woman is socially constructed. Of course, there are biological differences but much of a woman's experience has been constructed by men's views and expectations. From a young age, many women are expected to dress in feminine clothing, wear make-up and shave their body hair. If I asked you to imagine a woman named Sophia, 28, from London, you are less likely to envisage Sophia playing for Arsenal FC, working as an electrical engineer or as a professional fighter. Nearly half of mothers were stay-at-home mums in America in the 1960s, compared to a quarter today.[4] That's not to say there's a right or wrong choice but it is simply evidence that social constructs change over time.

Money is just a piece of paper. We have designed our society and global economy around generating more money, though it has no intrinsic value. Governments and central banks simply print it – or more recently generate digital numbers. The entire system is built on trust and a collective agreement on what the paper money or digital numbers represent. Race is also a social construct. You probably have an answer for what your race is, but race is not biological either. It's a social construct. A simple reflection of the changing view on race can be viewed through US history. Terms like 'race', 'white' and 'Black' emerged in Europe during the 1500s and made their way to North America. The invention of race, particularly white and Black, helped to justify the transatlantic slave trade and colonization in general, as slaves were not considered human. Slavery had existed for millennia, including in ancient Egypt, Greece and Rome, but it was never correlated with race in the same way. The very idea of whiteness is a modern invention. During the 19th century, the pseudo-science of eugenics further legitimized the social construct of a superior race. The social construction of race is evident in the US census. Finns were excluded from whiteness until the 21st century.[5] Germans, Greeks, Irish and Italians were viewed as 'not quite white'. Mexicans were viewed as 'white' until 1930. In 2000, the US introduced a multiple-race option in the census.[6] Until this day, people from the Middle East and North Africa are viewed as white in the US federal government's data. What is simply cultural and social difference has been interpreted as a social truth called race. A DNA test can tell you where your ancestors are from, but it won't tell your race. This is not the same as saying race doesn't exist. The racial category to which we're assigned can determine our experiences and prospects. It highlights how social constructs inform and shape our worldviews.

Karl Popper and falsification

But there is another view on how ideas spread. Fellow philosopher of science, Karl Popper, had a slightly different take on how knowledge develops. The traditional understanding of knowledge comes from observing and experiencing the world with a blank slate (tabula rasa), a tradition dating back to Aristotle and ancient Greece. Historically, knowledge has developed through inductive logic, reaching a general conclusion from a set of specific observations. Here's an example of inductive logic: every time you eat spicy food, you get stomach-ache. You observe a specific phenomenon (stomach-ache), you recognize a pattern (eating spicy food) and you arrive at a conclusion: spicy food upsets your stomach. In contrast, Popper developed the theory of falsification, which stated that a universal conclusion can be falsified with a single genuine refutation.[7] According to Popper, knowledge can never be proven, only disproven. The longer a theory stands the test of time, the more probably has a resemblance to truth. Unlike Kuhn, Popper doesn't reject absolute truth but simply posits that we don't know what is true or false. Through falsification, we become closer to the source of truth. The best possible sign is standing the test of time. It's an ambition for truth which guides us forward. Discovering false beliefs brings us closer to objective reality. There exists an inherent confirmation bias attached to exploring our existing beliefs and intuition. We humans suffer from confirmation bias: the tendency to seek out or interpret information in ways that reinforce our existing views, while ignoring any contradictory evidence. Popper's work emphasizes the power of the hypothesis. In many ways, science becomes a creative act of producing new theories and testing whether they can be proven wrong. Accepting the idea that your concept could be wrong enables greater progress.

Popper illustrated falsification through the now-famous 'black swan' story. For hundreds if not thousands of years, through observation, we assumed that 'all swans are white'. This conclusion was valid until 1667 when Dutch explorer Willem de Vlamingh discovered black swans in Western Australia. Popper famously said: 'No number of sightings of white swans can prove the theory that all swans are white. The sighting of just one black one may disprove it.' Therein lies the power of falsification. A single example can refute thousands of years of observation that can be undone in a matter of seconds. Such is the fragility of human knowledge.

Nassim Taleb and Black Swans

But why are we talking about black swans? The seminal work of Nassim Nicholas Taleb takes black swans from theory of knowledge into global events. He brings the logical metaphor of the black swan into the real world. When thinking about social change, it's worth examining the disproportional power of highly unlikely events. Contrary to media reports, the past can be a terrible indication of the future. There's little merit in using existing systems, which are reliant on known variables, constancy and logic to create information where there may be none. Taleb addresses such uncertainty in his book *The Black Swan*.[8] A Black Swan is an outlier outside the realm of expectation that, despite its low probability, fundamentally changes the course of history (unlike the bird). Most fascinating of all, a Black Swan is often rationalized with the benefit of hindsight, once there is sufficient data available. According to Taleb: 'rarity, extreme impact, and retrospective (though not prospective) predictability. A small number of Black Swans explain almost everything in our world, from the success of ideas and religions to the dynamics of historical events to elements of our own personal lives.' A combination of low predictability and high impact makes the Black Swan a mystery to most central institutions. We live in a random world full of uncertainty, variance and coincidence, and under such circumstances, knowledge can only take us so far. We only know what we know, not what we don't. Similarly, a highly probable event which doesn't occur is also a Black Swan. As mentioned before, it's the outliers, not the norm, which transform the course of history.

Black Swans are inherently unpredictable, therefore attempting to predict them is pointless. Like counting sand on the beach, to count the whole beach you'd need more than 300,000 people counting sand for their whole lives. And that's if the wind, storm or tsunami doesn't change the number of sand grains on the beach. The focus should be on adjusting to Black Swans or maximizing our exposure to the unknown. What we don't know is more important than our existing bank of knowledge. Entire disciplines post-rationalize the unpredictable world, including history, economics and psychology. More emphasis should be placed upon the unpredictable, what we don't know.

Unpredictable events

On 11 April 1992, three young men in jumpsuits performed at a music competition. The leader of the band was Seo Taiji, who was previously in a heavy metal band before starting a new band called Seo Taiji and Boys, combining Korean lyrics with African American hip-hop, Europop and R&B. This was a completely new sound, blurring genres and, with it, shattering the status quo within Korean music: namely folk songs, pop ballads and trot. When the song *Nan Arayo* (I Know) debuted live on the South Korean TV channel MBC the group received heavy criticism from the judges and the country's music establishment. Seo Taiji and Boys received the lowest score of the night. Understanding the historical context of South Korea in the early 1990s is important to this story. The Korean War had ended less than 40 years earlier. The country changed hands from military dictatorship to democracy in 1987 through nationwide protests and the June Democracy Struggle. Travel bans and censorship laws were lifted in 1989. The country was entering a new era of modernization. Even though the group didn't win the competition, the next day everyone was talking about the performance. Young people couldn't stop talking about it at school. Seo Taiji and Boys challenged the existing paradigm and introduced K-pop to the world. As one YouTube user remarked: modern Korean history could be divided into before and after Seo Taiji and Boys, just like the Silla and Goryeo periods.[9]

Today K-pop is an undeniable cultural phenomenon. What started as an act of rebellion and disregard for the existing ways of producing music has become a global movement. In 2019, BTS became the first group since The Beatles to earn three number 1 albums on the Billboard 200 Chart in less than a year.[10] BLACKPINK is the most subscribed channel on YouTube ahead of Rihanna, Taylor Swift and Ariana Grande. Interestingly, most K-pop songs are in Korean with the odd English word thrown into the mix. And K-pop artists have more fans globally than within the country. The K-pop fandom is diverse, dedicated and passionate. As Lee Soo-man, Founder of SM Entertainment – affectionately nicknamed 'President of Culture' – said, traditionally 'soft power' came from economic supremacy, but the Korean model is 'culture first, economics second'.[11] What began life as Korean pop is now Korean everything – Korean food, cosmetics, drama series and more. This further demonstrates the value of soft power and the unpredictability of Black Swan events.

This phenomenon even has a name, the Korean Wave (*Hallyu*), which began gently on the shores of neighbouring Japan and China but has since taken the world by storm. Of course, using Nassim Taleb's third criterion for Black Swan events, the rise of K-pop is considered common knowledge thanks to the benefit of hindsight. On a recent trip to South Korea for work, I found time to explore the country and visited the Demilitarized Zone (DMZ), the border with North Korea. From the DMZ you can use binoculars to watch North Koreans farming in nearby fields. On the South Korean side, tourists could purchase DMZ T-shirts and chocolate. This was one of the most surreal experiences of my life. During the visit, our tour guide mentioned in passing that both sides blast propaganda across their mutual border using loudspeakers – on the North Korean side, eulogies of Kim Jong Un and on the South Korean side, the latest K-pop hits. I will let you decide which strategy is more effective. Will K-pop disappear as a trend or get even bigger? The future is uncertain and unpredictable, but the impact of highly improbable events is clear.

Complexity and connections

If we want to challenge the status quo, we need to understand complex systems. But defining complexity is not easy. There are as many definitions as there are explanations. Definitions can differ across maths, science, economics and philosophy. Complex systems include ant colonies, social media and the human body. In complex systems, the whole is greater than the sum of its parts. A complex system is interactive, which creates a network effect and unpredictable behaviour. Complexity is proportionate to the interaction between the parts. Complex systems differ from individual systems.

This book is about social change, not personal change, though the two are often interrelated. Therefore, understanding complex systems is critical to mapping and challenging the status quo. Group behaviour is more complex and less predictable than individual behaviour. If I skip lunch, I might end up being hungry. Whereas, when Chairman Mao, the founding father of the People's Republic of China, decided to kill hundreds of millions of sparrows, he didn't expect it would lead to the greatest starvation in history with as many as 45 million people dying.[12] It turns out that locust populations ballooned without sparrows to eat them, destroying all the crops. Nature is an infinitely more complex system. Networks like nature are far more dynamic than individual behaviour. We can't afford to ignore complexity and connectivity when enacting social change. Our world is interconnected. It means we can buy Costa Rican pineapples from our local supermarket for 99p. But it also means it takes 71 days for Covid-19 to be declared a pandemic.[13] Complex systems are emergent and interactive, making them highly scalable. Social phenomena have a multiplicative effect. The outcomes within complex systems are open and unknown. Unlike simple systems, where cause and effect are obvious. The spread of norms, ideas and technology happens through the interaction of complex systems. If we can understand the tools and principles for understanding complexity we are more likely to become agents of social change.

Organizations are model examples of complex systems. It can be easy to view corporations as uniform entities with set business strategies, well-defined departments and employees with clear roles and responsibilities. On the surface, everything is certain, predictable and under control. In reality, corporations are a microcosm of different cultures and behaviours. You would only have to have a bad boss or a change in management to understand the complexity and unpredictability of corporations. The company might be based in Zurich and valued at $800 billion on the stock market, but it consists of 60,000 staff with different personalities across 46 countries and 32 languages. You will also probably notice how the culture and expectations are different across departments. Each department – marketing, sales, HR, operations, IT, finance, and legal – has its own ways of doing things, but the whole is greater than the sum. A screw-up in one department could blow up an entire company. Conversely, a single product or policy could transform the entire organization.

In 2000, Enron was a globally established business. It was the golden child of corporate America. The company had an annual revenue of more than $100 billion. Enron was named 'America's most innovative company' by Fortune for six consecutive years, from 1996 to 2001. It was the seventh largest company in the United States, which has the largest economy in the world.[14] Enron was an energy trading and utility company during an era of deregulation in the 1980s and 1990s. It was more valuable than Microsoft, Bank of America and AT&T. But then, a few months later, Enron went bust. Boom! The executive team had used fraudulent accounting practices to hide debts and inflate profits. The company had been creative with its financial statement, one of the only areas in business where creativity isn't recommended. The term 'Enronomics' came to describe the innovative and fraudulent techniques a parent company deploys to distort economic reality.

At Enron, compensation, including bonuses, was based on the firm's stock price – with big bonuses for leadership teams. The company was unrealistic about what employees could achieve within a short timeframe. Complex systems can generate snowball effects, and Enron's accounting firm Arthur Andersen, which was one of the 'Big 5' accounting firms, also went down. The firm was found guilty of obstruction of justice for shredding documents and being complicit in the debacle. The Big 5 became the Big 4 (though Arthur Andersen's consulting arms still exist as Accenture). Just like that, thousands of employees' jobs and investors' savings were lost. Shareholders sued banks like Barclays Bank, JPMorgan Chase, Citigroup and others for $40 billion. Enron changed how Americans viewed the stock market. The Enron scandal resulted in a wave of new protective measures to improve corporate transparency, specifically, the Sarbanes-Oxley Act, which stipulates a board to oversee audit reports for public companies.[15]

The internet is a man-made complex system that can give rise to unexpected phenomena. At the time of writing, there are 5.3 billion internet users worldwide, which amounts to 65 per cent of the global population. One feature of complex systems is non-linearity. Simply put, the interaction between the components can lead to a disproportionate outcome when compared to the input. Small actions can have unexpected and drastic effects on the system's behaviour. The internet and social media – just like the world at large – are non-linear. Actions aren't additions but multiplications. In linear systems $1+1+1+1 = 4$ whereas 5.3 billion users' actions and interactions are non-linear and therefore every action can spark new reactions and feedback loops. The possibilities are endless. Consequently, we're unable to understand the system by examining individual actions. Complex systems show emergent behaviour, which arises from the interactions between parts of the system. We cannot predict behaviour from individual elements; complex systems need to be understood at a systems level. The system has the capacity for adaptation. Agents update their behaviour in response to feedback from other individuals and the collective system. It has a feedback loop, a mechanism to either deliver positive or negative feedback. Another important component of complex systems is their ability to evolve. Through independent actions and group interaction, the system is updated, creating new patterns at a system and individual level.

During the pandemic, a 20-year-old factory worker in Italy lost his job. He was from an immigrant Senegalese family living in Chivasso in Northern Italy. Like many of us, he started spending more time on TikTok during lockdown. And soon began posting content under the name Khaby Lame. Khaby was mostly making fun of silly and unnecessary life hacks. The videos were reactions to existing videos, without saying a single word. In the first month, he gained nine views and two subscribers. But during lockdown, Khaby's animated reactions won the hearts of millions of fans worldwide. He was on a mission to 'make people smile'. His videos were recorded on his phone with close to no production value. Unlike other creators focused on specific niches, with dedicated talent management and production teams, Khaby's funny, non-verbal videos transcended language and cultural borders. At present, Khaby is the most-followed creator on TikTok with more than 160 million followers and counting. He is now the face of Hugo Boss, responsible for launching football kits for Juventus and a judge on the TV show *Italia's Got Talent*. As the world becomes more interconnected, people can achieve international stardom overnight. But the fame can also fade just as fast.

In complex systems, one unit can disproportionately affect the whole, in a non-linear way. Social media and the rise of the creator economy are prime examples. Social media promised the democratization of voices, content and talent at an unprecedented scale. However, the promise hasn't materialized. Success in complex systems is random, explosive and disproportionate. On Twitch, 1 per cent of streamers earn more than half of all revenue.[16] The top 1 per cent of podcasts receive 99 per cent of downloads.[17] In contrast to the meteoric rise of Khaby, there are 50 million creators globally, but 96 per cent don't make enough money to reach the poverty line.[18] The same is true of films, books, footballers, musicians and many more cultural phenomena.

Such distribution seems extreme, but such variance can also create the conditions for social change.

Foucault and power relations

Now that we've explored the properties of complex systems – random, interconnected, emergent and non-linear – we need to understand the theory of power. What is power? How is power generated or distributed? Here we turn to the work of Michel Foucault.[19] In classical sociology, power was viewed as the exploitation of the working class by the ruling class. In the 20th century, Antonio Gramsci expanded this definition of power from physical and economic domination to cultural domination. An outspoken critic of Benito Mussolini and fascism, he was arrested and imprisoned for 11 years, where he wrote *The Prison Notebooks*.[20] Gramsci's central contribution was the notion of cultural hegemony, or the way power is established and reinforced through the ideas of the ruling class. Unlike previous definitions, power is expressed by the consent of the majority, not through physical force. The dominant ideology enters our collective consciousness and becomes 'common sense', further entrenching the status quo. Cultural hegemony is 'when an ideology becomes so normalized that it is difficult or even impossible to reflect on it'. The worldview of the dominant class becomes the accepted cultural norm. Modern examples include English being the de facto global language, the Americanization of everything, and maximizing shareholder value at the expense of society, consumers and employees. Power is nothing more than ideas and relationships.

Michel Foucault's idea of power was somewhat different. The traditional notion of power is physical or mental domination. However, Foucault stated that this is merely the failure of power. If a government cracks down on protests, this isn't the presence of power but the failure of power. A truly powerful government wouldn't need to exercise its authority. The most dominant form of power is invisible, subtle and pervasive. Foucault called this normalized power, which constructs values and norms that shape individual and group behaviour. Power isn't something that is only wielded by repressive governments – power is everywhere. Power relations exist in every aspect of life; they define the 'norm' and create the 'deviant'. Normalized power includes family, school and work relations. Power in Foucault's view is not just top-down, it is all-pervading. This power model is a perpetual struggle for normalization and resistance. It can be tempting to view social change through the prism of structures, systems, technologies and solutions. However, power relations can define the probability of social change. If we can understand the origins and structures of power, we will be able to create new opportunities for social change.

The social power map

If we accept the notion that power is everywhere then understanding, identifying and reshaping power relations is critical for social change. But how can we visualize the invisible? How can we make the implicit explicit? How can we turn theory into action? Challenging the status quo begins with mapping out power relations. Social power mapping is a useful way of visualizing complex systems and power dynamics. The more accurately we can define the status quo, including individuals, groups and institutions, the more probably the occurrence of social change.

1 **Define the status quo**

   Change is possible, but we need to be selective in where we apply our energy and resources. Defining the status quo can be a strong foundation for mapping power relations and commencing your journey to create social change.

2 **Power mapping**

   Creating social change is complex. Thinking about structures, processes, theories, problems and solutions is insufficient. To create meaningful social change, we have to understand how complex systems and networks operate.[21]

3 **Determine the relationships**

   This is the point in the process when things become more dynamic. Most traditional change plans focus on structures, not social networks or relationships. Addressing the interactive dimension of systems is what enables and disables social norms. We can't achieve social change by focusing on structural qualities only. The relationship between individuals and groups is equally important. Don't worry if the map gets messy.

4 **Develop first-mover actions**

   It's not easy riding a unicycle and juggling at the same time. Remember, systems are complex. There are so many different actions, scenarios and interventions we could tackle. But attempting to do everything is a fruitless battle. A more effective strategy is identifying a first move. This could be a group with more power, connections or needs. The best place to start is within your circle of influence. What's the one action you can take today?

ACTIVITY

1 **What is the status quo you are trying to change?**

  o What's the problem with the status quo?
  o What are you looking to change? Why?
  o What are you hoping to achieve?
  o What are the barriers to change?

2 **Map out the key players and the power relations between them**

  o Who are the key players?
  o Who are the main individuals?
  o Who are the main groups?
  o What are the main institutions?
  o Who else is involved?

Write down all the agents you can think of. It's important not to discount any groups at this point, even if you think they are oppositional or lack influence. The process works best when you map out the entire process and allow room for unknown unknowns. Remember the disproportionate impact of Black Swans? We can't afford to discount any players at this stage of the process. Once you've listed all the individuals, groups and institutions, it's time to visualize the map.

3 **Identify relationships**

  o Identify the connections between all actors.
  o Map out the flow of interaction in a visual way.
  o Analyse the power relationships, including positive and negative.

4 **What's the one action you can take today?**

What's the first action you can take within your circle of influence? Think of no more than one action that would influence decision-makers and involve more players in the process.

5 **Action plan**

You should now have an action plan with the following ingredients:

  o A clear definition of the status quo.
  o A map of key players and relational power-lines.
  o First-mover action for social change.

Your action plan doesn't need to be perfect. We are talking about a work-in-progress outline which you can refine through action, feedback and exploring the upcoming chapters. The main purpose is to articulate your thoughts and ideas into words that can eventually be shared with others.

Notes

1   Body Shop. Our story, nd. www.thebodyshop.com/en-au/about-us/our-story/a/a00002 (archived at https://perma.cc/D655-HZ2V)

2   T S Kuhn (2012) *The Structure of Scientific Revolutions*, 4th edn, University of Chicago Press, Chicago

3   S Sipihrī (2011) *Water's Footfall*, Omnidawn

4   J Galley. Stay-at-home mothers through the years, US Bureau of Labor Statistics, September 2014. www.bls.gov/opub/mlr/2014/beyond-bls/stay-at-home-mothers-through-the-years.htm (archived at https://perma.cc/V6R6-UVFK)

5   P Kivisto and J Leinonen. Representing race: Ongoing uncertainties about Finnish American racial identity, *Journal of American Ethnic History*, 2011, 31 (1), 11–33. doi.org/10.5406/jamerethnhist.31.1.0011 (archived at https://perma.cc/NY7L-B2VA)

6   A Brown. The changing categories the US census has used to measure race, Pew Research Center, 25 February 2020. www.pewresearch.org/short-reads/2020/02/25/the-changing-categories-the-u-s-has-used-to-measure-race/ (archived at https://perma.cc/7PKK-RNUG)

7   K Popper (2002) *The Logic of Scientific Discovery*, Routledge Classics, Abingdon

8   N N Taleb (2008) *The Black Swan*, Penguin Books, London

9   Old Song TV. [New song stage] A debut stage of shock and fear that everyone remembers! Seo Taiji and Boys – I Know: 1992 Scoop TV Entertainment, YouTube, 2020. www.youtube.com/watch?v=Zr-9NlWLr5g (archived at https://perma.cc/V539-7C42)

10 K Caulfield. BTS scores third no. 1 album on Billboard 200 chart with 'Map of the soul: Persona', Billboard, 21 April 2019. www.billboard.com/pro/bts-map-of-the-soul-persona-no-1-album-billboard-200-chart/ (archived at https://perma.cc/Q2TF-NGKY)

11 T Adams. K-everything: The rise and rise of Korean culture, *The Guardian*, 4 September 2022. www.theguardian.com/world/2022/sep/04/korea-culture-k-pop-music-film-tv-hallyu-v-and-a (archived at https://perma.cc/VE56-8KWS)

12 T Branigan. China's Great Famine: The true story, *The Guardian*, 1 January 2013. www.theguardian.com/world/2013/jan/01/china-great-famine-book-tombstone (archived at https://perma.cc/6S7D-XM6A)

13 D Cucinotta and M Vanelli. WHO declares Covid-19 a pandemic, *Acta Biomedica: Atenei Parmensis*, 2020, 91 (1), 157–60. doi.org/10.23750/abm. v91i1.9397 (archived at https://perma.cc/9R73-WEGK)

14 Fortune 500. A database of 50 years of FORTUNE's list of America's largest corporations, CNN Money, 2001. money.cnn.com/magazines/fortune/fortune500_archive/full/2001/ (archived at https://perma.cc/2RMS-PN99)

15 M Maurer. Arthur Andersen's legacy, 20 years after its demise, is complicated, *Wall Street Journal*, 31 August 2022. www.wsj.com/articles/arthur-andersens-legacy-20-years-after-its-demise-is-complicated-11661938200 (archived at https://perma.cc/4KCX-GUSM)

16 E Bentley and K Kim. Twitch streamer earnings increase for top gamers, data from Hack shows, *Wall Street Journal*, 9 October 2021. www.wsj.com/articles/twitch-streamer-earnings-increase-for-top-gamers-data-from-hack-shows-11633802185 (archived at https://perma.cc/D7WA-WRDD)

17 S Fischer. The podcast business is booming, but few are making money, Axios, 25 January 2021. www.axios.com/2021/01/25/podcast-business-booming-few-making-money (archived at https://perma.cc/WM2S-5CZH)

18 M Grothaus. 96.5 per cent of YouTube creators don't make above the US poverty line, Fast Company, 28 February 2018. www.fastcompany.com/40537244/96-5-of-youtube-creators-dont-make-above-the-u-s-poverty-line (archived at https://perma.cc/BAZ7-3RWW)

19 M Foucault (1975) *Discipline and Punish: The birth of the prison*, Random House, London

20 A Gramsci (1971) *Selections From The Prison Notebooks*, Lawrence and Wishart, London

21 A Tang. Power mapping and analysis, The Commons Social Change Library, nd. commonslibrary.org/guide-power-mapping-and-analysis/ (archived at https://perma.cc/JT2V-GVDL)

3

Craft your mission

In the 1960s Swedish scientists discovered that most people suffer from lactose intolerance. A student at the University of Lund, Rickard Öste, started to experiment with removing lactose from milk. After testing barley and rye, Öste invented oat milk, and in the 1990s, together with his brother Björn, he created his own brand – Oatly. Until 2012, Oatly was a small Swedish brand with 50 employees operating in a highly technical, uninteresting and niche category. But then, the board hired a young CEO who prioritized defining and articulating the company mission. Oatly positioned itself as an activist brand on a mission to challenge big dairy. If you want to turn your mission into a movement, you need a common enemy to rally against. For Oatly this was the Swedish dairy lobby and big food companies. The simplicity of the Oatly mission has produced an entirely new category and made plant-based milk mainstream.

A mission is something we might associate with Jesuits evangelizing about religion, James Bond defeating evil villains or the *USS Enterprise* exploring new worlds in *Star Trek*. But we don't have to discover a new planet to be on a mission. Missions can offer individuals and companies direction, inspiration and meaning. The automatic response when thinking about social change is to look outward, but the spark for social change begins with you. Change starts from within before it can manifest externally. The first person we can understand, support and transform – if necessary – is ourselves. That's not to say we should prioritize individual actions above collective wellbeing. On the contrary, our personal mission can and should serve a cause greater than ourselves.

The idea of dedicating our lives to a single mission can seem scary and confusing in equal measure. It sounds like a big commitment, especially if you're unsure where to start. The following chapter will guide you through how you can create or update your personal and business mission. Being intentional about how we allocate limited time, energy and resources can be a rare achievement in our busy world. A mission statement can convert your personal values and vision into positive social change.

Getting in the zone

Discovering your mission statement isn't about constructing an imaginary story. This isn't about becoming the next Superman or Wonder Woman, unless that's what you want. In contrast, mission statements are an act of introspection and self-reflection. The mission should be a distillation of who you are, what you stand for and your unique contribution to the world. Most people struggle to find headspace to tackle their daily to-do lists, let alone articulate and realize their mission. There are 1,440 minutes in a day. The average person will spend 26 years sleeping, 13 years working, 11 years staring at screens, 1 year on romance (if they are lucky) and 4.5 years eating. Our time on this planet is limited, but distractions are unlimited. Having a mission will allow you to channel your energy, talents and expertise into zones which you care about, and the world needs most. This isn't about being selfish. Sure, you will still have to make time for everyday activities like going grocery shopping, picking up the children from school and washing the dishes. But you also have the right to be intentional about your life. The opportunity cost of not designing our mission and desired impact is that we might end up spending most of our existence responding to the never-ending list of tasks, projects and jobs which fall outside our mission. We somehow subconsciously know when we're not working towards what brings us meaning, even if we haven't explicitly defined our mission: the feeling of intense dread and anxiety on Sundays before heading back to work; that gut feeling which tells us not to accept the new project or job offer; and the general malaise of coasting and not fulfilling our full potential.

The work of Mihaly Csikszentmihalyi and his book *Flow* brings rigour to the notion of having a personal mission.[1] The Hungarian went on a quest to discover the root causes of happiness and creativity. Csikszentmihalyi noticed that money only boosted happiness up to a certain point, before happiness began to plateau. If you are rich and miserable, more money won't make you happier.[2] As shown in Maslow's hierarchy of needs, once we have fulfilled our basic needs like food, clothing, shelter and financial stability we begin to search for greater meaning. Maslow called this self-actualization, where personal potential is realized. Nevertheless, there are people and communities with little to no material wealth who are happy and endeavour to make others around them happy. Conversely, there are people blessed with money, power and good looks who are unhappy and make others around them miserable.

A large proportion of entrepreneurs experience deep and prolonged sadness after selling their business, even when the valuation is a life-changing sum of money. After years, if not decades, of hustle, selling the company leaves an unfillable void. It represents the loss of meaning and personal identity. In comparison, Csikszentmihalyi spent time with artists, scientists and creatives and discovered that they found work meaningful, despite not expecting fame or fortune. His central conclusion was that happiness was an internal state of being. When observing artists, he noticed that they were more focused on the process than the end outcome. The motivation was intrinsic, and they entered a state of flow. This can only happen when we have control over our thoughts, behaviours and experiences.

Csikszentmihalyi defines flow as a state in which people are so immersed in an activity that nothing else matters, irrespective of the cost and for its own sake. There exists a distinction between pleasure and enjoyment. Although pleasure is an important part of the quality of life, eating a super-size pizza, drinking alcohol and spending hours on Netflix don't bring us happiness. In excess, pleasures can dull the mind and prevent us from escaping our comfort zone and achieving a state of flow. Enjoyment, on the other hand, derives from an internal feeling of accomplishment, momentum and impact. Enjoyment can be enduring; pleasure is fleeting. You might not get pleasure from going to the gym, but you might enjoy being healthy. You might find writing excruciating, but you enjoy sharing your ideas with the world. You might be scared to present to your wider team, but you enjoy learning new skills. In a flow state, our skills and the challenge match. External goals become immaterial. We create because it makes us happy.

The search for happiness

Most of us have experienced flow in our lifetime, when we become so immersed in an activity, we lose track of time and space. A flow state shouldn't be confused with finding something easy. It's not the same as binge-watching your favourite series on Netflix. Flow is a dance between your skills and the size of the challenge. The flow state is no different to playing a computer game. If the game is too easy, we'll get bored and stop concentrating. And if the game is too difficult, we might give up and switch off the console. Achieving a flow state is a delicate balance. The best moments aren't relaxing, they stretch our limits in a voluntary effort to experience or accomplish something meaningful. We all have the potential to spend more time in flow and less time being passive and indifferent. To achieve a state of flow, our goals need to be challenging but attainable. The challenge should be within our reach. Flow is the answer to a more flourishing life, stretching our abilities and reaffirming our mission. Our mission doesn't have to depend on external motivations. Our consciousness can determine our quality of life.

Csikszentmihalyi outlines eight components of achieving a flow state after interviewing surgeons, professors, assembly line workers, young mothers, retired people and teenagers from the USA, Korea, Japan, Thailand, European cultures and a Navajo reservation. There seems to be a shared human experience. Whether it was the elderly Koreans meditating or Japanese teenagers swarming in motorcycle gangs, the feeling of flow was almost identical:

- a task with a reasonable chance of completion
- clarity of goal and immediate feedback
- deep concentration and transformation of time (speeding up/slowing down)
- the experience is intrinsically rewarding
- a correspondence between challenge and skills
- effortlessness and ease
- no concern for the self but the sense of self emerges stronger after the flow
- a sense of control over the action

Finding meaning

Getting into flow sounds wonderful, but how can we discover our mission? Unless we identify the things we deeply care about, we cannot allocate attention to them. Viktor Frankl's main preoccupation was the quest for meaning. He was an Austrian psychoanalyst, which is like being a Soviet gymnast, Kenyan marathon runner or Jamaican sprinter. Unlike most modern academics, Frankl's experience as a Holocaust survivor was the basis for his theories. During World War II, Frankl spent three years at four different concentration camps: Theresienstadt, Auschwitz, Kaufering III and Türkheim. His father died of starvation. His mother and brother were murdered in the gas chambers and his pregnant wife Tilly died of typhus in Bergen-Belsen concentration camp. Frankl had endured immense pain and unimaginable inhumanity when he was liberated in 1945. Within nine days, Frankl wrote his most famous book, *Man's Search for Meaning*.[3] The book is split into two sections. The first section is about Frankl's experiences in concentration camps, and the second details the universal lessons he learned from the experience and introduces his new theory, called logotherapy. Until then, psychotherapy was built on the theories of fellow Austrians Sigmund Freud and Alfred Adler. Sigmund Freud, who is regarded as the father of modern psychology, argued that humans are driven by pleasure and repulsed by pain. Through this lens, pleasure is the driving force of human activity. This is called a will to pleasure. Alfred Adler contended that the desire for power is the motivational force in human behaviour. Through this lens, we are driven to overcome inferiority and therefore strive for superiority in three main areas: love, work and society. This is called a will to power. In the creation of logotherapy, Frankl took human psychology somewhere different to Freud and Adler, beyond the realms of primitive needs, desires and weaknesses. Frankl argued that humans are driven by the desire to find meaning and purpose. This is called a will to meaning. Through his experiences in concentration camps, Frankl realized that humans seek to find meaning even in the most miserable circumstances. It was not pleasure, success or power that motivated people but finding something to live or die for. Frankl himself lost his entire family during the holocaust but what kept him alive was his love for his wife – whom he was separated from – helping his fellow prisoners and reconstructing his book, which the prison guards had confiscated. Logotherapy identifies three ways of finding meaning in life:

1   Create something of importance. This could be writing a book, starting a new project or baking some bread.

2   Experience something wholeheartedly or have meaningful interactions. Like watching the sunrise, reading a book or spending time with friends.

3   Consider our attitude towards unavoidable suffering. This is a central insight in Frankl's work: we might not be able to control our circumstances, but we can control our response to the situation.

At the concentration camp, if you didn't listen to orders you would be killed. People couldn't control their environment. The only thing they had control over was their reaction. Between a stimulus and response there is a gap. In one of the darkest moments in modern history, Viktor Frankl discovered a ground-breaking insight. We don't always control what happens in life, but we can always control our reaction to the life events. Choosing our attitude to external events is the last of the human freedoms. In 1963, a young Stephen Hawking was diagnosed with amyotrophic lateral sclerosis (ALS) and given five years to live. The average life expectancy for ALS is only 14 months. Hawking could have easily chosen to give up on his dreams and ambitions. Instead, he selected the last of the human freedoms – choosing his attitude and response to the devastating news. Hawking went on to reshape our collective understanding of gravity, black holes and cosmology. He continued his work for 55 years with the incurable condition: possibly the longest-surviving ALS survivor. Hawking won the world's respect and changed society's perception of people with disabilities. None of this would have happened if the 21-year-old Stephen Hawking had accepted his fate. He would never have found his mission and would not have become one of the most influential scientists of the 20th and 21st centuries.

Humans are the only species that ask 'Why?' We are compelled to seek meaning and purpose. Even our closest ancestors, chimpanzees and bonobos, are not able to ask questions. Apes can recognize themselves in the mirror, learn sign language and make tools, but they can't ask questions. Our ability to ask questions is inextricably linked to our progress as a species. Dogs are curious about new stimuli: what is it? But they don't ask why it exists. We are the only species on the quest for meaning. The distinction between meaning and success is an important one. Finding meaning and crafting your mission is a creative endeavour. Success shouldn't be the primary motivation. Discovering your reason for being can make life more worthwhile. Happiness and success might be by-products of pursuing your mission. But they should not be the main objective. Not having a mission, explicit or implicit, can make life feel directionless. What makes life beautiful is that meaning looks and feels different for each person. We cannot compare or compete when it comes to meaning. Our mission, like our life experiences, personality, genetics and fingerprints, makes us unique. We can only find our mission through personal experience, social interaction and experimentation. In his later work, Frankl reflected that, once the struggle for survival had subsided, the question that emerged was: survival for what? It's time to discover your mission.

Your personal mission statement

1 **What are you passionate about? What do you enjoy doing?**
   What could you do for 5, 10 or 50 years without losing interest and fulfilment?

2 **What is your unique gift to the world? What is your area of expertise?**
   If you're unsure about your unique gift and expertise ask three of your friends, family or network.

3 **Who are you serving?**
   Your mission isn't about you. It's about sharing your gifts with the wider world. The aim is to serve others. But, at the same time, the more we serve others the more we gain. This is the essence of value creation.

If you're still not sure what your passion and expertise are you can begin by finding role models that inspire you. The purpose isn't to copy others but to acquire a taste and develop a compass of what 'good' looks like for you. You can create a mood board that will eventually inform your personal mission statement.

Company mission

In the business world, mission statements were in vogue in the 1980s and 1990s thanks to Peter Drucker and fellow management consultants. What was once ground-breaking has become standard business practice. Almost all Fortune 500 companies have a public-facing mission statement. It has become a corporate rite of passage. Words like mission, vision, purpose and values are often used interchangeably in business communications. I have no interest in exploring the semantics. As controversial as it sounds, they all serve the same purpose. Different companies use different terms – depending on the agency or consultancy they collaborate with – to communicate their mission. The essence of a mission statement includes: why do you exist as a company? What makes you unique? And how does it serve others? The benefits of mission statements are well documented. A clear company position with guiding principles can focus efforts on a shared strategic direction. Everyone on the boat can row towards the same destination. Mission statements can align stakeholders with different needs and interests: employees, customers, investors and society at large, building momentum and movement towards a more desirable future. Effective mission statements combine inspiration with aspiration. Thinking back to flow states, our collective skills match the size of the challenge. A compelling mission can increase employee engagement and improve overall business performance. Companies with strong mission statements are more likely to outperform competitors – similar to having a website, its presence isn't a gain but its absence is a loss. In summary, company mission statements can engender stronger business performance, employee engagement and anti-fragility. Profitability isn't an exciting enough mission for most people (except shareholders, who are incentivized accordingly). Business performance should be a by-product of the value and benefit we deliver to the world. Here we should unpack the meaning of the word 'company'. A company is an organization formed by a collective of individuals with a common purpose, whereas a business refers to any profit-generating organization. Sometimes, it can be easy to forget the difference. In America, companies have the same rights as a natural person: free speech, free religion, equal protection and property rights. Companies seek missions, businesses seek profits.

What's not to love about company mission statements? Well, most are a bunch of generic buzzwords and grandiose platitudes but lack substance. Competitors in the same industry – and companies in different categories – arrive at similar conclusions and declarations. It ends up being a C-suite game of purpose bingo, facilitated by the same thought leaders their competitors used to create a mission statement. There's very little differentiation. No key to success ('secret sauce'). A true mission statement should reflect the product, service and ideas your company shares with the world. Missions don't need to be created; they already exist, we simply need to capture and articulate them. The objective shouldn't be to share some fancy words and pictures using a press release. We simply need to articulate our internal mission to the outside world. Missions aren't manufactured; they are discovered, cultivated and communicated. A mission statement is the distillation of a company's intentions and actions. The journey begins with employees. It is impossible to create a genuine mission statement without employee input and contribution. Company employees are the ultimate acid test for mission statements. You will know straight away if the mission rings true based on employees' instinctive reactions. The greatest breakthroughs happen when employees feel connected to the company's mission. And the biggest issues arise when internal teams don't feel aligned with the company's directions. The disconnect results in a deterioration in employee morale and business performance.

Getting it wrong

Getting a mission statement wrong can cause more harm than good, especially if your mission isn't grounded in the realities of the product or service. The mission and your actions become out of sync. Like break-dancing to classical music or karaoke singing at an annual board meeting. When a company's statements are incompatible with its actions, it loses the trust of customers, employees, investors and the public. Mission statements might have been the fashionable thing to do in the 1980s, a new and pioneering way to stay ahead of the competition and get featured in business journals. In today's fast-moving world, mission statements are a tool for accountability. There's nowhere to hide. To paraphrase Ice Cube: you have to check yourself before you wreck yourself. Remember Enron? Its values were communication, respect, integrity and excellence. Shell's mission statement is to power progress together by providing more and cleaner energy solutions, despite being one of the biggest climate change polluters. Phillip Morris's mission statement is to deliver a smoke-free future and transform for good, despite being the world's largest tobacco company. People are more aware than ever before. Communication without action is counterproductive to building trust and a long-term relationship with communities. For International Women's Day, most companies were posting on Twitter (now known as X) their appreciation of women in their business. An infinite feed of proclamations supporting and advocating their workforce. Francesca Lawson and Ali Fensome decided to expose the hypocrisy by creating a bot that highlighted the companies' gender pay gap.[4] The bot used publicly available information from a government database to record differences in pay between men and women in UK companies. When one of those companies tweeted about International Women's Day, the bot re-tweeted them with the data on their gender pay gap. As information becomes more accessible, companies will have no choice but to be transparent.

Many younger employees refuse to work at companies whose behaviour doesn't reflect their mission. Employee activism is fast becoming one of the defining features of the workplace. This is when employees speak up against their company on issues that impact workers, customers, the environment or society at large. A recent survey by Paul Polman shows that nearly half of Millennials and Gen-Z have resigned from a position because the values of the company did not align with their own values.[5] Unlike previous generations, Gen-Z is pushing back on the traditional 9 to 5 culture and exploring multiple income streams. The motivation is to challenge capitalism and maintain a healthy work–life balance. Climbing the corporate ladder is no longer aspirational. Polman's employee barometer report identifies three ways that companies can start to engage the future workforce. First, companies need to show greater ambition and take steps to be less bad. Second, business leaders need to do a better job of communicating the action being taken. Finally, employees should be empowered to help you on the journey. Young people want to be active participants in creating positive social change. Companies' commitment to climate and social justice will attract not only consumers but employees too. Leaders unable to transform their business will lose out on the best and brightest talent – including partners and suppliers – which will directly impact business results. A meaningful mission statement cannot be a top-down initiative from leadership.

Getting it right

A powerful mission articulates a shared vision and motivates employees. The two begin to build a symbiotic relationship. But, despite the proliferation of mission statements, less than a third of employees feel connected to their company's purpose.[6] A sorry situation, since companies are underperforming and employees feel underappreciated. This is a missed opportunity. The purely transactional relationship of exchanging hours at work in exchange for cash is redundant. All things being equal, employees value purpose more than traditional incentives like salary and promotions. Not that workers don't expect a fair payment, they do, but that is only the minimum requirement. People want meaning from work; after all, we're spending one-third of our lives there. A great purpose should be built around the needs of your customers and wider society. Employees are the living embodiment of the relationship between the company and its customers. A mission statement can be co-created with your employees, customers and community. It doesn't need to be a top-down management initiative which doesn't connect with the rest of the company. If you want to build an effective mission statement, build it with those who are closest to the customer, or, better yet, with the final customer. Your mission should be easily memorable and actionable for all members of the company. Can the receptionist remember the mission? How about the delivery driver? Or the customer service representative? This is the litmus test of a mission statement.

A good place to start is by asking employees, customers and even strangers why the company exists. What makes the company unique? Who do we serve? Don't focus on stats, this is a qualitative exercise. Encourage, collect and collate as many personal stories, anecdotes and experiences from employees and customers as possible. This is a much better reflection of the company's will to meaning than the views of the leadership. At this beginning stage, we want to gather as much information as possible. Afterwards, you should allocate a group to make sense of and create themes from all the content, before facilitating a creative session to explore the themes and discuss ideas. A major consideration, especially in bigger companies, is avoiding 'death by committee'. Too many chefs in the kitchen make for an overcooked soup. The key is to gain input at the right moment while keeping everyone informed along the journey. But if everyone is involved in every aspect, it will culminate in a Frankenstein mission statement which serves to appease all parties, and delight none. Blandness is the enemy of creative participation. You have to be willing to make a stand and share what makes the company unique. If another company can create the same mission and it still rings true, then the statement is too generic. The message needs to be simple, memorable and single-minded. We all live busy lives and attention is one of the scarcest commodities. The mission statement should cut through the noise.

Crafting a mission statement is only the beginning of the journey. The hard work begins once you've defined the company's reason to exist. Now you need to eat, sleep and breathe it. A mission statement is only as valuable as our collective ability to realize it. If customers see that your actions are in contradiction to your words and if your employees are unable to realize the mission due to internal blockers it will create resentment. The company has to allocate the necessary time, attention and resources to make sure the mission is being realized. If you are not investing in your mission, then it's nothing more than some words on a PDF document. The emphasis and prioritization of the mission starts with leadership. The leadership team have to set an example through their actions and priorities. Will they make tough decisions informed by the guiding mission? Once the C-suite is playing an active role in realizing the mission, more work needs to be done socializing the mission to busy middle management and the rest of the business. This cannot be a one-time announcement. The message needs to be repeated – positive actions celebrated, and harmful behaviour reprimanded – to turn beliefs into behaviour. Your mission is a living and breathing organism. It should be nurtured, reviewed and updated accordingly. A company mission isn't static. It can push leadership, employees, investors and customers to do better. It can be a coach that stretches ambitions and capabilities. If you've ever watched the film *Rocky*, a mission is a bit like Mickey, who was the boxer Rocky's coach. He would push Rocky beyond his comfort zone, motivate him to keep running when he was out of breath, chase chickens and keep practising his jab. There was always a healthy balance between where Rocky was (contender) and where he wanted to be in the future (world champion). Crucially, Mickey wanted to make sure that Rocky could take care of himself outside of the ring (beyond business). Companies and people are no different.

IKEA

Ingvar Kamprad grew up in poverty on a small farm in rural Sweden. He started selling matches by the time he was 5 before upgrading to selling fish. When he was 17, Kamprad started IKEA on his family farm – selling pens, wallets and nylon stockings. He then focused on selling pens, but there wasn't enough demand. The venture wasn't profitable. Towards the end of the 1940s, IKEA started experimenting with selling furniture. Unlike other manufacturers, Kamprad sought to purchase the most affordable furniture on the market, without compromising on quality. IKEA managed to maintain a low overhead thanks to Ingvar's family providing free labour and storage. In the mid-20th century, furniture was an expensive commodity, the pursuit of a privileged few. And, even then, most families kept furniture for a lifetime and passed it down to future generations. Yet Kamprad's frugal upbringing offered him a unique insight into customers compared to the rest of the furniture industry. The ordinary people, like the families, farmers and small businesses he grew up with – and sold matches and fish to – were careful with how they spent their money. Most couldn't afford the luxury of buying expensive furniture. IKEA offered 'your dream home at a dream price'. This was the IKEA mission. The company instigated all sorts of innovations, like a catalogue with text and images, and there was a showroom for customers to view the items before making a purchase. Kamprad gave each piece of furniture a special name because his dyslexia didn't allow him to recall names. Beyond question, the most revolutionary invention was the IKEA flatpacks. It could be argued the invention of the flatpack, more than anything else, transformed the fortunes of the emerging retailer. IKEA's first employee, Gillis Lundgren, accidentally invented the concept after struggling to fit a table into his car and realizing the best option would be to remove the legs. Flatpacking allowed IKEA to increase the volume of sales and reduce the cost. Before flatpacks, shoppers had to go into the store, select the product and wait many weeks or months for delivery. IKEA allowed customers to pick up the furniture directly from the factory, saving labour time required assembling products, allowing more stock to be stored in the warehouse and eliminating delivery costs. Mission accomplished!

Just as things were looking promising for IKEA, the Swedish Federation of Wood and Furniture Industry managed to persuade loggers to cut all business interactions with the company. Furniture manufacturers were unable to compete with the company's low prices. IKEA didn't have a business without wood. It was like being a bakery without access to flour. Most business owners would have called it quits, but not Ingvar Kamprad. He managed to source wood from communist Poland – with significant cost savings. The IKEA story is well told in business circles. Perhaps an element less well known is that, during IKEA's international expansion in the 1970s, Ingvar Kamprad published his vision and ideology in *The Testament of a Furniture Dealer*.[7] The manifesto begins with a clear mission statement: 'To create a better everyday life for the many people'. Kamprad stated that IKEA has decided to side with the many. Central to the manifesto was the idea of 'democratic design' – creating furniture for the many, not the few. The letter includes nine principles to ensure IKEA remains true to its mission at crucial moments in the company's history. The lesson here is that reinforcing and updating missions is more critical than creating them. Kamprad emphasized the importance of frugality of course. He viewed expensive solutions as a sign of mediocrity. Equally, he valued the power of simplicity, citing over-planning as the most common cause of corporate death.

Most of all, Kamprad embodied the IKEA mission. He lived a frugal existence, re-using his teabags, driving an old Volvo car and opting to fly economy class despite being worth $58.7 billion. This isn't an endorsement, but simply an example of living and breathing the company's mission. IKEA has become the largest furniture retailer in the world. The company is on a mission to be climate-positive by 2030 (in a quest to save money on energy of course). What people don't know is that IKEA is the third largest charity in the world. Critics say this is a tax avoidance loophole since it makes billions in profit tax-free. Either way, it would be congruent with the company mission.

Oatly

As mentioned earlier, in the 1960s Swedish scientists discovered that most people suffer from lactose intolerance. Experts estimate that about 68 per cent of the world's population has lactose malabsorption.[8] A student at the University of Lund, Rickard Öste, was fascinated by this topic and started to experiment with removing lactose from milk. After testing barley and rye, Öste invented oat milk. Oat milk was mainly for people with allergies and lactose intolerance. It is more sustainable, since oat milk requires less water than almond milk and produces less CO_2 than cow's milk. Initially, the company supplied oat milk to bigger food companies but there wasn't enough interest or demand. In the 2000s it created its own brand. It was named Oatly.

Until 2012, Oatly was a small Swedish brand with 50 employees operating in a highly technical, uninteresting and niche category. The company was built by scientists and developed a corporate image and way of doing things along the way. But then, the board hired a young CEO with an entrepreneurial background. His name was Toni Petersson, and he had no experience or background in the food industry. The first strategic focus for Toni was defining and articulating Oatly's mission and reason for existence. A company is nothing more than a collection of people coming together to further a shared mission. There had to be a reason for people to go to work when it's cold and raining (which is often the case in Sweden). Toni placed sustainability at the heart of the strategy. The new Oatly mission became the centrepiece of all decisions and the foundation for all future actions. The mission was bigger than the brand and alternative milk category. It was about responding to wider societal change. The food industry was the primary cause of deforestation. More than 15 per cent of CO_2 emissions come from animal products including milk. And 38 per cent of the world's land was being used for agriculture. Oatly positioned itself as an activist brand on a mission to challenge big dairy. It went from a non-dairy alternative to a nutritional health company. The mission was to produce and deliver oat-based products that have high nutritional value and low environmental impact.

But how can you make a niche movement desirable? Toni Petersson hired John Schoolcraft as the Global Chief Creative Officer. John quickly set up the Oatly Department of Mind Control. The team were obsessed with building a cool company culture and shifting mindsets from a boring food processing company to a fun lifestyle brand, living proof that defining your mission and building a movement doesn't have to be boring. It was a strategy built around a single diagram which has influenced all marketing decisions since. Schoolcraft divided the business world into two camps. The first was 'good' and 'evil' – you're either serving the world or you're damaging it. The second was companies that are 'scared sh*tless' and those that are 'f*cking fearless'.[9] Schoolcraft contended that 90 per cent of companies are too scared to do any work which is creative or memorable because of fears of how the CEO, shareholders, competitors and media would react.

Oatly differentiated itself by doing good and being fearless. There would be no way for Oatly to grow an unknown category – where most people haven't even tried oat milk – if it produced unmemorable marketing campaigns. Oatly needed to punch through the noise and get noticed. In the early days, the department cajoled the CEO, Toni Petersson, to sing 'Wow, no cow' in the middle of an oat field while playing an eclectic keyboard and doing cooking challenges with his mum. All of this made Oatly feel less like a faceless corporation and more like a collection of real people. Oatly built an emotional connection which was unthinkable in the food and drinks industry. The brand understood that oat milk is not inherently interesting, so it attempted to enter and be part of people's everyday lives. It was about being more human, real and relatable. Oatly found its voice, and this helped to amplify the mission in interesting and entertaining ways. Early in this process, to create the capacity and internal change required, Schoolcraft produced a wooden book called 'Change' – every single employee got a copy – outlining the new mission. But, as shared earlier, words and documents are not enough. It is actions, not words, which expedite change. Oatly revealed new packaging which demonstrated the new direction to employees more than any words could, especially in a company full of logical academics and scientists.

The greatest catalyst for the Oatly mission was getting sued by the Swedish dairy lobby. If this happened to most 'scared sh*tless' companies, they would back down and publish a public apology to prevent any further damage. But since Oatly is 'f*cking fearless' the company published the full 172-page lawsuit on their website, sharing it with the public. It became a David vs Goliath story, and little-known Oatly started grabbing all the headlines. The brand even started taking full-page ads explaining why they've been sued. Oatly went from niche to mainstream because of the lawsuit. The company tapped into the challenger brand mentality. If you want to turn your mission into a movement, you need a common enemy to rally against. For Oatly this was the Swedish dairy lobby and big food companies. Challenger brands gain their energy and resources from being against the establishment. What makes the Oatly story fascinating is that the product hasn't changed. The plant-based company has simply upgraded its mission and followed through with actions. The simplicity of the Oatly mission has produced an entirely new category and made plant-based milk mainstream. Oatly has a 44 per cent to 76 per cent lower climate impact than comparable cow's milk.[10] It was one of the first companies to add a carbon footprint to its products, inspiring others to follow suit. The company has faced criticisms following its global expansion. It is now part-owned by Blackstone with investors including Oprah Winfrey and Jay-Z. What cannot be denied is Oatly's ability to create new norms through its mission, creative direction and human touch.

Fridays for Future

The Fridays for Future movement started in the summer of 2018 when a 15-year-old Greta Thunberg decided to skip school and protest outside the Swedish Riksdag (parliament) holding a placard reading *Skolstrejk för klimatet* (School strike for climate). Greta was demanding urgent action on the climate crisis. In the beginning, Greta was a solo protester holding a cardboard sign outside the giant stones of the Swedish parliament. At first glance, the odds of making an impact were close to none. Yet the size of the challenge didn't discourage Greta. She missed school for almost three weeks ahead of the Swedish elections. In Sweden, missing school was against the law, but Greta was on a mission, and nothing would stop her. Eventually, she was joined by friends, family and fellow school strikers. People started to notice and started talking to her and showing support. Media outlets started to interview her to understand why she was doing this. Greta was able to share her mission around the world. Momentum gathered, and soon enough 20 young people were protesting, and then 100. After the Swedish elections, Greta and her fellow students went back to school. However, they continued to miss class on Fridays to protest. This became the Fridays for Future movement. They created the hashtag #FridaysForFuture and encouraged other young people all over the world to join them.[11] In a famous speech at UN Climate Action Summit Greta said: 'I should be back at school… How dare you. You have stolen my dreams and my childhood with your empty words.' The Fridays for Future movement gained traction because Greta was leading through her actions, not words. She was tapping into the collective anxieties of an entire generation that felt older generations were ruining their future and not taking the climate crisis seriously enough. The movement has a clear mission to make those in power take climate change seriously and act accordingly. Students from all around the world are fighting for a more sustainable future and against incapable global leadership.

The Fridays for Future movement has mobilized more than 3.8 million people globally across 3,800 cities.[12] Young people are demanding climate justice from Oranjestad to Kabul. It is the biggest climate protest in world history, and has taken place in 185 countries. Mass movements build awareness, change public perception and create new behaviours. According to a study by the Swiss Federal Institute of Technology Lausanne (EPFL), almost a third of Swiss people changed their daily habits because of Fridays for Future climate strikes.[13] The changes were most prominent in transportation, buying and recycling habits. It shows that collective action has a direct impact on society. And to think it all started with a 15-year-old girl holding a placard outside the Swedish parliament. It can be easy to view Greta Thunberg and the Fridays for Future protests as an inevitable development. But going back to Black Swans and the work of Nassim Taleb, the movement seems inevitable only in hindsight. At the time, Greta's protests seemed futile and inconsequential.

ACTIVITY

1 **What's your vision for the future?**

   o IKEA wanted to make furniture more accessible.

   o Oatly had a vision for a more sustainable milk alternative.

   o Fridays For Future demanded better climate leadership.

2 **Who are you fighting against?**

   o IKEA is against expensive furniture.

   o Oatly challenged the dairy industry.

   o Fridays For Futures is fighting against climate change.

3 **What is your unique gift to the world**

   o IKEA championed democratic design for the many, not the few.

   o Oatly is more human (less corporate) than other food companies.

   o Fridays for Future is about youth participation and global solidarity.

Combining your vision for the future with who you are fighting against and your secret sauce will generate your mission statement, a monumental step in turning your purpose into business and social impact.

Notes

1 M Csikszentmihalyi (1990) *Flow: The psychology of optimal experience*, Harper and Row, New York

2 M A Killingsworth, D Kahneman and B Mellers. Income and emotional well-being: A conflict resolved, *Proceedings of the National Academy of Sciences of the United States of America*, 2023, 120 (10), e2208661120. www.pnas.org/doi/10.1073/pnas.2208661120 (archived at https://perma.cc/MSJ4-393C)

3 V E Frankl and H Lasch (1962) *Man's Search For Meaning: An introduction to logotherapy*, Hodder and Stoughton, London

4 C Colvin. How one bot's crusade to expose the UK gender pay gap went viral, HR Dive, 7 March 2023. www.hrdive.com/news/gender-pay-gap-bot-twitter-2023/644402/ (archived at https://perma.cc/UH9U-VP77)

5 P Polman. *Net Positive Employee Barometer: From quiet quitting to conscious quitting*, Paul Polman, February 2023. www.paulpolman.com/wp-content/uploads/2023/02/MC_Paul-Polman_Net-Positive-Employee-Barometer_Final_web.pdf (archived at https://perma.cc/EZ8S-7VNJ)

6 S Blount and P Leinwand. Why are we here? *Harvard Business Review*, November 2019. hbr.org/2019/11/why-are-we-here (archived at https://perma.cc/9VM9-SHFL)

7 I Kamprad. *The Testament of a Furniture Dealer Including a Little IKEA Dictionary*, IKEA, 1976/2018. www.inter.ikea.com/-/media/interikea/igi/financial-reports/english_the_testament_of_a_dealer_2018.pdf (archived at https://perma.cc/6VYE-TMZE)

8 C L Storhaug, S K Fosse and L T Fadnes. Country, regional, and global estimates for lactose malabsorption in adults: A systematic review and meta-analysis, *The Lancet Gastroenterology and Hepatology*, 2017, 2 (10), 738–46. doi.org/10.1016/s2468-1253(17)30154-1 (archived at https://perma.cc/GFC7-7LXY)

9 Slush. John Schoolcraft of Oatly on how to crack consumer marketing without a marketing team, YouTube, 2019. www.youtube.com/watch?v=YK0ez-pF5Q8 (archived at https://perma.cc/2TR7-Z9R9)

10 Oatly. Product climate footprint explained, Oatly, nd. www.oatly.com/en-gb/ oatly-who/sustainability-plan/climate-footprint-product-label (archived at https://perma.cc/ANU2-3ACZ)

11 Fridays for Future. Who we are, Fridays for Future, nd. fridaysforfuture.org/ what-we-do/who-we-are (archived at https://perma.cc/TGN6-27N4)

12 Fridays for Future. Strike statistics: List of countries, Fridays for Future, nd. fridaysforfuture.org/what-we-do/strike-statistics/list-of-countries (archived at https://perma.cc/TNA6-XXUM)

13 L Fritz et al. Perceived impacts of the Fridays for Future climate movement on environmental concern and behaviour in Switzerland, 2023, *Sustainability Science*, 18, 2219–44. doi.org/10.1007/s11625-023-01348-7 (archived at https://perma.cc/952V-ATD2)

4

Find your community

Humans are inherently social beings. We are wired to connect with other people; natural selection prefers humans with a stronger propensity to look after family members and collaborate in groups. From an evolutionary perspective, we have relied on cooperation to survive and thrive. There's safety in numbers, whether you are a human, a herring or a hyena. The human brain is designed to form and maintain relationships with others. Many of our conscious and subconscious decisions are driven by the primary need to belong. We have designed human civilization around the need to belong. In most cultures, the family is the main unit where early socialization happens. Afterwards, schools encourage children to make friends and learn in groups. Many of us end up working for a company, which is an association of people working towards a shared mission. Along the journey, we might find a partner, marry and form our own family. The desire to belong is universal across all human cultures. It is a fundamental human motivation which can explain much of our actions and hidden preferences.

Conversely, social exclusion harms our mental and physical health. Loneliness can be as damaging to health as smoking 15 cigarettes per day.[1] And people who experience social isolation have a 32 per cent higher risk of early death.[2] Scientists using MRI scans have proven that the pain of social rejection is not much different from physical injury.[3] Anyone who has been picked last in sports at school or dumped by a romantic partner would know the feeling. In one experiment people who recently experienced an unwanted break-up were asked to view a photograph of their ex-partner while they re-lived being rejected – a brutal experiment, if you ask me. The research discovered that powerful social rejection activated the same brain regions as physical pain. No wonder we use the term 'broken heart'.

Social rejection causes several emotional and cognitive consequences and an increase in anger, anxiety, depression, jealousy and sadness. The emotions are as strong, even when we are rejected by people we don't like. African American students experienced the same pain of rejection when they were told that the people rejecting them were members of the Ku Klux Klan. In another study, participants were paid money when they were rejected, but the payments didn't reduce the pain of social exclusion.[4] All of this points to an undisputable truth: human beings crave social acceptance, whether we acknowledge it or not. In the most extreme scenario, an analysis of 177 mass shooters in the US has identified social isolation as the most important external indicator leading up to the attacks.[5] Likewise, the UN has concluded that social exclusion fuels global terrorism. Social exclusion can promote the radicalization of individuals.[6]

Why do humans want to belong so badly? Our wellbeing is dependent on our connection with others. This isn't a personal choice but a biological reality. A lonely human being would not have survived six million years of evolution. We have relied on the support and protection of the group for survival. Modern life and developments in technology afford us the ability to live a solitary existence. But natural selection makes loneliness a painful and unhappy experience. Historically, social rejection from the wider group was a near-certain death sentence. You would be eaten by wolves, attacked by competing tribes or collapse from malnutrition. In most modern societies social rejection is no longer a matter of life or death, but the physiological response associated with rejection remains unchanged. The need to be accepted, belong and be part of a community is buried deep inside our biology. We are happier and healthier when part of a community. We thrive when we feel seen and accepted. Building a community has been humankind's most effective tool for collective progress.

Early adopters

Finding your community is critical to creating and accelerating social change. Visionary leaders can see beyond the status quo, but such ideas can only be actualized through collective effort. How do ideas spread? The diffusion of innovation theory attempts to answer this question. The theory was first invented by E M Rogers after observing how farmers in rural communities were adopting hybrid corn seeds, new tools and farming techniques.[7] At first glance, the model seems irrelevant for a book focused on using marketing to create social change. But the theory, much like its origins in Iowan farming practices, helps to explain how innovation goes from niche interest to mass appeal. Every norm, idea and technology we take for granted today started life on the periphery, not the mainstream.

Coffee was used by Sufi mystics to aid concentration and stay awake all night so they could chant the name of God. More than 500 years later the beverage is enjoyed by hipsters in Shoreditch, Williamsburg and Nyhavn. Coffee is the world's most popular drink – with more than two billion cups consumed every day. The caffeinated stimulant maintains workforce productivity and upholds global capitalism. Like most innovations, coffee started on the edge of conventional society. Hip-hop was started at a block party in the Bronx. The music started to spread through word of mouth and mixtapes distributed by local DJs like Grandmaster Flash and DJ Kool Herc and shared across different communities. Before long, hip-hop culture was embraced by middle-class America, producing a multi-billion-dollar industry. Personal computers were almost exclusively used by technical scientists, mathematicians and engineers. When the machines became more user-friendly, computers gained mass adoption. Similarly, your objective is to get your mission to connect with a small number of die-hard advocates who will help you spread the message as quickly and widely as possible.

The diffusion of innovation theory has five main stages of adoption. The first group are the innovators, who love taking risks and experimenting. Innovators are not afraid of getting things wrong. While only 2.5 per cent of the population, they have a disproportionate impact on the emergence and collapse of new ideas since they are the first group to experience them. The second group are the early adopters, who are opinion leaders and trend-setters. They feel comfortable with change and adopting new ideas but need to understand how to get started. Early adopters are 13.5 per cent of the population. Then we have the early majority (34 per cent), late majority (34 per cent) and the laggards (16 per cent).[8]

New ideas follow a similar pattern of adoption. It would be a waste of time if you allocated the same level of resources to communicating your mission with all groups concurrently. Attempting to engage everyone with your mission would be a fruitless activity. You stand a better chance by following the innovation curve. Begin with innovators and early adopters. These groups are more receptive to new ideas, even if the mission is still a work in progress and you haven't figured everything out yet. In truth, if your innovation worked perfectly, they might not be interested. Early adopters are more open to experimentation and would go out of their way to adopt new norms and behaviours – even if it means exerting some extra effort. They gain their sense of identity from being different and rebelling against mainstream culture. When PayPal first started, the company focused all efforts on eBay super sellers. This was the first and most important group they could communicate with. The founders of Airbnb started by renting out their own apartment to get the ball rolling. Spotify started with influential music bloggers in Sweden who loved the experience. When you have launched or updated your mission, it pays to focus finite resources on a niche audience. Unless you have an unlimited budget, employees and time – and even then – going mass won't bring you closer to your mission. Moreover, the speed of adoption is faster than at any other point in history. We live in a more interconnected world. In the Middle Ages, it might have taken 300 years for a trend to move from one continent to another. Now the same process can happen within minutes.

The rate of adoption is speeding up. It took more than 30 years for electricity to reach a 10 per cent adoption rate in America. But it took the internet five years to reach the same penetration rate. The main lesson is to take your time and work your way through the different stages of adoption. The process is like a small snowball that turns into a giant avalanche as it gains more mass and surface area. Focusing your mission on the people, groups and organizations most aligned with your mission will build some early momentum which will then expand into mainstream audiences. Where would you like to start your mission?

Marketing to tribes

For centuries, the relationship between corporations and people was purely transactional. Companies would produce and promote a product that customers would purchase and consume. Under this arrangement, companies had complete control of the message and consumers had no way to share their ideas. The relationship was top-down and unilateral. However, the emergence of social media has reversed the balance of power. Today, it's ordinary people, not companies, who are dictating how they engage with brands. A brand is no longer what companies tell people, but instead what people tell their friends. That's why more organizations are investing in building communities.

For a long time, demographic information (such as age, gender and location) was the only way companies could segment their audience. Today that is no longer the case. The wealth of consumer data now available means brands can layer attitudinal and behavioural insights on top of demographic data to paint a far richer, more nuanced picture of real people. At the same time, a decline in globalization has given birth to a new social order. The world is no longer a global village, but a theatre of disparate tribes. The digital age has enabled the creation of modern tribes, united by shared passion points, rather than age or location. Unlike the punks, hippies and goths of yesteryear, these new tribal allegiances are invisible. Modern tribes inhabit a virtual multiverse on TikTok, Reddit, Twitch and Discord. Traditional advertising is a prime example of mass marketing in an increasingly fragmented world. Many business and marketing leaders exclaim: 'We need to connect with Gen-Z.' The problem is that Gen-Z is the largest and most diverse generation globally. We're talking about more than two billion people. There's as much diversity within generations as there is between them. To think otherwise strips people of individual agency. For example, Donald Trump and Barack Obama are both Baby Boomers. Jay-Z and Elon Musk are both a part of Generation X. Lionel Messi and Mark Zuckerberg are both Millennials. And Greta Thunberg and Kylie Jenner are both a part of Gen-Z. As you can see, age alone is a poor determinant of individual identity or needs. We live in a post-demographic world, where patterns of behaviour can no longer be predicated by statistics. Therefore, we need to move away from traditional demographic segments towards tribes: individuals gathered around a shared passion.

The same logic applies to marketing for social change. Connecting with people with shared values, interests and passions is more effective and enjoyable than attempting to reach everyone. Historically, connecting with people, communities and activities was restricted by geographic proximity. Those living in rural areas had less choice than those living in big cities. But the notion of geographic proximity has collapsed. Niche interests have developed global fandoms thanks to the internet. There are millions of sub-communities covering anything you can imagine. Reddit is perhaps the greatest example of online communities united by peculiar interests. Subreddits include communities dedicated to r/rarelobsters, r/jazznoir and r/showerthoughts. On the face of it, these communities feel small and unsustainable, but if we reflect on the global population and variety of different people, personalities and cultures there's something for everyone.

When we think about our mission, it can be tempting to attempt to change everything at once. Despite noble intentions, such a strategy can end up being counterproductive. Beginning with a small number of advocates who are passionate about the mission will generate more impact than going mass market. The biggest challenge to new ideas, projects and movements is the entrenchment of the status quo and people's subconscious resistance to change. Building momentum with a small but highly engaged tribe can be a powerful way to build social proof and create early momentum. If you're going to the gym for the first time, it might make sense to start with the 10kg weights and work your way up. If you're going to a networking event it might be wise to start the evening reconnecting with people you already know. And if you want to disrupt an industry, you will launch a start-up with people that believe in the same idea. To create change, we don't need perfect conditions. We don't even need to get everyone to believe in our mission. We simply need to find and collaborate with a minimum number of people equally as passionate about the cause. Energy is more transformative than numbers. In fact, having too many people involved can be counterproductive to building a movement, especially in the early stages when decisions need to be made. It's better to have an agile speedboat than a giant shipping container. You can build and actualize the mission at speed, without tonnes of cargo weighing you down.

100 true champions

In 2008 Kevin Kelly, founding executive editor of *Wired*, wrote a prescient blog titled '1,000 true fans'.[9] The article circulated in Silicon Valley, before reaching the furthest corners of the world. Kelly went against the conventional viewpoint of what it takes to become a creator. At the time, broadcast media was still the dominant mode of communication and social media was growing in stature. Therefore, success was viewed as reaching millions of people via television, becoming a *New York Times* best-selling author or getting listed on the Stock Exchange. The prevailing mantra was 'Go big or go home.' In contrast, Kelly posited the idea of 1,000 true fans and a new definition of success. He realized earlier than most that technology would democratize and distribute access to different communities. This was before the invention of the creator economy, when platforms like Kickstarter, Patreon and OnlyFans didn't exist. Thanks to digital technology, people are no longer passive consumers, but creators. There are more than eight billion people in the world today. Even if your interest was extraordinarily niche – one in a million – there would still be 8,000 people who would share the same passion as you. A gamer in Hyderabad can find followers in Santiago just as easily if not more than someone in their own city. Finding people equally as passionate about Medieval archery, pickling food or bookbinding might have been challenging before the invention of the internet. The demand might have existed, but we simply had no means to connect with others outside our local neighbourhood.

In the creator economy, passion and true connection supersede likes, views and reach. Unlike broadcast media, individuals can build viable businesses and movements from a small number of dedicated fans. The strength and depth of affinity are more important than the number of fans. A true fan is someone who would camp outside to be sure of obtaining a new *Star Wars* movie on release day. Likewise, most outsiders might say to WWE fans that wrestling is fake, but the fans are enthralled by the storylines and drama – in many ways no different to ancient plays or modern drama series. Harley-Davidson superfans get tattoos of the logo to show their allegiance to the group. Being a superfan is all or nothing, there is no middle ground. It can be characterized by an unwavering commitment to the mission. Gaining 1,000 true fans doesn't need to be the end goal. It can be the beginning of the journey. It simply realigns what's needed to progress and make an impact. Creators no longer need a million followers to become successful. Direct access to 1,000 true fans is all you need to make a living. It also allows you to learn from the process, gain valuable feedback and build an advocacy engine. Imagine 1,000 people who are passionate about championing the mission within their networks. Kelly calculated that you only need to make £100 profit from each fan to make £100,000 per annum. The concept demonstrates that it's easier to dominate a niche than compete in a broad market. You are better off testing your newly built ship in your local harbour before attempting to sail across the Indian Ocean. Starting small can also serve as a playground for experimentation, co-creation and new innovations in ways not possible when engaging with mass marketing. Global multinationals like Coca-Cola are not set up in a way to connect and engage with 1,000 superfans for several reasons. Many mass brands see little value in connecting with niche communities when they can reach millions of people with a single advert. And they are not operationally designed to offer such a human touch. Starting with superfans can place challengers in a favourable position.

Bringing it back to marketing for social change, your mission needs 100 true champions to build a movement. A major barrier to social change is the belief that actions need to be enormous in scale, global in reach and leave an everlasting legacy. The size of the challenge is the first and often most intimidating obstacle that prevents people from getting started in the first place. Alternatively, if we start with the premise that our message is not meant for everyone – and that's okay – we can then begin to focus efforts on the people most passionate about the mission. Change happens when a small group of committed people believe they can upend the status quo. You don't need a million people to build a movement. All you need is 100 champions who are equally passionate about the challenge and share the same vision for a better future. If you were to add one champion every day starting today it would take just over three months to have a powerful movement of 100 champions aligned towards a common goal.

Historically, social change has never started with a Big Bang moment, although it often feels like that when you view it via a rear-view mirror. In the same way, billion-dollar companies feel like overnight successes. The reality is somewhat different. Social change starts with a small number of people who are no longer willing to tolerate the status quo and have come together to build a better alternative. Many global companies – even the ones that feel like overnight successes – started life as start-ups with a handful of relentless individuals. Facebook started at Harvard University before expanding to other colleges. The suffragette movement was started by Emmeline Pankhurst, her daughters Christabel, Sylvia and Adela Pankhurst, and a small group of women based in Manchester. In 1966, three men walked into a bar in New York, stated they were gay and ordered drinks. When they were denied service, a 'sip-in' movement was started and within a year the law was changed. Movements start small and build momentum through action and connection with other champions who share the same worldview. The aim shouldn't be to build a community – the individuals, groups and organizations already exist – we simply need to create an outlet and opportunities to connect.

Building 100 true champions is not about being the hero but rather offering a platform for people who are equally dissatisfied with the current situation but not sure how to channel their ideas and energy. Organizing a small but mighty collective is the recipe for creating social change at a local and global level. The 100 champions already exist – you simply need to share your mission and hold space for them to contribute.

Emotional connection

We tend to think of ourselves as logical creatures. But humans are not as logical as we might imagine. We are primarily driven by emotion, not reason. We use logic to justify and make sense of our decisions. It is estimated that 95 per cent of human decisions are made unconsciously by the emotional brain system. I'm pretty sure we have perfectly reasonable explanations for why we chose our partner? Decided to remain single? Why we choose to go to a certain restaurant? And why we picked our current career? The motivations might sound reasonable when we look back and post-rationalize, but much of it is nothing more than a series of emotional responses to stimuli. Brands and marketing agencies have long realized that stories are a more powerful way to build an emotional connection than cold, hard facts. To paraphrase Maya Angelou, people will forget what you said to them, but they won't forget how you made them feel. It is emotions, not statistics, that build social movements. Without an emotional connection, Apple is just another tech company. Coca-Cola sells carbonated drinks and Hermès sells leather bags. A company's ability to connect a product with a human emotion differentiates them and builds brand equity compared to competitors.

Apple is perhaps the ultimate example of building an emotional connection. The company was struggling to stay afloat and was operating at a loss between 1994–97. It was on the brink of going bankrupt. When Steve Jobs returned to Apple, he set out to reinvent the struggling business. Jobs got rid of 70 per cent of Apple's product line and simplified the portfolio. Apple then worked with TBWA to launch the iconic 'Think different' slogan. This was more than an advertising campaign. It captured Apple's mission, building an emotional connection with the audience. 'Think different' tapped into early adopters' belief that they are creative and think differently, compared to the rest of society. The campaign was launched with the iconic 30-second spot 'Here's to the crazy ones', which showed that people who buy Apple are fundamentally different. They have no respect for the status quo. They are deemed to be crazy by the rest of society. But they end up changing the world through their creativity. The advert included excerpts from Albert Einstein, Thomas Edison, Mahatma Gandhi, Pablo Picasso and more. The promise was that if you bought an Apple product, you would be joining a community of creative pioneers. Better than any brand before it, Apple was able to communicate and sell an emotional benefit: creativity and a sense of belonging. Notice that in the advert there was no mention of processing power, storage space or price. Apple was appealing not to logic but to human emotion. It realized that it was selling a feeling, not a product. A powerful mission transcends functionality, building a potent subconscious emotional connection. Incredibly, in a study by Duke University, when 341 students were shown either Apple or IBM logos the participants who were exposed to the Apple logo produced 30 per cent more ideas – and more creative ideas – than those shown the IBM logo.[10] How we feel can be a bigger determinant of decisions than what we think. Emotional connection works even when we don't think it does, making it a compelling but largely invisible lever in the quest to create and accelerate social change.

Conventional economic theory states that people make decisions based on demand and supply. But we don't make decisions on price alone – there are social and emotional factors in play. Balenciaga has produced a $1,600 bag which is almost identical to a 75p IKEA bag. In blinded trials, professionals can't find a difference in taste or aroma between standard and super-expensive wines.[11] Branded painkillers have no extra benefit despite being ten times more expensive than unbranded ones. In all three scenarios, human logic and rational economics won't be able to find an acceptable explanation for consumer behaviour. But when viewed through the lens of social status and validation, buying luxury goods makes emotional sense. There is no better case than diamonds. Contrary to popular belief, diamonds aren't particularly rare. Tanzanite is 1,000 times rarer than diamond but simply doesn't have the same marketing budget and emotional connection.

One of the most famous examples of emotional benefit in marketing is De Beers' 'Diamonds are forever' campaign. It might be hard to believe that proposing with a precious stone wasn't common practice until the mid-1900s. Buying a diamond ring seems like a logical next step when planning to propose and get married to your partner – although the practice is declining with younger generations due to ethical, environmental, preference and financial reasons. Diamonds have no inherent value. And so, the diamond consortium De Beers recruited Philadelphian advertising agency N W Ayer & Son to make diamond engagement rings the social norm in America. The agency connected diamonds (a stone) with an emotional benefit (love). Soon enough, the size of the diamond gifted started to correlate with the size of the man's – based on the heteronormative standards of the day – success and affection. This manufactured a new social expectation for young women. If your husband doesn't get you a diamond ring does he even love you?

Hollywood stars, newspaper photos and prestigious 'role models' – what we would call influencers – reinforced the emerging norm.

In 1946, a young copywriter at N W Ayer & Son, Mary Frances Gerety, came up with the tagline 'A diamond is forever'. The campaign didn't focus on diamonds but connected the stone to the enduring love between couples. It forever solidified the emotional benefit of love with the costly signalling of buying diamond rings. Diamonds became psychologically and socially associated with marriage. The emotional benefit prevented married couples from reselling their ring after marriage since this would lower diamond prices and damage De Beers' profit margins. In 1940, only 10 per cent of first-time brides were receiving diamond engagement rings, while in 1990 that number skyrocketed to 80 per cent. Adage named it the #1 slogan of the 20th century.[12] Diamonds serve no utility; De Beers accomplished this by building an emotional connection for a product people don't need by linking it to an emotion we can't do without.

On the flip side, we have the climate crisis – the greatest threat the world has ever faced and a major opportunity to build a more desirable future. We know human activity is destroying our planet. More than 234 scientists and 14,000+ research papers have told us this through the Intergovernmental Panel on Climate Change (IPCC) reports. And yet knowledge is not materializing into urgent action. The problem is that facts don't change our minds, emotions do. Unlike multinational corporations, climate action doesn't have a marketing budget. The climate movement – except for grassroots movements like Extinction Rebellion, Fridays for Future and a few others – has struggled to connect on an emotional level with mainstream audiences. The message has been restricted to an elite number of scientists, academics and middle-class people in developing countries. Using human stories, communicating emotional benefits and going beyond scary headlines might do the climate movement wonders. Just because climate change is a serious issue, doesn't mean we have to tackle it in boring ways. The use of comedy, entertainment and social proof could drastically improve the adoption of more sustainable practices. As shown through the above examples, humans are motivated by feelings and emotions, not statistics.

When reflecting on your mission, highlighting the problem and offering a rational solution is likely to produce a less than favourable response. If we want to inspire people to join the movement, we need to go beyond rational facts and figures. This is also evident in charity donations, where people are more likely to donate if the campaign is focused on a single person's story than a larger number of unnamed victims. This is known as the identifiable victim effect. To paraphrase Joseph Stalin, one death is a tragedy but a million deaths are a statistic. We need to understand primary human emotions and needs. Like the need to connect and belong. The desire to stand out from the crowd. Or be successful. What would compel people to join your mission? The answer should be at the heart of your action plan.

Identity and self-expression

When building, leading or advocating social change, we don't have to be the heroes of the story. Movements can be a vessel for identity, creativity and self-expression. This is evident in our relationship with brands. When choosing a brand, we aren't only choosing a utility, but also an outlet to express our values, beliefs and personality. Psychologists call this self-signalling. Of course, some products and categories lend themselves better to self-expression. Your clothes probably say more about you than your choice of yoghurt. But that too is up for debate. Research from BBH Labs shows that Orangina drinkers have more in common with each other than do Millennials with each other.[13] The brands we choose are an external signal of our internal motivations and desires. There's an entire discipline, semiotics, dedicated to the systematic study of signs and making sense of them. Semiotics can be split into two components. The signifier is the conceptual material form, such as images, words and sounds. The signified is the meaning conveyed by the signal. Buying a Lamborghini and driving a fast car is the signifier. The signified is the driver's eligibility for pro-creation. If the driver can afford a Lamborghini, they will most likely be able to provide sustenance for their offspring. Buying Puma signifies that you want to take your own path and don't want to follow the majority of people who prefer Nike or Adidas. And if you wear Patagonia, you are signalling either your commitment to the environment or your prestige as an investment banker. A North Face wearer could be an outdoor enthusiast, drill rapper or journalist operating in a war zone. Signs can be polysemic. Like language, meaning differs based on situation and context. Remember, we all want to belong. This is a fundamental need which drives our conscious and subconscious decisions.

Building an emotional connection and feeling part of a community is as much what we are not as it is what we are. In many ways, brands have become our main avenue to showcase our beliefs and feel part of something bigger than ourselves. Belief in consumer brands is replacing religious faith and the declining power of the nation-state. According to Gallup, wealthy nations rank high on quality of life, whereas countries with low GDP rank higher on meaning.[14] In Western countries, individualism is the dominant ideology – further compounded by virtual interactions and social isolation. Young people seek a collective sense of belonging. Previously, the Church played a central role in our collective identity. It offered guidance and a believable narrative. Local communities acted as a hub for distributing, debating and opposing views. The community was the root of conformity and rebellion. In the 21st century, we express ideology through our interactions with brands. We have swapped Zeus for Apple, Vishnu for Nike and Buddha for Starbucks. A compelling mission could fill the void in people's lives and move us towards a more meaningful future beyond hyper-consumption.

Building a movement

Until now, we've identified the ingredients required for finding your community. It starts with accepting the fundamental human drive to connect, understanding how ideas spread from early adopters to the mainstream, how tribes with shared interests and worldviews can create change, and establishing 100 champions and the need to create an emotional connection with your mission because facts won't motivate people into action. But how can you build a movement of 100 true champions? What steps can you take to identify, onboard and mobilize your early adopters? The journey begins with a small but important mindset change. The tribe that cares about your mission already exists. You don't need to create a movement from scratch. You can start by finding and connecting with them. If there are 2,000+ members dedicated to Minions, then I'm sure there are 100 people committed to your mission. The objective should be to start small. Who are five or ten people you can share your mission with? This allows you to practise and refine your message. You can gain qualitative feedback and see people's reactions. You will see people's automatic responses, understanding which parts resonate more and which parts need further work. Oftentimes, the parts you are least confident about can have the biggest impact.

Listening to your tribe is more impactful than spending days, weeks and months planning. Rapid testing is a better use of your time than producing a grand strategy which never sees the light of day. There's great comfort in researching, creating and refining plans. But it can be nothing more than deferring the inevitable and scary step of sharing your mission with the world. Sharing your mission can make you feel vulnerable. This is why most people never share their ideas with the world. There's always something that needs to be done before they are ready to launch. You will never be ready. This is as good of a time as any to start. The first step can be small. You can start with exploration, having conversations and understanding people's needs, desires and motivations. What would motivate them to join the movement? At this stage, you are trying to gain as much intelligence as possible to boost the efficacy of your mission and shape your future engagement strategy. Once you understand why, you can begin to hold space and organize events and forums for people to connect and share ideas.

A thriving community is self-activating. It should be able to operate and create without your input. If you can create space for people to connect and collaborate, then the mission will take a life of its own. Community members will take ownership and feel responsible for the mission. They will feel proud to be part of the community. The mission will become intrinsically linked with their identity and sense of self. And that's how movements are built, powered by a small but growing group of advocates sharing the message with their networks. As we know from marketing, word of mouth outperforms all other kinds of advertising. We simply need to give people something they feel is worth shouting about.

ACTIVITY

1 Early adopters

- o Who are your early adopters?
- o Who is most open to your ideas and mission? Why?

Beginning with people who share your worldview creates early momentum before reaching more mainstream audiences.

2 Road to 100

- o How can you connect with 100 true champions?
- o What are the key activities that will help you connect with 100 true champions?
- o Where can you connect with people who are equally passionate about the challenge and share the same vision for a better future?

Remember this is about creating a relatively small number of deep connections, not meaningless scale. If you connect with one champion every day, within three months you will have a powerful movement of 100 champions aligned towards a common goal.

3 Emotional connection

What is the emotional benefit of joining your mission? The most powerful way to create social change is by building an emotional connection, not delivering cold, hard facts.

o Apple make people feel more creative.

o De Beers connected diamonds with love and commitment.

o Coca-Cola has associated itself with happiness.

Notes

1 A Novotney. The risks of social isolation, *American Psychological Association*, May 2019, 50 (5), 32. www.apa.org/monitor/2019/05/ce-corner-isolation (archived at https://perma.cc/5KQW-R9NJ)

2 F Wang et al. A systematic review and meta-analysis of 90 cohort studies of social isolation, loneliness and mortality, *Nature Human Behaviour*, 2023, 7, 1307–19. doi.org/10.1038/s41562-023-01617-6 (archived at https://perma.cc/3HNS-WT9X)

3 E Kross et al. Social rejection shares somatosensory representations with physical pain, *Proceedings of the National Academy of Sciences of the United States of America*, 2011, 108 (15), 6270–75. doi.org/10.1073/pnas.1102693108 (archived at https://perma.cc/5JAJ-C3PG)

4 E D Wesselmann, J S Nairne and K D Williams. An evolutionary social psychological approach to studying the effects of ostracism, *Journal of Social, Evolutionary, and Cultural Psychology*, 2012, 6 (3), 309–28. doi.org/10.1037/h0099249 (archived at https://perma.cc/2H3R-R3XV)

5 S J West and N D Thomson. Exploring personal crises observed in mass shooters as targets for detection and intervention using psychometric network analysis, *Society for the Improvement of Psychological Science*, 17 December 2022. doi.org/10.31234/osf.io/63xyt (archived at https://perma.cc/2LBE-QV9R)

6 M Pfundmair et al. How social exclusion makes radicalism flourish: A review of empirical evidence, *Journal of Social Issues*, 28 June 2022. doi.org/10.1111/josi.12520 (archived at https://perma.cc/V2H5-GYKJ)

7 E M Rogers (2003) *Diffusion of Innovations*, 5th edn, Free Press, New York

8 W LaMorte. Diffusion of Innovation Theory, Boston University School of Public Health, 2022. sphweb.bumc.bu.edu/otlt/MPH-Modules/SB/BehavioralChangeTheories/BehavioralChangeTheories4.html (archived at https://perma.cc/H8QT-H9CA)

9   K Kelly. The Technium: 1,000 true fans, Kk.org, 2008. kk.org/thetechnium/
1000-true-fans (archived at https://perma.cc/QB98-DEHX)

10 Duke University. Logo can make you 'think different', ScienceDaily, 30 March
2008. www.sciencedaily.com/releases/2008/03/080328085918.htm (archived
at https://perma.cc/BD2Z-LRK6)

11 R T Hodgson. An examination of judge reliability at a major US wine
competition, *Journal of Wine Economics*, 2008, 3 (2), 105–13.
www.cambridge.org/core/journals/journal-of-wine-economics/article/abs/
an-examination-of-judge-reliability-at-a-major-us-wine-competition/15EF999F
BAC63C5FB6DCF1C2F4BB6655 (archived at https://perma.cc/84J9-U5V9)

12 Ad Age. Ad Age advertising century: Top 10 slogans, 1999. adage.com/article/
special-report-the-advertising-century/ad-age-advertising-century-top-10-
slogans/140156 (archived at https://perma.cc/FE5T-2CDE)

13 BBH Labs. Puncturing the paradox: Group cohesion and the generational
myth, nd. www.bbh-labs.com/puncturing-the-paradox-group-cohesion-and-
the-generational-myth (archived at https://perma.cc/H63T-HET2)

14 E Ortiz-Ospina and M Roser. Happiness and life satisfaction, Our World in
Data, 2017. ourworldindata.org/happiness-and-life-satisfaction (archived at
https://perma.cc/XNA3-G4RX)

5

Rise to the challenge

Until now, we have covered the best-case scenario of creating your mission and building a movement. The ideal blueprint for how things should progress under perfect conditions. But nothing in life works according to plan. Your mission needs to interact with the randomness of the outside world. Ask any military general, business owner or wedding planner. No plan survives first contact with the enemy. Nonetheless, the planning process gives you the best possible chance to prepare and respond. We can't address challenges if we are unaware of their existence. In business, transformation projects fail because leadership is unable to bring the rest of the organization on the journey. In society, movements fail when they are unable to build a critical mass. The inability to build a coalition can be one of the biggest barriers to achieving business and social impact.

New ideas feel scary

New ideas are usually opposed by people who are content with the status quo. We should recognize that some people don't want things to change. And you won't convince them no matter how hard you try. A better strategy would be to identify, onboard and collaborate with early adopters. If you work for a big organization, it will be almost impossible to make everyone happy. So why even try? And if you work independently or in a smaller company decision-making will be faster but you will still need to convince the outside world of your mission to achieve a critical mass. In larger corporations, embracing change is an existential challenge. When you read CEO interviews, you would think that most global corporations encourage innovation, celebrate failure and reward experiments. But if you've worked in a big company, you would know that most executives are risk averse. In general, the bigger the company the lower the risk tolerance. Big companies have more to lose. More costs, more employees, more profits and bigger losses if things go wrong. Yet, unlike start-ups and individuals, most large companies have sufficient cash reserves, resources and headroom to take bolder risks.

The word risk carries a negative association in the business world. Many managers believe that risks should be avoided as much as possible. In truth, most of the value created in business emerges from innovation and risk-taking activities. There is a positive correlation between risk and reward. The level of reward is proportionate to the level of risk associated with the activity. As a company ages, it drifts from its original mission. Leadership doesn't want to rock the boat or mess with the winning formula. When interns question the existing ways of working or suggest new ideas, they might hear 'This is the way it's always been done.' Funnily enough, many of the original ideas of the founders of the company would have been rejected by the risk-averse attitudes of the management and employees at the company. Walt Disney might have struggled to get Snow White commissioned. Samsung might not have been able to pivot from selling dried fish to electronics. Wrigley's would never have discovered customers preferred gum more than the soap he was selling because the finance team would have viewed offering free chewing gum as a frivolous expense. New ideas, navigating unpaved roads and shifting away from the past is scary. The move from the known to the unknown can feel deeply uncomfortable. However, change is the prerequisite for future growth and progress. The only way to expand our understanding is by exploring new territories.

You can't make everyone happy

If you wait for everyone to get on board with the mission you will be waiting forever and things will never change. At some point, you will need to commit and go for it. You'll need to set a direction of travel and see who joins your ship for the journey. There's no point waiting for permission. People are never going to agree on a particular course of action. Nothing meaningful has come from consensus decision-making. Loss aversion, status quo bias and vested interests are too-powerful forces. Early on, you are looking for commitment, not consensus. Who is really with you? And who can be persuaded?

In modern business books, we are encouraged to be open, collaborative and receptive to the needs of colleagues. This is important. Hierarchal and authoritarian change has a short lifespan. People won't feel a sense of agency to make decisions or contribute to the mission. At the same time, you will have to accept that it's impossible to please everyone. Even in democratic elections, not every citizen is happy with the outcome, but a decision is made. Attempting to reach a consensus drains valuable time and resources, slowing down your movement and preventing your mission from reaching a wider audience of people who can be persuaded. If your goal is to make everyone happy then you have failed before you've even started. It's like scheduling a meeting without an agenda to guide the discussion. You will end up talking about everything but achieving nothing.

Playing it safe

Making everyone happy creates a culture of mediocrity. Leaders should proceed with a single vision for the future. Not everyone will agree with the vision. You should listen to others, understand their concerns and see things through their lens. The problem is if you build in everyone's feedback at this early stage – before you've acted and received real-world feedback – it will dilute the original vision. Everyone might be mildly satisfied, but no one will be excited about your mission. Marketing campaigns offer a fascinating window into how consensus breeds mediocrity.

Historically, the main purpose of marketing has been to get people interested in buying products or services from the company. But most marketing campaigns go unnoticed. I'm sure no one enters a job – including marketing – and purposefully chooses to do a bad job. Most marketing professionals, whether brand or agency-side, want to make an impact. But the fear of getting it wrong and losing their job prevents them from taking creative risks and standing out. Marketing campaigns often include numerous teams, multiple stakeholders and considerable budgets. The risk of messing things up prevents marketers from achieving the primary objective of getting noticed. There are lots of passionate people involved in the process with a clear audience, message and creative direction. Sadly, design by committee, multiple review rounds, focus groups and senior leadership input turn a creative campaign designed to make maximum impact into a corporate soup produced to please everyone and attract no one. Too many cooks spoil the broth. The world is awash with boring, samey and unremarkable campaigns that go unnoticed. Global advertising is expected to surpass $1 trillion in 2024 but 91 per cent of digital ads are looked at for less than a second.[1] An inordinate waste of time, energy and resources born from a culture of playing it safe. In marketing and when advocating for social change (unlike the fields of medicine, law and engineering) conservatism is the enemy of progress. Not taking risks is the biggest risk you can take. It's the equivalent of staying home, not going to the party and expecting to find the love of your life.

The big idea

Mediocrity is the enemy of business and social impact. Modern marketing has traded imagination for validation, the magic of human storytelling for highly polished, pasteurized and predictable work. In many marketing departments it has become easier to make a business case with a dashboard of questionable statistics than an original idea based on gut instincts and human emotions. The big idea has been replaced by version number 134. Early on in my career, my mentor and legendary adman George Lois taught me the importance of the 'big idea'.[2] A big idea is a platform that gets people to think and act differently. It taps into a universal human truth. Advertising used to be packed with big ideas. The period covering the 1960s to the 1980s was the golden age of advertising. You only have to look at 'Think small' by DDB, 'Just do it' by Wieden+Kennedy or 'Buy the world a Coke' by McCann Erickson to understand the power of creative advertising. What these ads had in common was a big idea, and in today's world big ideas are far and few between. The big idea isn't created; it already exists in the world – we simply have to be interested enough to discover it.

Creative ideas can make communication more effective. This is as true in marketing as it is for social change. We should always endeavour to avoid mediocrity. The priority should be getting noticed and then being distinctive, which requires defying conventions, taking risks and being comfortable with making mistakes. When George Lois's advert for Xerox was banned because of complaints from competitors. Lois remade the advert and invited the Federal Communications Commission (FCC) to the new advert where they hired a chimp to press two buttons and demonstrate the ease of use of a Xerox photocopier. The big idea was that the photocopier was so simple that even a monkey could use it. The campaign was so successful that eventually Xerox became a synonym for photocopying. Conformity breeds indifference, but creativity drives business and social impact. What's your big idea?

Small teams, big dreams

In the 1950s, Britain was experiencing a fuel shortage because of the Suez Crisis. Petrol was scarce so the President of the British Motor Company briefed automotive designer Alec Issigonis to create a fuel-efficient vehicle. Issiggonis invented the world's first Mini. The magic of the Mini was its surprisingly spacious interior relative to the vehicle's size. It was one of the first cars to be front-wheel drive, which opened 80 per cent of the floor space for passengers. The team that designed the Mini was small, consisting of 10 people. Three engineers, Issigonis, two engineering students and four draftsmen. Proof that a small number of committed people can punch above their weight. The Mini was born from crisis, imagined by a visionary leader and brought into reality by a small but mighty team of experts and fresh minds. In contrast, the Pontiac Aztek represents the summit of design by committee. Arguably the worst-looking car ever produced, the car was meant to represent General Motors' (GM) ambition to be innovative and future-facing. GM was criticized for never doing anything new so the board decreed that 40 per cent of new cars would be 'innovative'.[3] The Aztek started with a question: what if you took a Camaro (mid-size car) and a Blazer (SUV) and put them in a blender? The design team took inspiration from the versatility of North Face jackets (which wasn't yet a mainstream brand). But to save money and increase profit margins, GM used a cheaper minivan platform, ruining the unique selling points of the original design. The proportions were all wrong. GM ignored the early negative feedback from focus groups and decided to roll ahead with the launch – failing to share the response with the executive team. The idea of the Aztek was interesting but the team lost sight of the original vision. The irony is that the Aztek met all the internal indicators of success like budget, timeline and ways of working. But the teams forgot a simple but important external objective: would people want to buy the car?

Death by committee

Design by committee is the biggest killer of progress. When an idea, project or mission is first born, like a new-born baby it needs to be looked after, fed and nurtured. Early-stage feedback can undermine the formation of a strong foundation. Naturally, the bigger the company, the more stakeholders involved. Everyone is keen to share their perspective. When the baby is first born, you will need to protect it and provide it with sufficient time and space to walk. Designers, product managers, strategists and creatives will be familiar with death by committee. Trying to communicate with everyone prevents us from connecting with anyone. Better to bring one product to market that fulfils a genuine need than botch 1,000 concepts together and become overwhelmed with the scale of the task, with no sense of direction or prioritization. When you mix all the colours you end up with a neutral grey. Having more contributors increases complexity and hinders direction and speed. All meaningful projects begin with a mission and small team of believers, before reaching the mainstream. We shouldn't confuse consensus with collaboration. Design by committee is the tyranny of the many and the creation of nothing. The biggest leaps in human progress come from imagination, before collaboration makes the idea accessible to more people. The key is to start small and build momentum. If you start big with loads of stakeholders, you might never get past the drawing board. At the same time, we don't want to design by dictatorship, either. Nothing good has come from totalitarianism. Begin with your mission, and don't forget why you started the project in the first place. Later, you can begin to open space for different voices and perspectives.

Understand the resistance

The second-worst decision after trying to please everyone is ignoring the resistance to change. Any new concept shaking up the existing equilibrium – no matter how dysfunctional – will encounter opposition. If your mission doesn't encounter challenges, then you're doing something wrong. Friction is growth and overcoming obstacles is an integral part of creating social change. If everyone is happy, then nothing has changed. As the proverb wisely states, you can put lipstick on a pig, but it is still a pig. Change is a messy process and unpredictable with exhilarating highs and jaw-dropping lows. Resistance is guaranteed, but success isn't.

The way you deal with resistance can increase your impact. In Chapter 1 we identified the various reasons people resist change in general. People are more comfortable with the familiar than the unknown. Leadership demands facilitating change. Nothing in business or life is constant. Everything is moving. Like nature, business and society have seasons with a different rhythm. Not adapting to changing seasons creates inertia, like a waterway that doesn't flow. How can you understand the reason for resistance? How can you inspire people to try new approaches? How can you get your team to explore a new product, proposition or community? The first step is understanding why people are not adopting your mission. There could be several different reasons, as outlined in the following sections.

Loss of freedom

The foundational reason for resisting change is not feeling like you have a choice over the decision. Having a choice makes people feel powerful – no choice makes people feel powerless. In laboratory experiments, animals learn to press buttons to get food. When offered the choice, monkeys and pigeons prefer multiple buttons to a single button. In similar experiments, when people were given the choice to bet at a table with one roulette wheel or two roulette wheels, most preferred the table with two roulette wheels,[4] despite the wheels all being identical. We like choice independent of the outcome. We like the freedom to choose. Research has shown that lack of control at work – limited freedom on how you work – in combination with high work demands can increase risks of diabetes and death from cardiovascular diseases. The freedom to choose is deeply connected to our self-preservation instincts. Thinking back to our ancestors, limited variety and choice could be a death sentence. Two mating partners would increase your chances of an offspring. Four plum trees would be better than two trees that might be devastated by locusts. Eight spears were better than four when it came down to tribal war.

Too much choice can be equally debilitating. Analysis paralysis can occur when there is too much choice, such as when ordering food at a restaurant with a 100-page menu, or attempting to choose a date from 75 million profiles on Tinder. More choices won't always lead to better outcomes. Enough choice can liberate people, but too much choice can suffocate them. The role of the leader is to make people feel involved and offer a clear direction forward. Too much choice can shut the human brain down. Ambiguity creates uncertainty and a relapse into the status quo.

Lack of communication

The mission might be clear for you and a coalition of early adopters. The real challenge is getting people outside of your immediate bubble to believe in the mission. Of course, you're passionate about the change. It's your baby. This is known as the IKEA effect, where people place a disproportionately high value on things that they create. You will need to remember that other people will have different interests or priorities. They might have family issues, be struggling with debt or thinking about what to eat for lunch. One speech or presentation isn't going to change people's minds. People might forget everything once they move into their next meeting. You will have to maintain a regular cadence of communication. The greatest campaigns in marketing and politics repeat a single message until it's etched into people's memory. The rule of seven has existed in marketing since the 1930s when Hollywood studios realized they had to expose viewers to advertising an average of seven times before people committed to watching a movie. The principle has applications beyond consumer marketing. People need to hear your message at least seven times before they take action. Repetition creates familiarity and trust, the opposite of novelty, which can generate doubt and uncertainty. We are more likely to get bored with our message than our audience. Most marketing campaigns 'wear in' because of habituation, but marketers end up pulling the campaign because they've viewed it a million times. Whereas consumers have better things to do with their lives.

Similarly, political campaigns can be won or lost on repetition. Cunning political strategists understand that most people lead busy and overwhelming lives. They would be lucky if they could wedge a single message into people's minds. The French Revolution had 'Liberty, equality, fraternity'. Lenin had: 'Bread, peace, land'. Tony Blair had: 'Education, education, education'. Obama had: 'Yes, we can' and Trump had: 'Make America great again'. Throughout their campaigns they effectively repeated their core message again and again. Communication becomes even more important as your mission moves from theory into action. This is where you can communicate how each decision can support or undermine the new collective vision for the future. Use every single chance to communicate the mission with your teams. Just make sure communication doesn't turn into propaganda.

A crucial element is communicating why things need to change and painting a picture of a better future than the current reality. The best form of communication is action and leading by example. Nothing kills a movement more than the leadership not living and breathing the mission through their actions. People will learn more from your actions than your words. Communication is not just words. We communicate through actions.

Loss of identity

A small change can break our worldview. The current way of doing things might not be fair, effective or enjoyable but at least it's familiar. Changing the existing order can make people lose their orientation. A new pillow might make it harder to sleep. A new haircut might feel strange for your partner. Moving offices could mean building a new daily routine. Here, we're not necessarily against the change, we simply don't understand our place in the new order. It's the role of leadership to comfort people and help them acclimatize to the new reality. People build mental and physical habits, rituals and connections. Breaking this cycle can make them question their place in the new world. Who am I? How can I navigate through this change? Where should I start? You might be comfortable with the unknown, but some people need more support than others. The process requires unremitting patience and empathy for where people are coming from. A useful approach is anchoring the new with references that people are familiar with. For example, reminding people that the new product still requires the same skills of selling and negotiating the team has been using for the last 12 years. Sharing how new wellbeing practices support employee satisfaction and retention, which has always been a business priority. If you move house, make sure the new house has the same doormat to create a semblance of familiarity. The objective here is to make the new feel familiar.

No incentive

We must give people a reason to abandon the old and embrace the new. It doesn't have to be financially motivated, but there does need to be an incentive. Understanding incentives is key to understanding people. If you're trying to encourage new behaviour, your guiding mission will only take you so far. You must make sure incentives are aligned. Behaviours are influenced by incentives. We are more likely to continue a behaviour if rewarded and less likely to continue a behaviour if punished. If a comedian receives blank stares when they tell a particular joke they are less likely to perform it again, but if the audience laughs they might well repeat it. Rewards and punishments shape our actions.

In theory, we can encourage or discourage a behaviour by changing its consequences. For example, if your child is not performing at school you can respond with reinforcement or punishment. This is known as 'Skinner's Box', named after American psychologist B F Skinner. The theory is almost

100 years old but as influential today as when it was first invented. Skinner created a machine where he would place pigeons and a button. The pigeons had the choice to peck at the button. The animal learns that pressing the button and displaying specific behaviours led to rewards or punishments. (Note: Skinner used the word reinforcement, not rewards, since it would reinforce a behaviour.) When the ratio of incentives changed so did the pigeons' behaviour. Gambling devices and computer games use Skinner's Box to manipulate the reinforcement schedule. The gambling device can reward you at certain points to keep you gambling (and spending money). The experiment showed how positive reinforcement, negative reinforcement and punishment can change animals' behaviour.

We humans, however, are differ from rats and pigeons. It turns out we tend to lose interest in activities after we get rewarded for them. Offering people more cash, bigger bonuses and shiny prizes doesn't generate long-term motivation. Rewards are often an offering to get people to do things that they don't want to do. We might pay someone more money to stay in the job, offer our kids sweets if they finish their homework, or treat ourselves to a holiday after an exhausting year of working. Rewards can also make us expectant, and we usually go back to our default once the reward schedule ends. Like a sugar baby that moves on to the next target once the sugar daddy or mamma has run out of cash. The intent wasn't there in the first place – they were only with them because of the monetary reward. Neuroscience shows that punishment won't motivate people to act, either.[5] Being demoted, receiving negative feedback or facing public humiliation is less moving than positive reinforcement. A study on hygiene at a New York State hospital brings this point to life.[6] The study wanted to encourage staff to wash their hands more frequently to prevent the spread of disease. There were signs everywhere warning about the consequences of not washing your hands. Patients might die from infection. And yet, cameras revealed only 10 per cent of staff washed their hands before and after visiting the patient's room, despite knowing they were being recorded on camera. The researchers then introduced a digital board that produced a positive message like 'Good job!' every time they washed their hands, and the improved hygiene score would show up on the LED boards. Hygiene rates jumped from 10 per cent to 82 per cent by week 16 and, more impressively, the new behaviour was increased and maintained, reaching 88 per cent by week 75. In general, positive reinforcement is more effective for inspiring action, and punishment is a more useful deterrent. If we look at the most extreme case, however, which is often useful when studying social behaviour, the death penalty doesn't deter criminal activity. Why is that? Until now, we have only covered extrinsic motivators.

The most powerful incentive is intrinsic. Life is more meaningful when we gain satisfaction from the activity, irrespective of the outcome. We write not because we want to be the next Leo Tolstoy, we run not because we want to be the next Haile Gebrselassie. We produce art without planning to become the next Frida Kahlo. The act of creation brings joy to our lives. If your mission can tap into people's intrinsic motivations, it would be a more powerful incentive than any external reward or punishment. How will this change feed into people's intrinsic motivation? Meta-analysis shows that positive feedback inspires people to keep going, whereas external incentives can undermine our sense of accomplishment and drive.[7] This is known as the overjustification effect. Take, for example, reading for leisure (intrinsic) vs reading for an exam (extrinsic), when our passion (intrinsic) becomes our business (extrinsic), or supporting a charitable cause (intrinsic) vs being emotionally blackmailed to donate (extrinsic). Working with people's intrinsic motivations means your mission is surfing the wave. Everything becomes easier, and you will end up paddling and struggling less.

Politics

There are times when change is not in the interests of others. They don't want you to change things. Your desire to create change is perceived to directly harm their position, status or interests. In any organization consisting of people from different backgrounds, personalities and agendas, there will naturally be a diversion of interests. In workplaces, this manifests itself as office politics. In society, it is exhibited as so-called 'culture wars'. Your responsibility as a leader is to avoid and overcome such division. Politics is more likely to occur when there isn't a clear and unified vision of the future, leaving space for ambiguity and differences of opinion. If your mission is open to interpretation, it will become open to translation. Even when groups view or experience the same situation, they can still emerge with a different perspective. Like Catholics and Protestants in Christianity, Sunnis and Shia in Islam, and Orthodox and Reform in Judaism. In the world of business, differences can be even more pronounced as parties might not even agree on the same principles. Politics can divide teams and destroy morale. Leaders need to address this problem immediately. A politicized environment emerges when incentives aren't aligned and if people feel threatened by change or when undesirable behaviour isn't disciplined. Your role should always begin with trying to understand people's motivations, attempting to align incentives and building bridges. If the behaviour persists you will need to encourage radical communication and transparency. A healthy culture is one where teams can disagree and discuss decisions in public, not behind closed doors in fragmented factions. Amazon has a 'Disagree and commit' management principle whereby employees are empowered to disagree with decisions but once a decision has been made everyone must commit to implementing it.

Kick out any political behaviour and unfair policies or practices that go against company values. Demand accountability for actions. Office politics is inevitable, but it can be a positive force if conducted in a transparent, democratic and just way that promotes new ideas, and delivers additional rigour to future activities. A more decentralized organization reduces the likelihood of destructive workplace politics, allowing more people to share ideas, collaborate and make decisions. There needs to be an agreement on collective goals. If certain people have interests outside of the group goals, future success will not be achievable unless you can align interests or remove the obstacles to progress.

Legitimate concern

Not all resistance is negative – people and groups may have legitimate concerns about the effectiveness of the vision for the future. The ability to listen, hold space and receive constructive feedback, including criticism, is critical for success. Humans don't like criticism, it can make us upset, defensive and emotional. But feedback is a gift – constructive criticism helps us gain fresh insights that might be missing from our bubble of believers.

Don't surround yourself with people who think the same and have no original ideas, provocation or challenges. It might feel good for the ego, but it won't help with moving the mission forward. This could be compared to yes-men and yes-women who float around presidents, CEOs and football managers. They are easier to be around and make you feel good, but they won't challenge your thinking, even if you are making a big mistake. History is dotted with the dangers of yes-men and groupthink. As you build or facilitate the movement, it becomes essential to make space for disagreement, divergent perspectives and constructive criticism. The inability to deal with criticism could become an impediment to creating long-lasting change. If someone has a question or critique of the movement, others might also share the same sentiment. Feedback can help the movement grow by understanding blind spots, weaknesses and areas for improvement. An open culture also creates a more honest relationship, where members can feel comfortable and empowered to ask questions and make their feelings known rather than masking them or airing them privately.

Feedback is a gift, and criticism usually comes from a good place from people who care and want to see the best possible outcome. The key is to not take the criticism personally as an attack on your character or abilities. Take time to understand where the challenge is coming from. Ask open and clarifying questions to understand more about the problem. Feedback is one of the best tools for personal, business and social change. Make sure to thank people for sharing with you, even if you don't agree with everything. How can you encourage a culture where criticism is viewed as an opportunity to grow?

You

Most change programmes fade because of an inability to recognize the existing culture and social undercurrents. As we spend an increasing amount of time, effort and resources, we become engrossed in our mission. We become so busy thinking about change, but forget how others might feel about the change we are instigating. Unintentionally, we forget about the feelings, needs and vulnerabilities of others who haven't been immersed in the journey of change as much as we have. How might others feel about the change? How will this decision impact their future? How can I best support this person or group? Change collapses when we haven't thought about others, and they aren't included in the story. If you don't care about others, they won't care about you. Leadership should prioritize collective benefit over individual benefit. It should be a pleasure to actively listen, understand and support people on their journey of development and growth.

When the suitcase with wheels was invented in the 1970s (5,000 years after the invention of the wheel in Mesopotamia) it faced serious backlash from men. It was obvious rolling suitcases were a great idea. They would make the transportation of heavy suitcases much easier. But men refused to carry rolling suitcases because they were 'unmanly'. Women were expected to travel with their husbands and have their men carry suitcases. It wasn't until the 1980s that rolling suitcases became mainstream. This might have happened sooner if manufacturers had understood the underlying resistance which went beyond the technology. We might not have had the rolling suitcase if companies hadn't found ways to overcome men's resistance to wheels threatening their manhood. Without understanding the needs and concerns of others, new ideas will fail to build traction.

Reluctant leadership

I have talked a lot about leadership throughout the last chapters. Depending on your disposition, the term might feel natural or alien to you. You might be thinking, 'Yep, that's me.' Or, 'I'm not a leader, and this isn't for me.' Leaders notice and embrace change before others, and that's you. It's why you are reading this book and looking to bring others on the journey with you. What do you imagine when you think of a leader? A powerful president, the CEO of a Fortune 500 company or a revolutionary leader? Some of the greatest leaders and most impactful movements have emerged from unlikely places. This is the essence of reluctant leadership – you are not leading for fame and fortune, but because you recognize the need for change. Naturally, you might have reservations. Are you the right person for this mission? Yes, your reluctance is precisely why you should proceed forward. The greatest leaders possess a unique mix of humility and empathy with a dash of self-doubt. They have no yearning for power, only progress. Being too humble might make it hard to communicate the mission confidently and inspire others to join the movement. People who don't place their self-interest above the collective interest make for the best but also the most reluctant leaders. Joseph Campbell's book *The Hero's Journey* talks about the call to adventure, when we are called to do something new and radical.[8] Have you ever had a call to adventure that's scared you? Moving to a new city? Starting a new job? Leaving your family home? In every heroic movie, book and throughout history, the call to adventure pertains to the refusal of the call. This is when the hero refuses to step up to the occasion. Luke Skywalker initially refused to join the force and fight against the Empire. Neo initially refused to join the Matrix. Simba initially refused to become King and fight against Scar. Along the journey, you'll face great hardship and might even doubt your abilities. Just remember this too is part of the process. Accept it, but keep moving forward.

Nike dream crazy

In 2016, 49ers quarterback Colin Kaepernick refused to stand during the US national anthem. Kaepernick made the conscious decision to take the knee in protest against racial injustice and police brutality following the shootings of Alton Sterling, Charles Kinsey and Freddie Gray.

When asked about his decision, Kaepernick said that he wasn't going to stand up to show pride in a flag for a country that oppresses Black people and people of colour. He explained that this is bigger than football and it would be selfish to turn a blind eye. Kaepernick went on to point out that there are bodies in the street and people are receiving paid leave and getting away with murder. This was in reference to a series of African American deaths caused by law enforcement that led to the Black Lives Matter movement – he further added that he would continue to protest until he feels like '[the American flag] represents what it's supposed to represent'.[9]

Kaepernick's action sparked a movement within the NFL. At one point in 2017, more than 200 NFL players took the knee, sat or raised their fist during the anthem. It can be difficult to grasp, in retrospect, how controversial taking the knee was in 2016. Kaepernick was booed on the pitch. The 49ers planned to release him so he opted out of his contract and every single team in the NFL refused to give him a contract. The move would mean the end of his playing career. Despite the backlash, Nike decided to make Colin Kaepernick the hero of its 'Just do it' campaign titled 'Dream crazy'. It featured the former NFL quarterback and the slogan: 'Believe in something. Even if it means sacrificing everything. Just do it.'

Nike, a mainstream brand, enjoyed by most Americans, received heavy criticism from politicians, the media and consumers. The sports brand risked angering the NFL, older and more conservative communities. But ultimately Nike decided it was a risk worth taking given the credibility the brand would gain with young, urban and progressive communities. The backlash was real. News channels showed clips of people burning their Nike trainers. Shares in Nike dropped by 3.2 per cent by the next day, but Nike held their nerve. They didn't pull the ad; much like Kaepernick, they held on to their beliefs, even if it came at a cost. The campaign seemed like a disaster. Donald Trump infamously tweeted: 'What was Nike thinking?'

The gamble paid off in the long term – it increased Nike's share price by 5 per cent and earned Nike a cool $6 billion.[10] This isn't the first time Nike has made their stand clear. The launch campaign for 'Just do it' by Wieden+Kennedy featured an octogenarian runner who ran 62,000 in his lifetime, directly addressing ageism and making the brand appealing to more consumers beyond its young and trendy fanbase. In 1995 Nike's advert 'If you let me in' tackled gender inequality in sports. Naturally, this was in the brand's best interest since it would further open the sports market to

50 per cent of the population. It also shows that business and social impact can be connected. In the same year, the company released the first campaign with Ric Munoz, an openly gay runner with HIV.

Critics might argue that Nike made a calculated bet on its audience. I would tend to agree. You can't be everything to everyone. Nike made a stand both socially and commercially. You can only do this if you don't fear the consequences of your actions. It also epitomized the Nike mission and values. Just do it.

ACTIVITY

Now that we have covered the main reasons why people resist change let's explore practical ways to deal with resistance.

1 **Communicate the mission**
   Communicate a vision for the future that is more attractive than the current reality. You might personally feel that the need for change is clear, but not everyone is as close to the mission as you. Keep communicating the message through words and actions at every opportunity. Remember, people need to hear your message at least seven times before they take action.
   Your mission needs to answer the following questions:

   o Why is change needed?
   o How will the change be better for people?
   o How will the change be better for business?
   o How will the change be better for society?

2 **Active listening**
   Once you've got your point across, now is the time to hold space and listen to people's thoughts, ideas and resistance. Change can be scary for people for numerous reasons. The first step in turning sceptics into believers is to understand their concerns. Unless you know why people are resisting change, there's nothing you can do to support them or change your approach. Remove your ego, put yourself in the audience's shoes and ask open, clarifying and non-judgemental questions. Becoming defensive will put people's barriers up and prevent dialogue. Active listening improves our chances of meeting people's personal, professional and social needs. Sometimes, it will require flexibility to adapt our initial approach based on feedback. You need to identify the reason for resistance and create a plan to overcome the challenge.

Holding space and active listening will help you understand where people are at on the social change journey. You can use the following questions to spark conversations:

o How do you feel about the change?
o What are you concerned about?
o How can I support you on the journey?

3 Bring people on the journey

Change can be exciting for some, but overwhelming for others. Your mission should invite and involve people, not tell them what they should do. Human beings value autonomy and making personal decisions. Studies show we feel less inclined to change our behaviour if we don't feel like we have a choice over the decision. Once you've understood people's worries and incentives, you need to bring them on the journey. This is not the same as death by committee. By now, you should have created a vision for a better future and assigned roles and responsibilities. However, there should be enough room in the process to include ideas, thoughts and involvement from new people. The mission should be 80 per cent complete but leave enough room for people to create their own stories and actions. No one wants to be dictated to. Why not involve your audience in key milestones in the process? And I'm not talking about fake participation, where people pretend they are open to new ideas but steamroll in with their existing plans. In contrast, develop genuine forums for people to share ideas, feedback and stories. Change is not only about the 'why' and 'what' but also the 'how'. The best change initiatives make people feel like they are creating the change, rather than the change is happening to them. Projects don't fail because of technical reasons but because we fail to factor in social interaction and adoption.

Here are some ways you can get people involved and invested in the mission:

o Ask for people's ideas and thoughts.
o Share early ideas and get feedback (sharing is better than presenting).
o Create a mechanism to crowdsource ideas and share progress on collective goals.

4 Start small

Most change agents are remarkably ambitious. They always overestimate the amount of time and effort required to achieve collective goals. That's not a bad thing. We just need to combine big thinking with small bitesize actions to build trust, engagement and buy-in from people and groups. We should help people build confidence and new stories. People will be unsure about their place when things change. How will the change impact my life? Do I have the skills? Where do I stand? Starting small builds confidence, capacity and social proof. If my goal is to go to the gym, lifting 10kg weights gives me the confidence that I might be able to lift 15kg weights and eventually 20kg. Conversely, beginning with 100kg weights, failing to lift them while everyone stares at me at the gym may discourage me from going to the gym again.

Here are some questions that might make it easier for people to get started:

o   What's the smallest change people can get started with today?
o   How can we help people build confidence and proof around this new story?
o   How can we break down long-term ambitions into smaller actionable goals? For example, turning five-year plans into a 12-week cycle.

5   Keep going

When you look at business transformation or social change, it seems to happen suddenly. Most change initiatives gain traction over time. They can feel small, slow and insignificant. Small ripples can turn into enormous tsunamis. The trick is to keep believing, listening and adapting your approach based on real-world feedback. How do you maintain interest after the honeymoon period? This is the true task of the leader. It takes patience, urgency and consistency.

Here are some questions to explore as you begin to engage with different people and groups:

o   How can we maintain momentum after the launch?
o   How can we improve our approach using the feedback we've received?
o   How can we celebrate small wins?

6   Make a stand

There comes a point where you need to draw a line in the sand. It's important to understand people's resistance to change. It's equally important to actively listen and bring people on the journey with us. The truth is, however, there will be people who will never join our mission. And that's okay. We must be comfortable with this reality. There comes a point where we must make a stand for what we believe and what we are fighting against. We have to show through actions and not words what we stand for.

There are many examples of brands standing for something. These brands are more memorable, famous and engaging. Even those who don't like the brand have feelings towards them. The same cannot be said about 98 per cent of brands in the market that are dull, boring and unremarkable.

Your mission should be the ultimate decision-making framework. It should make it easier to answer the following questions:

o What are our non-negotiables?
o How should we respond to this situation?
o How should we communicate our mission with the world?

Notes

1 WARC. Global advertising to top $1 trillion in 2024, as big five attract most spending, WARC, 24 August 2023. www.warc.com/content/feed/global-advertising-to-top-1-trillion-in-2024-as-big-five-attract-most-spending/en-GB/8558 (archived at https://perma.cc/QP2S-V5RE); T Hobbs. Marketers continue to 'waste money' as only 9 per cent of digital ads are viewed for more than a second, *Marketing Week*, 26 July 2016. www.marketingweek.com/marketers-continue-to-waste-money-as-only-9-of-digital-ads-are-viewed-for-more-than-a-second (archived at https://perma.cc/WA2L-4QEM)

2 G Lois (2012) *Damn Good Advice (for People With Talent!): How to unleash your creative potential, by America's Master Communicator, George Lois*, Phaidon, London

3 B Lutz and D Sherman. Complete acquiescence: Bob Lutz reveals how the Pontiac Aztek happened, Car and Driver, 14 October 2014. www.caranddriver.com/news/a15361262/complete-acquiesence-bob-lutz-reveals-how-the-pontiac-aztek-happened (archived at https://perma.cc/AED3-57ZU)

4 S Iyengar (2012) *The Art of Choosing*, Abacus, London

5 M Guitart-Masip et al. Action versus valence in decision making, *Trends in Cognitive Sciences*, 2014, 18 (4), 194–202. doi.org/10.1016/j.tics.2014.01.003 (archived at https://perma.cc/LV8J-HBMX)

6 D Armellino et al. Using high-technology to enforce low-technology safety measures: The use of third-party remote video auditing and real-time feedback in healthcare, *Clinical Infectious Diseases*, 2011, 54 (1), 1–7. doi.org/10.1093/cid/cir773 (archived at https://perma.cc/LG3C-LD7K)

7 E L Deci, R Koestner and R M Ryan. A meta-analytic review of experiments examining the effects of extrinsic rewards on intrinsic motivation, *Psychological Bulletin*, 1999, 125 (6), 627–668. doi.org/10.1037/0033-2909.125.6.627 (archived at https://perma.cc/M8YZ-U6ER)

8 J Campbell, P Cousineau and S L Brown (2003) *The Hero's Journey: Joseph Campbell on his life and work*, New World Library, Novato, CA

9 S Wyche. Colin Kaepernick explains why he sat during national anthem, NFL, 27 August 2016. www.nfl.com/news/colin-kaepernick-explains-why-he-sat-during-national-anthem-0ap3000000691077 (archived at https://perma.cc/FSL3-3J48)

10 K Gibson. Colin Kaepernick is Nike's $6 billion man, CBS News, 21 September 2018. www.cbsnews.com/news/colin-kaepernick-nike-6-billion-man (archived at https://perma.cc/L463-73ST)

6

Lead a revolution

Movements face a perennial dilemma. How to best respond to defunct economic, social and political systems? Should we reform them or spark a revolution? These kinds of questions emerge when existing institutions and systems fail to serve us. We seldom ponder reform or revolution if things are working smoothly. If your marriage is going well, you are less likely to think about marriage counselling (reform) or divorce (revolution). If you're happy with your car, you are unlikely to take it to the mechanic (reform) or consider buying a new car (revolution). And if you are thriving at work, you are less likely to change roles (reform) or switch industries (revolution). The desire for change stems from the dissatisfaction with the old way of doing things.

Reform or revolution?

Is there a difference between reform and revolution? We should start by thinking about the outcome we're hoping to achieve. A constructive revolution occurs when we are no longer able to create change within the existing framework. The general belief is that revolution and reform are in direct conflict. Reforms seek to improve the existing system, whereas revolutions seek to uproot it. The truth is that reform and revolutions work in tandem to create change. If you are a revolutionary, you are a reformist and if you are a reformist, you are a revolutionary. Change happens when we press existing systems as far as possible with the tools and resources at our disposal.

Radical change can emerge from small reforms. When it comes to your movement and actions, instigating reforms might feel small and insignificant in the grand scheme of things. But reforms can kickstart a much bigger process of change. In fact, most societal change has emerged from small, seemingly inconsequential reforms triggering large-scale change. We must throw away the romantic notion of change being this sliding-door moment, a big, once-in-a-lifetime event where people unite and everything changes at once. The idea of a big festival of change where everything is transformed within a 24-hour window is a myth. This distorted view of transformation, portrayed by Hollywood and encouraged by our limited understanding of butterfly effects, has restricted our imaginations and confidence to enact change. A radical overthrow of a government, change in business policy or improved human rights might look like the outcome of an overnight revolution, but in truth, much of human progress has been gained through hard-fought incremental reforms, culminating in long-term transformative change.

In some circumstances, system change is the only answer. Without revolution, people will suffer from social and economic injustice. But how do you create social change? You need to fight for reforms. Reforms create evidence of another reality, a viable alternative to the status quo. The struggle for reform can create the need for transformation. Pontificating about system change and radical revolutions without fighting for tangible improvements won't change anything. We must avoid becoming armchair change agents who talk about the ideal scenario without actively working to improve the existing reality. Reform and revolution should become best friends. Currently, those who are fighting for reforms are viewed with a side-eye by revolutionaries demanding more radical interventions. And revolutionaries are seen as unrealistic idealists. We need to ensure that revolutionaries support reforms and that reformists support the revolution. We can have both. They are simply different stages of the same process.

The Soviet Disunion

There are few better examples of how reforms can lead to radical transformation than the collapse of the Union of Soviet Socialist Republics (the USSR or Soviet Union). The Soviet Union was once a global superpower, occupying one-sixth of the Earth's land surface, including half of Europe and one-third of Asia. During the 1980s, the Soviet Union was suffering from economic stagnation. This was known as the Brezhnev stagnation, named after the Soviet leader Leonid Brezhnev, a relatively stable period, but characterized by a refusal to innovate, economic malaise and a growing technological gap between the USSR and the United States. The USSR was spending too much on the military and lacking development in agriculture, manufacturing and consumer markets. When Mikhail Gorbachev became the new leader of the USSR he set his sights on improving the system. The intention wasn't to overthrow the system but simply make sure it worked better. At the time, many Russians were struggling with poverty while corruption and nepotism were prevalent in the leadership. The only product that was cheap was vodka, leading to alcoholism and reduced productivity. Following Joseph Stalin's death, successive leaders – including Nikita Khrushchev and Alexei Kosygin – attempted to implement economic reforms and move away from totalitarianism. The state needed a new approach. But all attempts were defeated by the Central Committee (aka the Politburo) who always rejected any new ideas. Comparisons can be seen in the modern business world and civil society.

Gorbachev implemented two main reforms to modernize the Soviet Union. The first was known as *Perestroika* (Restructuring). This was an attempt to rejuvenate the stagnant economy of the USSR. In the Soviet economy, demand and supply were out of sync. Money was not being allocated where it was most needed. At that time, 25 per cent of GDP went towards military spending to compete with the United States.[1] Gorbachev made the move from centralized markets to a more decentralized model. All companies would still be owned by the state; however, they could now allocate budgets where they would make the most impact. The aim was to incentivize companies to increase productivity. *Perestroika* also allowed the establishment of private commerce. Small businesses were allowed to set their prices and keep their profits. This enabled the creation of small family-owned shops, cafes and restaurants, giving Russians their first taste of capitalism. The reforms also encouraged foreign investments in the shape of joint ventures. The first McDonald's had a grand opening in Russia's Pushkin Square on 31 January 1990 with approximately 38,000 customers waiting for hours to taste an American Big Mac. The second reform was known as *Glasnost* (openness). Ushering in a new era of transparency and freedom of speech, the aim was to address corruption and encourage dialogue. *Glasnost* led to the emergence of artists and journalists criticizing the government. Freedom of expression increased internal political pressure; examples included the popularity of the Gulag Archipelago. Mikhail Gorbachev implemented these reforms to modernize and maintain the USSR. What seemed like small reforms culminated in the collapse of the world's second-biggest superpower. It just goes to show, that reforms can indeed be revolutionary. In 1998, Gorbachev infamously featured in Pizza Hut's first TV commercial in Russia on Moscow's Red Square.

What happens next?

Revolutions are seen as a Big Bang moment, with millions of people uniting to bring about the triumph of good over evil. The disappearance of the old world brings with it the arrival of the new. But what happens next? The collective fight against the status quo is what created the initial energy and meaning. What happens when the good guys win? Creating social change and maintaining it are two different beasts. Comparisons can be made to having a baby and raising a child for 20-odd years. The idea of bringing a baby into the world is exciting, but the reality of looking after a human being is more ordinary, yet arguably more important. Revolutions can be easy to initiate but much harder to maintain. The most important aspect of social change is how it translates to people's daily lives. We can't have a big meeting about the company's new mission and then everyone goes back to business as usual. We can't distribute power without creating new governance. We can't advocate for social justice if oppressive institutions remain intact. Change cannot be an announcement, or only felt in the corridors of power. The transformation must be felt in people's everyday activities. They need to see it. They need to hear it. And, before you know it, they believe it. There needs to be a clear plan on how to convert a collective vision for a better future into everyday reality.

Occupy Wall Street

Occupy Wall Street looked destined to change America. The movement was born from dissatisfaction with economic inequality and corporate greed. Following the financial crisis of 2008, the US government bailed out the banks with taxpayer money. Ordinary Americans lost their jobs, homes and livelihoods, but there was no consequence for corporations. The message was, if the banks make money they keep it but if they mess up society bails them out. The bailouts affirmed the belief that government, corporations and public institutions are serving the interests of the 1 per cent and don't care about the rest of us. The early 2010s was a time of renewed collective awakening. We were witnessing the Arab Spring in North Africa and the Middle East, mass student protests against the government in the UK and anti-austerity protests throughout Europe. The Occupy Wall Street movement was the continuation of the dissatisfaction with the status quo on US soil, in the world's biggest economy and the epitome of 'free market' capitalism.

The protest started in New York City on 17 November 2011. It was born from a conversation between Kalle Lasn, co-founder and editor-in-chief of *Adbusters*, the anti-consumerist magazine, and Micah M White, who was the magazine's senior editor. They were inspired by how many Egyptians turned out to protest Hosni Mubarak's regime in Tahrir Square in January 2011. Lasn registered the website OccupyWallStreet.org and soon enough proposed a peaceful occupation of Wall Street to protest growing inequality. They promoted the protest with a poster of a ballerina atop Wall Street's iconic Charging Bull statue.[2] A symbolic location and a simple demand drew thousands of people to the mission. Soon enough, people from all around the world got involved. As news circulated via Facebook, Twitter, YouTube and word of mouth, more people joined the movement. New York police prevented protesters from reaching the Charging Bull, so the protesters moved to Zuccotti Park. There were roughly 1,000 protesters on the day and 300 people reportedly stayed the night. Momentum gathered quickly. Zuccotti Park became a mini-city and the home of the protest movement. The camp evolved to include amenities like a library, free meals and wireless internet. Residents donated bathrooms and laundry machines. There was a sense of community and collective participation that felt unprecedented. The city had its newspaper *Occupied Wall Street* and Ben & Jerry's provided free ice cream for protesters. The movement was a social phenomenon that brought people together, uniting them against a common enemy. Occupy Wall Street was so successful that the movement spread worldwide, motivating thousands of people to voice their frustrations against global economic inequality. New chapters were opening with Occupy London, Occupy Brussels and Occupy Tokyo. Occupy Wall Street started locally but somehow transformed into an international solidarity movement transcending age, geography and class. People from all around the world shared the same frustration against a ruling elite. Occupy Wall Street spread across 900 cities in 82 countries.[3]

Occupy Wall Street's main mission and fight was against economic inequality. It was a message that most ordinary people understood and experienced following the 2008 economic crisis. The movement's slogan was: 'We are the 99 per cent.' In 2011, 'The Protester' was named *Time* magazine's Person of the Year, a fitting reflection of the collectivist attitude and mood globally. The movement showed how people power can raise awareness about important issues. It proved that mass mobilization is possible in the digital age.

What happened to the Occupy Wall Street movement? Occupy Wall Street was incredibly effective at bringing people together to fight against the status quo. The Occupy movement, however, lacked leadership. There was no set of established demands or goals. There was no defined strategy. The movement created an important narrative, but it wasn't able to embed this energy into concrete actions. There was, purposefully, no social or political vision of a future that looked different from the current. In simple words, Occupy Wall Street knew what it was against, but it failed to outline an alternative. Rightly so, many of the protesters didn't want to turn Occupy into an autocracy. They wanted to be the antithesis of corporate governance. Not having any governance structure in place led to lots of conversations, but little meaningful action. America and the world are more unequal in 2024 than in 2011. Occupy Wall Street represents the pitfalls of not having the end goal in mind. However, the social and cultural impact of the Occupy Wall Street movement can't be understated. The movement laid the foundations for the Black Lives Matter and climate justice movements. What could Occupy Wall Street have done if they had the power to shape society? That's the question the movement failed to answer.

Shareholder primacy

For much of the 20th century, business has existed to maximize shareholder value. This is known as shareholder primacy – the belief that companies should primarily, or only, focus on maximizing profits for shareholders. It is also known as the Friedman doctrine, named after American economist Milton Friedman who advocated that a company's only social responsibility was to its shareholders.

The most emphatic legal case study on shareholder primacy comes from the 1919 Michigan Supreme Court case: *Dodge v Ford*.[4] In 1914, Henry Ford took the radical step of doubling workers' pay to $5 and reducing shifts from nine hours to eight hours. It's important to note, that this wasn't a benevolent move. It was a business decision. Ford understood that doubling worker's salaries would increase their disposable income. They would be more likely to buy a Ford car. And reducing work hours boosted productivity, happiness and loyalty to the company. When the Ford company slashed its dividends in 1916, the Dodge brothers, who were shareholders in the Ford Motor Company, sued the company for failing to deliver on its corporate responsibility. Ford's defence for lowering dividends was prioritizing employees and customers, with corporate profits a secondary motivation. Legal experts argue that Ford wanted to maintain a monopoly and prevent money flowing to the Dodge brothers, who had started their own company. Meanwhile, the construction of the new River Rouge – which was considered the world's largest factory – required profits to be put back into the business. Nonetheless, the verdict from the Michigan Supreme Court was telling, setting a landmark precedent in corporate governance: 'A business corporation is organized and carried on primarily for the profit of the stockholders.' Henry Ford was forced to pay $19 million to John and Horace Dodge. More than a century later, the debate continues: what is the role of a company? Does it only exist to make money for investors, or should it serve a greater purpose?

Negative externalities

Shareholder capitalism fails to account for the negative externalities caused by the business. In economics, a negative externality occurs when the production or consumption of a product doesn't include the true costs. For example, food company X opens a new manufacturing plant after lobbying to displace the local community. The energy-intensive manufacturing process spills toxic chemicals into the local river, which ruins the local crops. The chemicals used contribute to climate change and harm human and wildlife health. At the same time, profits skyrocket by 29 per cent and the food company experiences the biggest quarterly boost in its history. The business is successful, and the shareholders are happy, but they have failed to recognize the cost to society, the environment and future generations. The price of the product does not reflect the true cost of production and consumption. The business world is packed full of examples of negative externalities. They are the corporate version of sweeping something under the carpet and hoping nobody notices. If you brush too many things under the rug it becomes a mountain.

You might think this is a somewhat flimsy, imaginary example. Take the tobacco industry. Eight million people die each year, including 1.3 million people exposed to second-hand smoke.[5] According to the World Health Organization, smoking costs the global economy more than $1 trillion annually in healthcare expenditure and lost productivity.[6] Sure, governments have started to tax cigarettes, but it doesn't cover the full cost to society. Now let's take an even more lethal example. The biggest cause of early death in the world isn't smoking or alcohol. It's a bad diet. And yet the fast food (junk food) industry is thriving, while not absorbing any of the external costs it inflicts on society. A major study found that eating and drinking better could prevent one in five deaths around the world.[7] That's the other problem with shareholder capitalism – it doesn't factor in positive externalities. Shareholders won't directly benefit from planting trees, building schools and investing in local communities. At least, not in the short term. Most companies aren't incentivized to carry out activities that don't increase shareholder profits. Perhaps the greatest example of a negative externality is climate change. Damage from the global climate crisis is costing the planet $391 million per day.[8] That's $16 million per hour. And still, in 2022–23 fossil fuel companies logged record profits for shareholders. A prime example of how the true costs of products and services are not built into our current economic system. This is famously known as the tragedy of the commons, when individuals working in a self-interested way behave contrary to the common good of others by depleting shared resources through the action. The theory was first posited by British economist William Forster Lloyd, who described a hypothetical common where, if a herder grazed more cows, that person would accrue more profits, but if all herders followed suit it would lead to overgrazing and degradation of the land. The common land would be destroyed for everyone. No cow would be able to benefit from the resource. So, what's the solution? Establishing social codes that serve the interest of the common good. Privatization, but the party would need to pay the true price. Regulation to protect everyone's rights.

On profit

The word profit comes from the Latin 'to make progress'. But today, a country's progress has become one-dimensional, measured through gross domestic product (GDP), the total value of products or services produced within the country's borders. And yet, the most valuable things are almost impossible to measure. How do you measure love, happiness, culture or nature? We are reading the wrong charts. Progress measured through financial data is a relic of the Industrial Revolution. We need to look at more well-rounded ways of measuring progress whereby companies internalize the negative externalities.

Ancient cultures and traditions have a more multidimensional definition of progress, beyond maximizing profits for shareholders. They also think more long-term compared to the short-term view of capital markets and shareholders expecting quarterly dividends. In 1987, the UN Brundtland

Commission defined sustainability as 'meeting the needs of the present without compromising the ability of future generations to meet their own needs'.[9] Until the Industrial Revolution, most communities were living sustainably. The Bakhtiari tribe are a nomadic tribe who live in south-west Iran. They live in the Zagros mountains, 3,000 metres above sea level. Every year, the tribe would migrate their flock and family between summer quarters (*yaylāq*) and winter quarters (*qishlaq*), a practice known as transhumance. The migration takes between 20–40 days across 200 miles of mountainous terrain. The migration prevents overgrazing and the depletion of flora and fauna in one area, and the large herds of dung act as a natural fertiliser. Similar patterns can be seen in other communities. Traditional Swiss Alpine farming communities practise transhumance. The same can be seen with the Fulani people of the northern region of Nigeria.

Some historians suggest that the Iroquois Confederacy (*Haudenosaunee*), which translates to People of the Long House, in the United States is the oldest living participatory democracy in the world. Some historians have stated the Iroquois Great Law of Peace shaped and inspired the US Constitution.[10] The Iroquois Confederacy are famous for the seventh-generation principle which states: 'In our every deliberation, we must consider the impact of our decisions on the next seven generations.' Imagine how decision-making, business and our world would be transformed if corporations applied the seven generations principle? Inuits only hunt and fish as much as needed and respect wildlife populations, mainly because their life and culture depended on it. In contrast, if the current rate of industrial overfishing continues, the world's oceans will be emptied of fish by 2048.

Stakeholder capitalism

As a direct outcome of the Friedman doctrine – the only purpose of a business is to maximize shareholder profits – wealth and income inequality have increased. According to Oxfam's recent report, billionaires gain $1.7 million for every $1 earned by a person in the bottom 90 per cent of earners.[11] The divide between CEO and worker pay has never been higher. In economics, this is known as the wage ratio, which is the ratio of top salaries to the bottom salaries. According to the Economic Policy Institute, CEO pay skyrocketed by 1,460 per cent between 1978 and 2021.[12] In contrast, the compensation of the typical worker grew by just 18 per cent from 1978 to 2020. The average CEO of an S&P 500-listed company earns 272 times as much as their employee. In 1965, the ratio was 21 times as much. The numbers don't only point to the widening of the wealth gap but also the centralization of power in companies. When we look at climate change, environmental destruction and biodiversity loss, a widely reported CDC paper suggested that 100 companies have been the source of more than 70 per cent of the world's greenhouse gas emissions since 1988.[13] The need for a more inclusive economy and a habitable planet has raised questions about the legitimacy of shareholder capitalism. Even the staunchest capitalists are calling for more sustainable economic models. Stakeholder capitalism has been marketed as the solution to our social and environmental problems. Stakeholder capitalism has different names such as corporate social responsibility (CSR), environmental, social and governance (ESG) or ethical business.

Stakeholder capitalism is the idea that corporations have a responsibility to serve a wider community, not just shareholders. These stakeholders include employees, suppliers, customers, the planet and communities. The move to embrace stakeholder capitalism stems from pressure from inside the company, namely employees – and the odd activist CEO – and pressures from outside the company from consumers and civil society. Young people are demanding that corporations play an active role in society and, most importantly, refrain from causing harm. Some companies and business leaders are publicly advocating for a triple bottom line of people, planet and profit. That means companies should pay equal attention to their impact – whether positive or negative – on the planet and people. In the same way that corporations report on financial performance, they should apply effort and processes towards social and environmental reporting. Currently, most multinationals are not incentivized to report on their positive or negative impact on people and planet. Leadership, shareholders and reputation are mostly evaluated based on quarterly and annual financial profits and growth, unless other stakeholders are baked into a company's DNA with a clear governance model, daily operations and incentives.

Stakeholder capitalism can be critiqued for being an idealistic vision for a better future grounded in performative PR statements as opposed to structural change. It receives criticism from two camps. Proponents of shareholder primacy and the Friedman doctrine argue that focusing on social and environmental factors can distract boards and leadership from improving business performance and increasing shareholder value, ultimately increasing the risk of being outperformed by competitors who are solely focused on increasing profits. Others view stakeholder capitalism as a cynical move by the world's richest and most powerful people to further entrench existing power dynamics. This would give shareholders and corporations powers beyond the realm of business, allowing companies to dictate and shape social and environmental factors, without a democratic licence. Under this view, stakeholder capitalism doesn't make corporations more responsible, but more powerful and less accountable to external regulators and public scrutiny.

Advocacy for stakeholder capitalism includes the powerful Business Roundtable trade group, which includes 200 global CEOs of America's leading companies, stating that shareholder profit isn't everything. This sent shockwaves around corporate America. The *Wall Street Journal* called it 'a major philosophical shift'. Evidence suggests the statement was mostly performative, designed to please and appease the public, but didn't translate to action.[14] The World Economic Forum (WEF) produced the Davos Manifesto, which states 'the purpose of a company is to engage all its stakeholders in shared and sustained value creation'.[15] They believe that shareholder and stakeholder interests align in the long term. The problem is, few companies have legally embedded purpose into business operations. Part of the challenge is that there isn't a universal definition of stakeholder capitalism. It looks and feels different in each company. Some leaders in the financial world view it as a more long-term approach to ensuring shareholder value. For example, paying employees a fair wage or transitioning to renewable energy sources will mean the company can still provide dividends to shareholders in 10, 20 and 50 years. In other words, stakeholder capitalism protects the long-term interests of shareholders and minimizes risks. It is mainly a form of risk management. Such a perspective only views other stakeholders through the lens of maximizing shareholder profits. The second interpretation of stakeholder capitalism gives legitimate rights to stakeholders like employees, suppliers and local communities, independent of whether it maximizes profits for shareholders. The challenge emerges when the interests of different stakeholders directly clash, such as employee wages vs shareholder profits, or local community jobs vs environmental concerns. It can be tricky to navigate how to make decisions compared to the first view, which always prioritizes long-term shareholder value. The third view is improving outcomes for all stakeholders. Under such an economic system stakeholders like employees, suppliers and communities are not only viewed as a means to achieve higher shareholder value but as a constituent part of the company. The company exists to improve the outcomes of all stakeholders. The wellbeing of each stakeholder group is beneficial to the whole, not a nuisance to be minimized, mitigated or acknowledged. Challenges arise if CEOs and companies are competing in markets against other companies that only prioritize shareholder value. Moreover, many shareholders might protest the prioritization of non-shareholders in decision-making. You would need shareholder buy-in and support to initiate such a plan. This can be particularly challenging if left to the free will of corporations or during economic downturns.

The above has focused on reforms which enable the consideration of other stakeholders in the decision-making process. Employees, suppliers, communities and the planet are an addition to the main show, which is shareholders. But what happens if we decentralize and distribute power? What if non-shareholder groups like employees and communities were given voting rights? What if they had a seat in the boardroom? This could be the moment when iterative reforms give way to system change. Rather than hoping corporations and CEOs do the right thing, why not make sure stakeholders are represented in the company's governance? From a business perspective, involving a diverse range of stakeholders would increase employee engagement and innovation, and mitigate risks. This debate gets to the core of the question: what is the purpose of a company? And how can companies prevent becoming an organization with no sense of prioritization, collective organization and clarity on decision-making?

Patagonia

Yvon Chouinard was born in Maine; his father was a French-Canadian mechanic. He was one of the leading mountain climbers of the Golden Age of Yosemite Climbing. In 1957 he became dissatisfied with the quality of pitons (metal spikes used as a climbing aid), and decided to forge his own. Soon the word spread, and everyone wanted his improved steel pitons. Between climbing and surfing, he would sell his pitons for $1.50 each. In 1967 Chouinard entered a partnership with Tom Frost to produce climbing tools. The new and improved tools helped establish ice climbing as an official sport. By the 1970s Chouinard Equipment was the biggest supplier of climbing hardware in the United States. But it was ruining the rocks of Yosemite and other natural reserves. Chouinard and Frost made a conscious decision to scale down the profitable piton business because of the environmental damage, despite it representing 70 per cent of company revenues.[16] They introduced a disruptive invention into the market – aluminium chockstones, known as hex, which could be wedged into cracks rather than hammered into the rock face. They introduced clean climbing.

Today, Chouinard is better known for his outdoor and recreational clothing company, Patagonia. The journey started when Chouinard visited Scotland in 1970, bought some rugby shirts and managed to sell them instantly. Rugby shirts were made to be highly resistant and durable, making them perfect for rock climbing. The rugby collar also prevented the climbing sling from hurting people's necks. Call it fortune or destiny. Either way, the demand was evident, and the company began to grow and even started to support the marginally profitable hardware business. Two years later, Patagonia was selling rugby shirts from England, plastic raincoats and sacks from Scotland and boiled-wool gloves from Austria. This was a time when most mountaineers were getting soaked wearing traditional layers of moisture-absorbing wool, cotton and down. What started as a fantastic way to supplement the hardware business became the main business. Inspired by North Atlantic fishermen, Patagonia released the pile fleece jacket. Patagonia kept innovating with new materials and ways to protect and inspire outdoor enthusiasts. What's more, the outdoor products were colourful and fun, unlike traditional garments.

The business kept growing. By the 1980s sales were growing by 50 per cent every year.[17] Patagonia was one of the fastest-growing companies in the world. But in the 1990s, after decades of exponential growth, the company was in turmoil. An economic recession impacted the company's sales and Patagonia eventually laid off 20 per cent of employees. These were dark times at the outdoor company. This was also a moment of personal reflection for Yvon Chouinard. This was a slap in the face for a man who always rebelled against 'business as usual'. Knowingly or unknowingly, Patagonia had followed the traditional shareholder capitalism model of maximizing profits and growth above everything else. More products, more stores, more customers, more markets. In 1995, Chouinard wrote the Patagonia manifesto (remember the importance of having and maintaining your mission?). The manifesto, named 'The next 100 years', challenges the notion of bigger is better and growth at any cost. It questioned society's obsession with consumption. It called for a more sustainable approach to business, deciding to focus its efforts on the quality of products and longevity. A plan for the next 100 years, not the next quarter, half or full accounting year.

Following the manifesto, Patagonia led many innovative initiatives and campaigns, including donating 1 per cent of profits or 10 per cent of sales to the planet. In 2011, Patagonia launched its most famous 'Don't buy this jacket' campaign. The campaign was launched during Black Friday – an event which has come to symbolize overconsumption – and aimed to make the public aware of the environmental impact of consumerism. But it resonated with Patagonia's core tribe of outdoor enthusiasts and young people who were passionate about the future of the planet. The company launched a radical repair programme, where consumers can mail their broken clothes and Patagonia would repair it for free, allowing clothes to remain in circulation for as long as possible. Ironically, sales for Patagonia increased by 30 per cent in the following months after the campaign. The outdoor company has more than doubled sales since 2011, surpassing more than $1 billion in annual sales in 2019. In 2021, Yvon Chouinard updated Patagonia's mission to reflect the seriousness of environmental destruction. The old one was to build the best product, cause no unnecessary harm and use business to inspire solutions to the environmental crisis. The new mission became 'We're in business to save our home planet'. What's evident about the Patagonia story is the hunger for continuous innovation and adaptation. The company has a clear mission and values, and even if it doesn't get everything right, Patagonia is always evolving.

In a move which reflected the new company mission, in 2022 Chouinard announced a new ownership model. He was giving the company (valued at $3 billion) away to the planet.[18] Unlike other successful companies, Patagonia wasn't going public, being acquired by another conglomerate or being sold to a private equity firm. All profits from the company, at the time of the new governance model ($100 million per year), would go towards combatting climate change. Chouinard's family donated 2 per cent of all stock and all decision-making authority to a trust to oversee the company's mission and values. The other 98 per cent of the company's stock went to a non-profit organization called the Holdfast Collective, designed to protect wildlands and promote nature-based climate solutions. Every year, after re-investing money into the business, profits will be distributed to the Holdfast Collective. Chouinard made this move because he felt selling the company or going public would have compromised Patagonia's values. In many ways, Patagonia has flipped shareholder capitalism on its head. The company is using profits from product sales to pay dividends to its only shareholder, planet Earth. Critics have argued that Patagonia is still operating within the paradigm of consumerism. But there's no doubt that the move sets a precedent when it comes to reimagining the role of business.

Governance baby

At the risk of sounding like a Belgian civil servant, governance is the boring (but important) side of activism. You can't have social change without strong governance. Another example of a company redefining the traditional shareholder model is Ben & Jerry's. The activist ice cream brand was acquired by Unilever in 2000. Despite the purchase, Ben & Jerry's preserved the right to have an independent role in guiding its social mission to ensure brand integrity. Crucially, the Board of Directors are independent of Unilever shareholders and leadership. It means Ben & Jerry's makes decisions autonomously from Unilever. Since then, Ben & Jerry's has continued to grow the brand, consumer base and popularity with communities while maintaining its core mission and values, thanks to a clear brand positioning. How many other ice cream companies advocate for human rights, and social and economic justice? In 2020 the Ben and Jerry's Independent Board of Directors decided to stop selling ice cream in the Occupied Palestinian Territories. In an opinion piece in *The New York Times*, the company's Jewish founders stated, 'It is a rejection of Israeli policy, which perpetuates an illegal occupation that is a barrier to peace and violates the basic human rights of the Palestinian people who live under the occupation.'[19] Ben & Jerry's knew full well this would have an impact on the brand's profits but proceeded with the decision. Anuradha Mittal, Chair of the Board of Directors in 2018, told the *Financial Times*: 'Ben & Jerry's ice cream was travelling on roads that the Palestinians cannot use. It became clear that the presence of our product in the occupied Palestinian territory was inconsistent with our values.'[20] Unilever decided to sell the rights to the Ben & Jerry's ice cream business in Israel to its local licensee for an undisclosed fee. A couple of days later, Ben & Jerry's decided to sue its parent company, seeking to block the sale. There are rumours Unilever ceased paying Ben & Jerry's Board of Directors. The companies eventually settled the dispute, but the saga highlights the importance of governance when trying to create change.

It's the product, stupid

Part of the problem with the brand purpose debate has come from a misunderstanding of the role of purpose. Most examples of brand purpose have been nothing more than an exercise in communications. Multinational corporations have attempted to showcase their purpose through words, not actions. More importantly, glossy PR statements often fail to incorporate the most important aspect of a brand's purpose – the product or service you are producing. This is fundamentally the most direct, tangible and conclusive reflection of what the company stands for. Without designing a product or service which enriches business and society, everything else becomes irrelevant. There's little point in producing a harmful product and then working hard to wrap a social purpose around the product. And yet this is how brand purpose has been approached. People will choose the easy way without any structural change to the company's product, operation and governance. But the results are superficial and transparent, like not going to the gym and drawing a six-pack on your body with a pen. You won't fool anyone at the beach. Consumers and society have become increasingly sceptical of 'purpose washing'. Brand purpose begins with paying your taxes, looking after your employees and not destroying the environment.

Cancel culture

Over the past few years, 'cancel culture' has entered the mainstream lexicon, thanks to social media. The term has stimulated public debate across politics, culture and media. Cancel culture refers to the practice of withdrawing support for a person or company – often on social media – based on their views or actions.[21] The global pandemic further increased the cultural impact of the internet on society. Ever since the physical world went into lockdown, people have been spending a record amount of time online. At the same time, social isolation has further facilitated online interaction, thus sparking a renewed wave of social activism like the Black Lives Matter movement following the murder of George Floyd. Powerful algorithms continue to confirm our existing worldview, which in turn creates a polarized society where citizens are experiencing different versions of reality. All these factors combined make cancellation one of the most contested issues of the decade. What's more, this is likely to be the start of an enduring battle to maintain or reshape the prevailing narrative through which we live our lives, a battle that is bound to have major implications for business and society.

Critics of cancel culture view the movement as a modern form of mob rule. Cancellation prevents open debate, which has long been the foundation of democracy. After all, the ability to entertain different ideas and perspectives creates the conditions for social progress. Some of the greatest breakthroughs in human history have occurred when cultures have shared and exchanged contrary ideas. Whereas cancel culture can summarily execute opposing viewpoints without any due process or context. If we simply cancel all views considered offensive through the lens of modernity, what would we be left with?

Supporters view cancel culture as an important tool for achieving social justice. The internet, in particular social media, provides a platform for the historically underserved to share their views, opinions and lived experiences. In many ways, TikTok offers an outlet for groups excluded from traditional institutions such as politics, education, economy and media to have a say. Today, marginalized groups are no longer solely reliant on prejudiced establishments built for the privileged few. Every citizen with access to the internet can now write an opinion piece, share their story and speak truth to power. A single video has the power to plummet share prices, hold politicians accountable and force celebrities to admit to wrongdoings. Put another way, cancel culture represents the voice of the voiceless.

But there's also a deeper layer of social, cultural and historical context that can be applied to the cancel culture debate. It could be argued that cancel culture doesn't actually exist. Instead, the term has become a convenient red herring to silence legitimate protests and maintain the status quo. From this perspective, what we're seeing is an authentic attempt to right historical wrongs and push for meaningful change. For example, so-called cancel culture was instrumental in making the #MeToo campaign go mainstream, making sure that #BlackLivesMatter has been used on Twitter and Instagram since 2014 and rallying millions of people globally to protest against climate change. It could be argued that cancel culture is a synonym for legitimate criticism from groups who until recently lacked the means to express themselves.

More recently, the cancel culture debate has spilled over into the world of marketing and advertising. Historically, brands have stayed out of politics for good reason – taking sides can alienate a large chunk of their customer base. But in today's increasingly polarized climate not taking sides can be the bigger risk. Brands can no longer afford to remain neutral because neutrality is viewed as complicity. That being said, empty statements of solidarity no longer suffice either. The consumers of today are more informed and empowered than ever before. They expect you to turn your words into action. And if brands don't stick to their promises, consumers possess the knowledge, determination and platform to call them out. In short, there's nowhere to hide.

Two-thirds of consumers around the world will buy or boycott a brand solely because of its position on a social or political issue. Only a few years ago, the term 'boycott' was viewed as something confined to the radical fringes of society. But today boycotting has become a mainstream consumer reaction. And it's not only directed towards socially irresponsible brands but also towards brands seen to be overplaying their social and environmental credentials. Bud Light sales plummeted 25 per cent after backlash over its campaign with a transgender influencer.[22] The brand received unprecedented backlash from high-profile right-wingers including Ted Cruz, Ron DeSantis, Caitlyn Jenner and Kid Rock. At the time of writing, America's top-selling beer is no longer Bud Light. In a bid to win back its previous fanbase, Bud Light decided to attract rejecters with a camouflage print bottle to support families of military families. Unlike Nike's 'Dream crazy', Bud Light and AB InBev didn't take a stand. It didn't stand for anything, and failed to attract either group. The best way to avoid being cancelled is by making it clear what you stand for and what you stand against as an organization. In the race to reflect societal values, brands are becoming ever more reactive, but doing so can lead to consumer backlash unless the sentiment is backed by authentic action. On the flip side, companies that ignore the climate crisis and social inequality will struggle to attract new consumers and employees.

ACTIVITY

1 **Reform and revolution**

- o What's a small reform you can instigate today that might lead to a bigger change in the future?

Something that builds confidence and belief around the new story. Remember the Soviet Union collapsed following a series of reforms, not a revolution.

2 **Establish your demand**

- o What are your demands?
- o What are you hoping to achieve from the change?
- o How will you get there? What are the current barriers to change?

Remember the Occupy Wall Street movement and the dangers of not having a coherent vision and strategy.

3 **Build a governance model**

- o What is your governance structure?
- o Who is leading what?
- o How are decisions made?

Without a governance structure, your movement is less likely to be aligned and working towards a shared mission. A robust governance model would also improve decision-making, mitigate internal and external risks and increase accountability and trust in the movement. Governance is the boring but important part of activism.

4 What's your metric?

In the old world, companies existed to maximize profits for shareholders. This was the only lens through which leadership viewed progress, irrespective of the negative externalities.

o How will you be measuring progress?

o How will this be different to shareholder primacy?

o What are your annual and quarterly metrics? Do they include people and planet?

5 Proposition

If you are a business, the product or service you are producing is the most direct, tangible and conclusive reflection of what the company stands for.

o How can we make sure the product/service is more beneficial?

o What could be improved? How?

o How can we reduce the harmful impacts of the product?

Without designing a product or service that enriches business and society, everything else becomes irrelevant.

Notes

1 A Anisin. Military defection during the collapse of the Soviet Union, *Central European Journal of International and Security Studies*, 2022, 16 (2), 26–53. doi.org/10.51870/unyw3133 (archived at https://perma.cc/6NVU-PKJ9)

2 Adbusters. Occupy Wall Street, Adbusters, nd. www.adbusters.org/spoofs-ads/occupywallstreet (archived at https://perma.cc/UYZ2-4TKY)

3 S Rogers. Occupy protests around the world: Full list visualised, *The Guardian*, 17 October 2011. www.theguardian.com/news/datablog/2011/oct/17/occupy-protests-world-list-map (archived at https://perma.cc/3E73-R84G)

4 M Roe. *Dodge v Ford*: What happened and why? Harvard Law School Forum on Corporate Governance, 1 December 2021. corpgov.law.harvard.edu/2021/12/01/dodge-v-ford-what-happened-and-why (archived at https://perma.cc/M8XA-H3JZ)

5 World Health Organization. Tobacco, 13 July 2023. www.who.int/news-room/fact-sheets/detail/tobacco (archived at https://perma.cc/X4MX-JSA9)

6 World Health Organization. US$ 1.4 trillion lost every year to tobacco use: New tobacco tax manual shows ways to save lives, money and build back better after Covid-19, 12 April 2021. www.who.int/news/item/12-04-2021-

1.4-trillion-lost-every-year-to-tobacco-use-new-tobacco-tax-manual-shows-ways-to-save-money-and-build-back-better-after-covid-19 (archived at https://perma.cc/388V-N947)

7 BDJ Team. Bad diets killing more people globally than tobacco, study finds, 2019, 6, 8. doi.org/10.1038/s41407-019-0083-9 (archived at https://perma.cc/BCP3-LV65)

8 R Newman and I Noy. The global costs of extreme weather that are attributable to climate change, SSRN Electronic Journal, 2022. doi.org/10.2139/ssrn.4266618 (archived at https://perma.cc/DR3T-QVW6)

9 G H Brundtland (1987) *Our Common Future: Report of the World Commission on Environment and Development*, Geneva, UN-Dokument A/42/427

10 T Hansen. How the Iroquois Great Law of Peace shaped US democracy, Native America, PBS, 13 December 2018. www.pbs.org/native-america/blog/how-the-iroquois-great-law-of-peace-shaped-us-democracy (archived at https://perma.cc/2GTN-KELA)

11 Oxfam International. Richest 1 per cent bag nearly twice as much wealth as the rest of the world put together over the past two years, 16 January 2023. www.oxfam.org/en/press-releases/richest-1-bag-nearly-twice-much-wealth-rest-world-put-together-over-past-two-years (archived at https://perma.cc/5NK8-3G75)

12 J Bivens and J Kandra. CEO pay has skyrocketed 1,460 per cent since 1978: CEOs were paid 399 times as much as a typical worker in 2021, Economic Policy Institute, 4 October 2022. www.epi.org/publication/ceo-pay-in-2021 (archived at https://perma.cc/7CKH-8PD4)

13 P Griffin. *CDP Carbon Majors Report 2017*, CDC, July 2017. cdn.cdp.net/cdp-production/cms/reports/documents/000/002/327/original/Carbon-Majors-Report-2017.pdf?1501833772 (archived at https://perma.cc/3PRM-VLFS)

14 G Colvin. America's top CEOs didn't live up to their promises in Business Roundtable letter, researchers find, *Fortune*, 5 August 2021. www.fortune.com/2021/08/05/business-roundtable-letter-statement-on-the-purpose-of-a-corporation-stakeholder-capitalism-american-ceos (archived at https://perma.cc/P7LG-G6R5)

15 K Schwab. Davos Manifesto 2020: The universal purpose of a company in the Fourth Industrial Revolution, World Economic Forum, 2 December 2019. www.weforum.org/agenda/2019/12/davos-manifesto-2020-the-universal-purpose-of-a-company-in-the-fourth-industrial-revolution (archived at https://perma.cc/8KRZ-HXL2)

16 Patagonia. Company history, Patagonia, nd. eu.patagonia.com/gb/en/company-history (archived at https://perma.cc/G35B-XJJD)

17 Y Chouinard. Prosperity with less: What would a responsible economy look like? *The Guardian*, 4 October 2013. www.theguardian.com/sustainable-business/patagonia-founder-responsible-economy-with-less (archived at https://perma.cc/7A4D-KEPP)

18 D Gelles. Billionaire no more: Patagonia founder gives away the company, *New York Times*, 14 September 2022. www.nytimes.com/2022/09/14/climate/patagonia-climate-philanthropy-chouinard.html (archived at https://perma.cc/7CPY-P23Y)

19 B Cohen and J Greenfield. We're Ben and Jerry. Men of ice cream. Men of principle, *New York Times*, 28 July 2021. www.nytimes.com/2021/07/28/opinion/ben-and-jerry-israel.html (archived at https://perma.cc/7JZU-9W9N)

20 J Evans. Ben & Jerry's vs Unilever: How a star acquisition became a legal nightmare, *Financial Times*, 11 October 2022. www.ft.com/content/30efd993-8c23-4f1b-9385-132bbba3d863 (archived at https://perma.cc/ZUD5-D294)

21 K Bakhtiari. Why brands need to pay attention to cancel culture, *Forbes*, 2020. www.forbes.com/sites/kianbakhtiari/2020/09/29/why-brands-need-to-pay-attention-to-cancel-culture (archived at https://perma.cc/447F-ZZNH)

22 L Fickenscher. Bud Light sales plunge nearly 25 per cent in latest week as rivals steal away customers, *New York Post*, 23 May 2023. nypost.com/2023/05/22/bud-light-sales-plunge-nearly-25-in-latest-week (archived at https://perma.cc/SP37-8HMG)

7

Start collaborating

Competition can be good for business and society. There are many benefits to healthy competition. According to classical economics, perfect competition between many sellers produces better products, lower prices and more innovative solutions for consumers. The idea is competition for buyers means no party can risk having higher prices, a substandard product or poorer customer service. For example, if you had the choice to pick from three identical internet providers. Company A is $30 per month. Company B is $50 a month. Company C is $100 per month. Most buyers would opt for Company A and eventually, Company C will go out of business unless it lowers its prices or differentiates from the other two companies. Perfect competition creates an equilibrium between the price and the demand for the product and service.

The theory can equally be applied to examples outside of business. Like sports, international relations and neighbours. It could be argued that Pep Guardiola's Manchester City and Jürgen Klopp's Liverpool FC teams pushed each other to new heights. Both managers have admitted the rivalry has pushed them to think and play better football. Under the right conditions, competition can increase motivation, improve productivity and boost creativity. It forces teams to think more and find ways to outmanoeuvre their opponent.

The Space Race

Following World War II, the US and the Soviet Union competed in the Space Race. The objective was to achieve superior spaceflight capability. This was a competition between the world's two great superpowers, a rivalry between capitalism and communism. America and the Soviet Union raced to achieve supremacy in space, but it was also a symbol of superior ideology. It was a literal moonshot: a plan to do something that seems impossible. The USSR were the first to put a satellite into orbit in 1958 with *Sputnik 1*. Then the Soviets sent the first human, cosmonaut Yuri Gagarin, into orbit with *Vostok 1*. The US was falling behind so President John F Kennedy promised America would be the first to land a man on the moon before the end of the 1960s. The US increased NASA's budget and *Apollo 11* was launched into space on 16 July 1969. 'The Eagle' landed on the moon and Neil Armstrong became the first man to walk on the moon, ending the Space Race. Both states might not have allocated as much funding, human capital and political interest if they weren't competing for global dominance. The last time someone visited the moon was in 1972. In Renaissance Italy, Leonardo da Vinci and Michelangelo shared the same patrons and disliked but respected each other. On a micro level, one of the best predictors of whether people install solar panels isn't age, income or politics. It's whether your neighbours did it first. The study has been repeated in the US, Germany, Switzerland and the UK with the same conclusion – competition can keep you on your toes.

Imperfect competition

The problem is that economic models don't always reflect reality. Perfect competition is a figment of the human imagination; it doesn't exist in the real world. Economic theory posits that perfect competition occurs when there are many buyers and sellers. All companies sell the same product and market share has no impact on prices. A firm operating in perfect competition can't influence the price of their products. All participants in the market have complete information about products and prices. Capital resources (machinery, buildings and tools) and labour in perfect competition conditions are mobile. There is no barrier to the market – any company can enter or leave the market without restrictions.

Can you think of an example of perfect competition? Perfect competition is an economic unreality. The business reality looks somewhat different. Companies are always engaged in a type of warfare – fighting to control a bigger chunk of the market. After years of collaboration, Rudolf and Adolf Dassler separated and started two shoe companies. Adidas and Puma were born from this brotherly rivalry. Adolf (Adi) Dassler started Adidas and Rudolf Dassler started Puma. The brothers sued each other numerous times over the years over design and trademark issues, costing each other a fortune in lawsuits. The two factories were built in the same Bavarian town of Herzogenaurach – situated on opposite sides of the Arach river – forcing people to choose a side. The southern part was Puma and anyone wearing Adidas would be unwelcome. And the northern part was Adidas, where anyone wearing Puma would be viewed with contempt. If you worked for one company, you wouldn't be found dead going to the other side of the river. This was the corporate equivalent of the Bloods and the Crips. Each side had its own bakeries, bars and sports clubs. The two brothers remained rivals until the very end. Before their deaths, both brothers demanded not to be buried next to each other. Following their wish, Adolf and Rudolf are buried on opposite ends of Herzogenaurach cemetery. Both companies are still headquartered in Herzogenaurach, and still trying to steal market share from each other.

The Great Tea Robbery

Unlike in economic textbooks, competition resembles war, a winner-takes-all game to increase market share, crush your opponents and increase profits. There isn't a more fitting example than the Great Tea Robbery. For most of the 19th century the British East India Company was the biggest corporation in the world. It had more than 260,000 soldiers – twice the size of the British Army – after being granted a monopoly to trade with the East in 1600 through a Royal Charter from Queen Elizabeth I. In 1689, the East India Company started to import tea from Imperial China.

It's worth remembering that from 1080 to 1850 China was the richest country in the world. Tea drinking had been a ritual in China for thousands of years before it arrived in Europe. The British took a particular liking to tea; the beverage was adopted by royalty and the upper class, before reaching all parts of society. The British public was hooked, and the East India Company was the only supplier of the goods. Tea was a big hit and by 1813 import duty on tea accounted for 10 per cent of the British government's entire revenue.[1] Historians argue that income from tea sales helped with the urbanization and industrialization of the United Kingdom. There was one problem, however. Britain had a massive trade deficit with China. Britain was importing ever-growing amounts of tea from China, but there was nothing China needed in return. China was a rich, self-dependent and ancient culture. The country would only accept silver in exchange for tea and Britain was fast running out of silver. The British came up with a new master plan of selling drugs to China to balance out the trade deficit. The plan was to illegally smuggle in and sell opium for silver and then trade the silver for tea. This move was made possible after Britain colonized Bengal, the wealthiest region in India, which was industrialized. Bengal accounted for 12 per cent of the world's GDP. It was renowned for its industry and trade. Through economic exploitation, tax collection and contortion of the local economy, the East India Company managed to establish a monopoly on opium. The reliance on opium farming, slave labour and high taxes during a time of famine caused the death of 10 million Bengalis.[2]

China banned the trade of opium after the illegal smuggling of opium by the East India Company created a social and economic crisis. At the time, foreign traders could only trade at the port of Canton (Guangzhou). They were not allowed to enter mainland China. In 1839, Chinese official Lin Zexu was tasked with stopping the opium smuggling. He wrote a letter to Queen Victoria appealing to her moral responsibility to stop the opium trade. When his letter was not answered, British opium dealers were forced to hand over 2.37 million pounds of opium. It was thrown into the sea to show the government's determination to ban opium. The British responded by sending its powerful navy to force the Chinese government to pay reparations and make opium trading legal. The three-year war concluded with a humiliating defeat for China and the Treaty of Nanking (1842) which gave away Hong Kong to the British, dismantling the Canton system and opening five Chinese ports for foreign trade, and reparations for the destroyed opium, and ultimately the expansion of the opium trade in China. Opium addiction was a social and economic drain on Chinese society. Families spent a significant portion of their income on sustaining their opium habits, exacerbating poverty and economic hardship. By 1839, the East India Company's sale of opium to China paid for the entire tea trade.[3] More than a quarter of China's male population were hooked on opium by 1906.[4]

But that wasn't enough for the East India Company because China still dominated the global tea trade. The British had plans to create their tea empire in India and reduce their reliance on Chinese tea. In comes Robert Fortune, a Scottish botanist hired by the East India Company to steal information on how to grow and process tea. This is considered one of the greatest thefts of intellectual property in history. Fortune travelled into mainland China disguised as a Chinese merchant by the name of Sing Wa. He shaved his hair, leaving only a ponytail and a moustache, and wore traditional clothes. Chinese tea production was a meticulous process of plucking, drying, cooking, rolling, cooking again and sorting by quality. Fortune returned to Shanghai with all the tea samples he could carry. He sailed to India with eight tea masters and 13,000 seeds of the finest tea. And with it, the fate of the two Empires had shifted. The Chinese call this period the century of humiliation. The East India Company became the world's most powerful corporation in human history. Far from perfect competition, it was achieved through monopoly, drug dealing, corporate espionage, slavery and colonialism.

Monopolies

The opposite of perfect competition is a monopoly. Under imaginary perfect competition, firms must sell at whatever price the market determines, and profit margins are low. Whereas monopolies get to determine their own prices. The lack of competition allows it to control supply and demand. Have you noticed why a bottle of water costs $5 when on an aeroplane? The lack of consumer choice explains why airlines can afford to sell water at three times the market price. Ryanair water is twelve times more expensive than in the supermarket. They have a monopoly and know you can't walk outside the aeroplane and look for alternative options. Bottled water is 200 per cent more expensive at airports. The same goes with cinema popcorn; once you enter the theatre, you have no other options to source your kernels from. Cinemas generate higher profits from snacks than from selling tickets since 50 per cent of ticket sales go to the film studios. If you live in a small village and there's only one shop, you are at the mercy of the shop owner's prices. Monopolies can set the price and dictate the rules of engagement. The famous board game Monopoly demonstrates this brilliantly. We have all been there when someone buys all the property and starts building hotels. They begin to collect rent and we have no choice but to pay rent until we're out of the game.

At its height, Standard Oil controlled 90 per cent of oil refineries in the US.[5] Standard Oil was founded by John D Rockefeller in 1870 who employed a number of strategies to eliminate and absorb competitors. America was powered by oil, especially kerosene, which lit up homes more effectively than whale blubber. Rockefeller was a shrewd entrepreneur and innovator; other refineries would only keep 60 per cent of the oil that would convert into kerosene and dump the rest into rivers and lakes, whereas Rockefeller used gasoline to fuel the refinery and turned the by-products into lubricants, petroleum jelly, chewing gum and paint. He bought a forest and used his own wood to produce barrels for storing oil. Unlike other oil companies, Standard Oil controlled every aspect of the oil production and distribution process. This is known as vertical integration, reducing costs and encouraging economies of scale. Rockefeller expanded aggressively by buying out competing oil refineries, and if they refused he would undercut their prices, forcing their business to become unprofitable before purchasing the struggling corporations. Standard Oil negotiated favourable terms with railroads, obtaining discounts and rebates for transporting large volumes of oil. This made it difficult for smaller companies to compete on price because of transportation costs. Within the first three months of 1872, he bought out, shut down or bankrupted 22 of his 26 Cleveland competitors. This was named the 'Cleveland massacre'.

American writer and investigative journalist Ida Tarbell started exposing Standard Oil's unfair tactics, including the bribing of politicians and government officials. She took on Rockefeller, the world's richest man (worth 3 per cent of US GDP) and won. Ida Tarbell had seen her father's business get crushed by Standard Oil's anti-competitive tactics. These included Standard employees threatening stores to switch to Standard Oil, bribing railroad agents to provide data on competitors' shipments, and Standard Oil's reorganization as a trust, which restricted free trade. Ida Tarbell's 'A history of the Standard Oil Company' was published in *McClure's Magazine* from 1903 and 1905. The exposé completely changed the public's perception of J D Rockefeller, Standard Oil and monopolies in general. She revealed how 200 companies controlled almost everything in America. This gained the attention of President Theodore Roosevelt, who became known as the 'trust buster'. He created a Department of Commerce and Labor with an investigative agency called the Bureau of Corporations that would monitor companies for antitrust violations. In 1909 the US Justice Department sued Standard under a federal antitrust law, the Sherman Antitrust Act of 1890, for sustaining a monopoly and restraining interstate commerce. A couple of years later the Supreme Court upheld the verdict and declared Standard Oil an unreasonable monopoly. The company was broken up into 34 separate entities, which include ExxonMobil, Chevron Corporation and ConocoPhillips – some of which still have the highest revenue in the world.

Oligopolies

While on the topic of oil, there is growing evidence that ExxonMobil knew about the negative consequences of burning fossil fuels as early as the 1970s. A mountain of internal documents shows that the corporation's scientists correctly and skilfully predicted how global temperatures and carbon emissions would increase.[6] But, rather than taking the necessary action, they allocated resources to downplaying and discrediting the science. Of course, ExxonMobil might have prevented environmental destruction – and accelerated the transition to renewable energy – but remember these are negative externalities in our current economic system. The purpose of business in shareholder capitalism is to increase profitability. Many times, perfect competition is an obstacle preventing companies from maximizing profits. Another example of imperfect competition is an oligopoly, where a small number of firms control the market. Airlines, automobile manufacturers, media, technology and pharmaceutical companies are the usual suspects. These industries tend to be capital-intensive with significant barriers to entry. For example, you can't start an airline company or car manufacturer with $10,000. Meanwhile, patents enable pharmaceutical companies to set prices and keep out potential entrants to the market. Patents last for 20 years, companies require regulatory approval and get to sell the product exclusively for 12 years. In the US, pharmaceutical companies receive government funds and tax breaks. American taxpayers fund research into new drugs. According to Professor Mariana Mazzucato, 'Since the 1930s, the National Institutes of Health has invested close to $900 billion in the basic and applied research that formed both the pharmaceutical and biotechnology sectors.'[7]

If oligopolies collude, they can set prices by controlling the supply of products and services. Once a drug is ready to reach the market, pharmaceutical companies can set a price point to maximize revenue at the expense of accessibility. Companies attempt to extend the patent duration of drugs by making tweaks and preventing generic competition from entering the market. Of course, the patent system has produced some breakthrough inventions in the medical space. But it also incentivizes companies to prevent competition from entering the market and this can also prevent innovation. Studies indicate that the average price of drugs declines by 48 per cent following patent expiration.[8] You only have to look at the low price of paracetamol to understand the impact of increased competition. It prevents firms from setting their own prices. Perfect competition is meant to bring the best possible outcome for consumers. In practice, pharmaceutical companies prioritize financial returns to shareholders rather than helping people become healthier. The same concept applies on the international stage. Another famous oligopoly is the Organization of the Petroleum Exporting Countries (OPEC). Founded in 1960 in Baghdad, its 13 members hold more than 80 per cent of the world's proven oil reserves.[9] The group was created to regulate oil prices by coordinating increases or reductions in supply. This allows the nations to get the best possible price for oil.

Reality check

An abundance of historical evidence and economic reality shows there's no such thing as perfect competition when the main objective is maximizing profits. Numerous reasons prevent perfect competition and enable monopolies.

Firstly, the notion of a homogenous product goes against the foundational principle of marketing. The focus is purely on the production of the product, not on how the product is positioned and communicated. Marketing has the power to create a unique value proposition and product differentiation in the mind of the audience. Brands can charge a premium by creating a point of distinction. A white T-shirt might cost $5 but when you imprint a Gucci logo the value increases greatly. This is not a different product, but a different positioning and framing. This is simply because of the brand's story, reputation and association. Secondly, as demonstrated in nearly all examples, firms tend to be price makers, not price takers as claimed under perfect competition. There might be some competitor analysis at play, but the price is rarely set by the outside world. Thirdly, capital and resources aren't as fluid as outlined, allowing bigger corporations to determine and push down wages and benefit from economies of scale. Tesco or Walmart won't be buying stocks for the same price and cost of sale as a local corner shop or bodega. And low barriers to entry don't exist in every industry. Otherwise, I would have launched my football team. It is in the interests of the incumbent to keep potential players out of the market so that they can maximize revenue. Existing actors have no incentive to operate efficiently.

The internet

Until now, we've explored the cold-blooded world of dog-eat-dog competition. A setting reminiscent of an episode of *The Apprentice* or *The Wolf of Wall Street*. Such a mentality makes you feel like it's you against the world, whereby your neighbours, colleagues, employees, industry peers and other nations' betterment would directly create a negative outcome for you. Put simply, if others win you lose, but if you win they lose. I'm pleased to say that merciless competition isn't the only path to progress. Business and social impact don't have to be a zero-sum game. Within the traditional shareholder primacy paradigm, the winner takes it all and the loser won't be able to survive in the long term. However, there are conditions where all parties can benefit from new innovation without harming anyone in the market.

The internet was developed by the public. The US military created the Advanced Research Projects Agency Network (ARPA) to keep its technology a step ahead of the Soviet Union. ARPA's greatest innovation was packet switching, which allowed for the transfer of data between devices over a shared network. This was known as the ARPANET. Satellites helped to extend the network across the world. As the number of computers increased, it became more difficult to manage the process. Domain names were created, with each organization having its unique name. However, the internet was still restricted to universities, scientists, mathematicians and researchers. ARPANET was officially decommissioned in 1990 and handed over to private enterprise. The World Wide Web was created in CERN by Tim Berners-Lee in 1989, which helped to democratize the internet, making it easier to get information, share and communicate using hyperlinked text. The hardware, software and satellites for the internet emerged from public funds, not from private enterprise. It is an amazing example of human creativity and innovation. In the 1990s Microsoft launched several versions of Microsoft Windows and captured over 90 per cent market share of the world's personal computers market. It became a major monopoly, using public technology and commercializing it for corporate transactions such as the intranet. The privatization of the internet opened new possibilities for corporations. It became a new marketing channel to promote consumerism. Advertising revenue funds a free internet model, whether it is YouTube advertising, banner adverts while reading an online article or e-commerce websites promoting the latest sales. Is the internet a public or private space?

Imagine if companies competed to reduce access and increase ownership of the internet to maximize profits. We would lose so much value and billions of people would lose out on valuable resources. There are over 5.3 billion internet users in the world, meaning over 65 per cent of the world's population has access. In 2016, the UN declared that it considers the internet to be a human right. Specifically, an addition was made to Article 19 of the

Universal Declaration of Human Rights, Section 32, which states, 'The promotion, protection and enjoyment of human rights on the internet'.[10]

The internet has changed the world in immeasurable ways. So much so that it's now hard to imagine life without it. It removed barriers to communication; we no longer had to be in the same physical space to share ideas, communicate and connect with others. People can email someone in a matter of seconds, not weeks, months or years using postal mail. It has given billions of people access to the world's information. A school child in rural Bangladesh has the same access to information thanks to Google as a student in New York. We are also able to connect and build movements with other people who share our passions and interests. The internet and social media have given everyone a voice; much of the world's population had no outlet to share their message before the invention of the internet. Employees can now find jobs and access health tools on the internet. Small businesses can promote their work and reach new audiences. We can watch cat videos to brighten up our day. The internet has been so transformative that we almost don't think about it, like water and oxygen. Unlike the traditional of the winner-takes-all competition, the internet shows us that a rising tide lifts all boats. The lesson here is that certain products, creations and innovations can benefit all participants.

A global pandemic

Before the Covid-19 global pandemic was announced in 2020, vaccines would take several years to develop. The quickest vaccine to be invented before this was the mumps vaccine, which took four years. But the coronavirus vaccine shattered this record, taking only nine months to develop. The reason is a mixture of urgency – people were dying around the globe – and radical international collaboration. Governments, corporations and citizens understood the interdependence of a globalized world. There was no way the coronavirus could be contained to a specific region once it had taken hold, since the world is deeply interconnected. Frankfurt airport has connections to 330 destinations around the world. Companies, factories, shops and supply chains were shut down. People knew they could get the virus from others when in public places. The world is interconnected. Finding a vaccine for the coronavirus became a collective global goal. Governments, companies, non-governmental organizations (NGOs) and communities began collaborating. Scientists used past research from SARS and MERS viruses to get started. The science community around the world shared information about the novel pathogen to help increase understanding of the virus and develop tools to test for the coronavirus. The approach was collaborative, using pre-print and open-access journals. This helped to build a collective scientific understanding, share knowledge and receive feedback in ways not seen in other outbreaks. A discovery from the UK Recovery trial in the NHS led by University of Oxford scientists discovered that an inexpensive steroid pill, dexamethasone, reduced deaths from Covid-19 by up to a third. It's estimated that dexamethasone saved the lives of around 22,000 Covid-19 patients in the UK and one million lives globally by March 2021.[11] A staggering 19,389 articles about Covid-19 were shared in the first four months of the pandemic.[12]

Under normal circumstances inventing a vaccine can take 10–15 years. The discovery phase takes between two and five years and involves lots of lab research to induce an immune response. The pre-clinical stage takes up to two years and involves animal testing, and then you have the clinical development process, which is a staggered approach. Phase one is testing with 10–50 people over two years in trials. The next stage is testing hundreds of people in randomized trials, including placebo control groups and people with the infection. The final stage is assessing whether the vaccine is safe, which can take 5–10 years and thousands of people to take part in trials. It can then take another two years to receive regulatory approval on the vaccine's safety and efficacy. And finally, the vaccine is manufactured and delivered. A faster process would reduce the tragic loss of life and prevent the loss of $375 billion to the global economy every month. It was good for society and business. Research and clinical trials were fast-tracked thanks to global cooperation. Governments, the private sector and global health organizations worked together to fund vaccine research. The US government invested at least $31.9 billion to develop, produce and purchase mRNA Covid-19 vaccines, including sizeable investments in the three decades before the pandemic.[13] At least 98 per cent of the funding for the development of the Oxford/AstraZeneca vaccine – a partnership between the University of Oxford scientists and pharmaceutical giant AstraZeneca combining expertise in vaccinology and manufacturing – has been identified as coming from taxpayers or charitable trusts.[14] The private sector shifted their research and development efforts to focus on the coronavirus. Massive government funding de-risked the decision for pharmaceutical companies. This allowed for parallel development where scientists and pharmaceutical manufacturers worked on critical aspects of the process at the same time rather than sequentially. It also meant multiple vaccines were being developed by rival manufacturers, diversifying the chance of finding a vaccine and accelerating the overall timeline as the entire world waited for a solution. The BioNTech/Pfizer holds the Guinness Book of Records for the shortest time between the identification of a disease and the approval of a vaccine for widespread use.

The collaboration wasn't perfect. Going back to the realities of imperfect competition and companies seeking to maximize profits, the pharmaceutical companies – and certain governments – prioritized wealthier markets, refusing to share the intellectual property (IP) with other companies so more people could access the vaccine in developing countries. Poorer countries were placed at the 'back of the queue' when vaccines were rolled out. Wealthy nations bought the bulk of vaccines for internal markets. The governments of India and South Africa pushed for an IP waiver to allow third-party manufacturers to develop vaccines at an affordable price for local markets. The campaign for temporary relief and the establishment of 'the people's vaccine' was backed by more than 100 countries, organizations, scientists, Nobel Laureates and the World Health Organization.

Nevertheless, the Covid-19 vaccine lays a new blueprint for global health and science collaboration. Delivering the vaccine in under 12 months was a moonshot, a testament of human inventiveness, creativity and capacity to collaborate. Global Covid vaccination saved 20 million people in the first year.[15] Imagine if the same level of effort were to tackle the climate crisis or global poverty. More can be achieved if we pool our brainpower, resources and plans together.

'Walk This Way'

As the legend goes, one day 22-year-old record producer and co-founder of Def Jam Rick Rubin heard Run-DMC freestyling over a popular instrumental. Run-DMC knew the beat, which was popular among DJs and MCs in the underground hip-hop scene. They had no idea who produced the track or the lyrics. When Rubin told them it was 'Walk This Way' by Aerosmith the crew had no idea who they were. Hip-hop started as an underground movement of DJs, MCs and independent labels in New York. The music felt different, foreign and somewhat alien for listeners who were used to singing, not rapping. Run-DMC was one of the hottest rap acts of the 1980s, but they still struggled to break through into mainstream audiences. It was impossible to break out beyond the group's existing young, urban and multi-ethnic audiences and reach the suburbs. The group weren't getting any play time on pop radio stations. What's more, Run-DMC represented real hip-hop, they were brutally honest and tough, not pasteurized, watered down or cheesy, unlike other musicians trying to appeal to mass audiences. Rubin had grown up on rock musicians like AC/DC, Aerosmith and Black Sabbath. He had an idea how to bridge the gap between the two worlds. He asked Aerosmith if they would be up for collaborating with Run-DMC. The group said yes. At the time, Aerosmith was less popular following its peak in the 1970s because of quarrels, drug addiction and changing music tastes. Run-DMC were unsure about the idea. They didn't want the collaboration to dilute their message or focus. But after some convincing they agreed. Later, DMC stated that they were afraid the move would ruin their careers and street cred. Even after hearing the Aerosmith verse, he and DJ Run thought it was hillbilly gibberish.[16]

The collaboration ended up being transformative for both parties. For Run-DMC, it helped them break into mainstream audiences. The crossover made rap music palatable and enjoyable for white, middle-class and rural listeners. This became bigger than Run-DMC – it moved hip-hop from the underground into the mainstream. Rick Rubin had the foresight that rap could be an outright genre and found a way to bridge the gap. Run-DMC became the first Black and first hip-hop act to appear on MTV. 'Walk This Way' became the first hip-hop song to reach the Billboard 100. The collaboration was arguably even more fruitful for Aerosmith, as it opened a new generation of fans – kids who were more familiar with Bon Jovi, Guns N' Roses and Mötley Crüe – who learned about the rock band. The partnership also helped Aerosmith expand beyond America to become a household name in Europe. The iconic music video saw both bands in neighbouring studios before Steven Tyler smashed the wall. Defying convention, redefining music genres and illustrating the power of collaboration. Interesting things happen when we are open to new approaches and partnerships. Sometimes you need a mediator like Rick Rubin to bring two different worlds together.

The power of collaboration

Our society is gradually moving away from the exploitative practices seen with the East India Company, to competition, such as Adidas vs Puma. The next evolution is embracing the power of collaboration, a move that requires us to adopt an 'abundance' mindset. With a scarcity mindset, for you to win someone else has to lose. An abundance mindset views personal and professional interactions as a win–win scenario. A scarcity mindset might have been useful before the agricultural revolution, when our ancestors weren't sure where our next meal would come from. In the 21st century, there are enough opportunities and resources for everyone to thrive. As demonstrated, we can go further to achieve new heights if we can collaborate. The whole is always greater than the sum of its parts. Unlike the rat race, an abundance mindset allows us to celebrate the wins of others. Because other people's or companies' success doesn't detract from our own. We should be happy if our colleague is promoted, or if a company in our industry creates a new product or another movement working on the same mission gathers traction. In this new era of marketing for social change, collaboration is more valuable than competition. Partnerships are especially valuable if they are complementary. Think about Run-DMC and Aerosmith – one brought cultural relevance and the other a new audience. A complementary partner can also compensate for your weaknesses and vice versa. It should spark innovation, with new ways of thinking. You might be surprised to discover that even some of the fiercest rivals collaborate. Apple buys the majority of its OLED displays from Samsung. In fact, in 2017, Samsung sold Apple about 180 to 200 million OLED panels for the iPhone X which earned it more revenue than selling its own Galaxy S8 series phones. China is the top supplier of goods and services to America. Despite growing demands from politicians to 'decouple from China', the world's superpower is reliant on Chinese machinery, technology and appliances.

LEGO Foundation and Sesame Workshop

LEGO's mission is to inspire and develop the builders of tomorrow. The entire business is founded on children playing and exploring. Since 2015 the LEGO Foundation has worked with Sesame Workshops in India, Mexico and South Africa to give children in need the opportunity to learn through play. Following the success of the partnership, the LEGO Foundation awarded a $100 million grant to Sesame Workshop to ensure that young children affected by the Rohingya and Syrian crises have opportunities to learn through play and develop the skills needed for the future.[17] The Sesame Workshop – the name behind the famous *Sesame Street* TV show – is on a mission to help children everywhere grow smarter, stronger and kinder. The charity is working in partnership with BRAC, the International Rescue Committee and New York University's Global TIES for Children. Sesame Workshop will reach children affected by crises in Bangladesh and the Syrian response region with early childhood and play-based learning opportunities. The partnership brings LEGO into the humanitarian field where most children don't have the opportunity to play, explore and learn. Sesame Workshop can reach more young people with their play-based learning opportunities in some of the most underserved communities. The programme is designed to help over a million children learn from play. Sesame Workshop will share its successes and mistakes with the larger humanitarian community so that everyone can learn. The LEGO Foundation, which owns 25 per cent of the Danish toy and brick maker, was set up by the company's founding family and is devoted to projects that support children through play. The move is good for LEGO and for the communities – Sesame Workshop is both entertaining and educating. The most important aspect of any partnership, whether marriage, activism or business is a shared set of values and mission.

ACTIVITY

The shift from competition to collaboration is an intentional move. It represents a transition away from a scarcity mindset towards practising an abundance mindset. There are enough opportunities and resources for everyone to thrive. We can go further to make a business and social impact if we can collaborate with others. Here are some questions which might spark an intentional approach to collaboration:

1   Who can you collaborate with to make an even bigger impact?

2   What are the strengths that you can bring to a strategic partnership?

3   What complementary skills are you looking for from partners?

4   What is the cost of collaborating? For example, time, resources, creative freedom, etc.

5   What is the cost of not collaborating?

6   What would be the best way to structure the partnership? For example, equity, informal, joint venture, etc.

7   How can we agree on the scope and parameters of the partnership? Establishing a shared mission, values and expectations is critical to building a long-term and impactful partnership.

Notes

1   T Wiltshire (1997) *Old Hong Kong, Vol 1: 1860–1900*, Formasia Books, Hong Kong

2   A Mukherjee. Famine and dearth in India and Britain, 1550–1800: Connected cultural histories of food security, University of Exeter, nd. english.exeter.ac.uk/research/projects/famine (archived at https://perma.cc/WZ4K-6YW3)

3   Royal Museums Greenwich. Cutty Sark and the tea trade, nd. www.rmg.co.uk/stories/topics/cutty-sark-tea-trade (archived at https://perma.cc/3QU8-C75X)

4   UNODC. *A Century of International Drug Control*, 2009. www.unodc.org/documents/data-and-analysis/Studies/100_Years_of_Drug_Control.pdf (archived at https://perma.cc/MKS2-CHVE)

5   N Burclaff. Standard Oil established, Library of Congress, 2020. guides.loc.gov/this-month-in-business-history/january/standard-oil-established (archived at https://perma.cc/U2F8-H5WH)

6   G Supran, S Rahmstorf and N Oreskes. Assessing ExxonMobil's global warming projections, *Science*, 13 January 2023. www.science.org/doi/10.1126/science.abk0063 (archived at https://perma.cc/5G89-E9HM)

7   M Mazzucato. Op-ed: How taxpayers prop up Big Pharma, and how to cap that, *Los Angeles Times*, 27 October 2015. www.latimes.com/opinion/op-ed/la-oe-1027-mazzucato-big-pharma-prices-20151027-story.html (archived at https://perma.cc/7NLU-MHKP)

8   L Gorman. Patent expiration and pharmaceutical prices, NBER, 14 September 2014. www.nber.org/digest/sep14/patent-expiration-and-pharmaceutical-prices (archived at https://perma.cc/5XBP-FN7L)

9   OPEC. OPEC share of world crude oil reserves 2022, 2023. www.opec.org/opec_web/en/data_graphs/330.htm (archived at https://perma.cc/9DMD-68P7)

10 United Nations. Universal Declaration of Human Rights, 1948. www.un.org/en/about-us/universal-declaration-of-human-rights (archived at https://perma.cc/Y32D-8VBG)

11 NHS England. Covid treatment developed in the NHS saves a million lives, 23 March 2021. www.england.nhs.uk/2021/03/covid-treatment-developed-in-the-nhs-saves-a-million-lives (archived at https://perma.cc/7S5J-YZWT)

12 O J Watson et al. Global impact of the first year of Covid-19 vaccination: A mathematical modelling study, *The Lancet Infectious Diseases*, 2022, 22 (9), 1293–302. doi.org/10.1016/s1473-3099(22)00320-6 (archived at https://perma.cc/M3EX-9S6T)

13 H S Lalani et al. US public investment in development of mRNA Covid-19 vaccines: Retrospective cohort study, *BMJ*, 1 March 2023, erratum in BMJ, 14 March 2023. www.bmj.com/content/380/bmj.p587 (archived at https://perma.cc/9DGY-5K88)

14 S Cross et al. Who funded the research behind the Oxford–AstraZeneca COVID-19 vaccine? *BMJ Global Health*, December 2021. gh.bmj.com/content/6/12/e007321 (archived at https://perma.cc/XT8D-V98A)

15 C Watson. Rise of the preprint: How rapid data sharing during Covid-19 has changed science forever, *Nature Medicine*, 2022, 28, 2–5. doi.org/10.1038/s41591-021-01654-6 (archived at https://perma.cc/2BC2-8SJA)

16 G Edgers. The inside story of when Run-DMC met Aerosmith and changed music forever, *Washington Post*, 18 May 2016. www.washingtonpost.com/graphics/lifestyle/walk-this-way (archived at https://perma.cc/K2SD-KAKC)

17 Sesame Workshop. The LEGO Foundation awards $100 million to Sesame Workshop to bring the power of learning through play to children affected by the Rohingya and Syrian Refugee Crises, Sesame Workshop, 2018. sesameworkshop.org/about-us/press-room/lego-foundation-awards-100-million-sesame-workshop-bring-power-learning (archived at https://perma.cc/4FVW-B8RG)

8

From silos to systems

What do the Sahara desert and the Amazon rainforest have in common? At first glance, we might not find an immediate link between them. The Sahara desert is an extremely hot, largely barren and rocky landscape situated in Africa. The Amazon rainforest is a dense, moist and tropical forest in northern South America. But each year dust from the Sahara makes its way via 3,000 miles of the Atlantic Ocean and lands on the Amazon basin. It makes the perfect fertilizer. NASA satellites reveal that 27.7 tonnes of dust from the Sahara – enough to fill 104,908 semi-trucks – reaches the Amazon basin each year.[1] The sand contains 22,000 tonnes of phosphorus. As it happens, that's about the same amount of phosphorus that washes away from the Amazon soil each year. Millions of years after Africa and South America separated, the two continents are still interconnected.

We live in a complex and interconnected world where rock particles from the Sahara desert travel across the ocean – a large body of saltwater covering one-fifth of Earth's surface – to deliver nutrients to a tropical rainforest. It is estimated that 50 per cent of the dust comes from a single spot known as the Bodélé Depression,[2] a prehistoric lake which used to be filled with algae and other microorganisms. More than 7,000 years ago the lake dried out and receded, leaving tonnes of nutrient-rich dust behind. The Bodélé Depression is covered with crushed skeletons of diatoms which are a form of plankton. This sand is lighter than other sand found in the Sahara desert making it easier to pick up and carry in the air for weeks. The location of the depression, within a large mountain-rimmed valley, makes it more exposed to surface wind. Thanks to the dust particles, the Amazon rainforest acts as the natural air conditioner of the world by releasing 20 trillion litres of water into the atmosphere daily.

When absorbed in our individual lives – daily chores, work challenges and future ambitions – it can be easy to overlook the interconnected nature of relationships. Modern life has made the separation of the parts from the whole convenient. Systems thinking is a way of looking at the complexity of the world by looking at events as a whole and the relationship between the parts. When we look at the world's most complex challenges like climate change, global inequality and biodiversity loss, we have to view problems as part of a dynamic, interrelated system. Systems thinking is a fancy technical term for looking at the whole picture. There is an extraordinary level of interdependence in our world. We exist within a beautiful complex system consisting of many interconnected components. Taking a narrow view of problems limits our understanding of underlying structures, interconnected relationships and unintended consequences. Reductionist thinking, or the belief that we can explain things by breaking them down into parts, prevents us from identifying the root cause of problems. We don't have independent problems. But we insist on dividing the world into different units. When looking to create social change, we have to think in systems, not silos.

Systems thinking

The term 'systems thinking' can be misleading. When we think about systems, we usually think about a computer system or a business process, where fixed rules and formulas are used to identify, understand and tackle problems. A linear process where problems have a determined starting point and a sequence of steps leading to an ultimate solution. Systems thinking is not about thinking systematically, but it is based on the realization that everything is interconnected. Take a minute to think about your personal life. You are probably part of a family. Your family is a system with inter-related members. Simply understanding one member won't produce a complete picture of the entire family. Your family is probably part of a wider neighbourhood or community. Once again, simply focusing on a single family won't provide a comprehensive understanding of the whole community. Your community is likely to be part of a town or city and country. At each level, there are multiple webs of interdependence and layers of complexity. But the whole is greater than the sum of its parts. If we were to analyse the parts in isolation, we would miss out on the big picture. A comparison could be made to staring at a single piece of a jigsaw puzzle from 2,000 pieces and attempting to understand the whole picture.

Social reality, the acceptance of social norms, values and laws, including how we view the world, is interdependent. Industrialization, globalization and the internet have expanded interconnection. The average consumer in the USA consumes 9kg of chocolate per year.[3] Cocoa beans are the primary ingredients in a chocolate bar, which is sourced from Ghana, where farmers are underpaid for their labour. The sugar comes from sugarcane farmers in Brazil, which incentivizes the expansion of farming land and drives rainforest deforestation. The milk comes from dairy farms in the Netherlands, an industry which is a major polluter of nitrogen. Vanilla is sourced from Madagascar by children. The chocolate is then processed in Switzerland using aluminium mined and rolled in China. The chocolate is then branded and shipped across the world before reaching your local store. It would be normal to bite into a chocolate bar without thinking about the interconnected system which created the product. Therein lies the paradox. The more complex our world, the more important it is but less capable we are to understand the relationships within the system and make sense of the whole. If we tried to observe the underlying structures, patterns and connections between all parts of a system our brains would explode. We wouldn't have enough brainpower to get on with everyday activities. There are times, however, when it becomes useful to switch our systems thinking vision on, like a secret superpower which makes connections and sees a more broad-beam view of the world.

Categorical thinking

Humans enjoy boxes

Why don't we always think in systems? There is a perfectly reasonable explanation. The average person has 6,000 thoughts a day.[4] Without the ability to place objects and events into categories, our brains would be overloaded with information. We are hardwired to sort information into boxes. This is a valuable faculty which helps us process large volumes of data in a relatively short amount of time. Categorization allows humans to understand objects, ideas and events by grouping them based on similar features. Like most other human cognitive abilities, categorization was born from the need to minimize the risks when living in social groups and enhance chances of survival. Early humans gained immense value from being able to differentiate tigers from harmless giant sloths, poisonous red-capped mushrooms from nutritious edible mushrooms, and whether the community next door was friendly, collaborative and peaceful or hostile, competitive and homicidal. The ability to process information using pattern recognition and rules of thumb allowed early humans to make quick decisions and extrapolate. This was especially useful in an environment where risks were abundant but resources and time were scarce. Early human history was a struggle for survival. Expending time, attention and energy to explore systems might have been a fatal decision.

We still use categorical thinking to understand concepts. We often use past knowledge and experience to inform future decisions. There are 73,300 tree species in the world and – although 98 per cent of people can't name five tree varieties – we recognize a tree when we see one.[5] We might not know the name, origins and history, but we know what a tree looks like. Classification simply helps humans make sense of these objects which share similar characteristics. It can be useful to identify a police officer if a thief steals our wallet and recognize the waiter at the restaurant when we are hungry.

Imagine for a moment not having the ability to form categories. We would end up gauging individual items and experiences without set categories. Our minds and bodies would shut down like an old laptop trying to process a thousand tabs at the same time. We would struggle to convey shared meaning using language. We would be incapable of recognizing patterns, identifying objects and solving problems. For example, imagine if we didn't have a category for cars, we would end up spending millions of hours trying to understand each model. Society wouldn't function without our ability to translate information into easily understandable categories. The cognitive load would be too great. This is why humans place items, people and events into boxes.

Despite all the benefits mentioned and the understandable need to simplify our complex world, categorization can be dangerous because we don't only categorize objects, we also categorize people. This is a process where we group people based on social information. We make automatic assumptions about people based on their accents or dress codes using past information and subconscious mental categories. Italians are passionate, Americans are loud, Russians are intimidating, the British have bad teeth, Jamaicans smoke weed and so on. Categories can also create in-groups and out-groups, in simple terms people who are like us and those that aren't. The categorization could be based on sex, race, gender, personality and even values. We aren't always aware of our prejudice; categorization isn't a conscious tool used to discriminate but a subconscious mechanism to process information. A study in the UK showed that someone named Adam is three times more likely to be hired than someone named Mohamed.[6]

When the BBC sent two CVs with identical experience and skills to 100 employers Adam was offered 12 interviews, while Mohamed was offered four. Although the sample size is relatively small it supports similar findings where Muslim men were 76 per cent less likely to be employed than their white Christian counterparts.[7] On the flip side, when people are exposed to different cultures it can expand their idea of an in-group. A study produced by Stanford University found that when Egyptian footballer Mohamed Salah signed for Liverpool there was an 18.9 per cent drop in the number of hate crimes in the Merseyside area.[8] A footballer can change people's perception and categorization of social groups. The same is true with school children; studies show that when kids are labelled 'gifted and talented' or 'special needs' it fundamentally changes how they are perceived by teachers and wider society. The labels become a self-fulfilling prophecy.

Pros and cons of categorical thinking

Categorical thinking can be harmful in business, too. Brands are useful because they are decision-making shortcuts. Brands prevent us from having to navigate millions of unknown products and services. A brand helps consumers to process and understand the experience behind the logo; rather than having to experiment with 100 different kinds of toothpaste, I can rely on a single logo which delivers a minty fresh taste. Ever noticed when we travel to a new country our ability to buy products is elongated and distorted because we don't always have access to a shared understanding of the brand? Brands and agencies can be in danger of overselling the difference between groups using fancy segmentation strategies. Customer personas are not as accurate as they seem in presentation decks. People share more in common than we think, and communities behave differently from how companies think they do. Young people and people from lower socioeconomic backgrounds are more likely to buy designer brands. LEGO is primarily targeted at children but there's a considerable community of adults obsessed with the brand. Red Bull was initially marketed at extreme sports – skiing, mountain biking, windsurfing, skateboarding – but it is now equally picked up by people who party or need energy working on building sites or in offices. Birkenstock was the footwear of choice for doctors, nurses and chefs during long shifts because of the orthopaedic benefits, but it's now worn by trendy fashionistas in London, New York and Tokyo.

Categorical thinking creates silos within an organization. We begin to assume that the marketing team does creative stuff, the finance team only deals with the numbers and the sustainability team doesn't understand the commercial models. We begin to attribute group features to individuals. Categories can create a fixed worldview, which is unhelpful when the outside world changes. It means the company is unable to escape from existing patterns of thoughts and actions. Innovation requires the ability to find new patterns, break boundaries and create new connections. Future solutions don't fit neatly within existing categories. Cognitive entrenchment can prevent us from exploring new ideas and discoveries.

When the platypus was first discovered by English zoologist George Shaw in the 17th century, he believed it was a hoax.[9] Shaw precisely described how the platypus has the beak of a duck, the body of an otter and webbed feet. The platypus lays eggs like a reptile but feeds milk to its young like a mammal. It is the amalgamation of a bird, mammal and reptile. When the platypus was first discovered, scientists questioned not their existing mental categories but the existence of a new species. This is the danger of categorical thinking. It happens all the time in business.

The problem with silos

Silos are a natural outcome of a group of people collaborating. Start-ups don't have to worry about silos as much. It is much easier to communicate, collaborate and exchange ideas when everyone shares one room. But as organizations scale in size and across geographies, new structures need to be implemented to manage the process. The dynamics between a team of six people with a shared mission and a company of 10,000 employees spread across 42 offices and numerous time zones are vastly different. As companies grow, new structures are created. We start to see the formation of specialist departments, hierarchal leadership teams, regional headquarters and multiple business units.

There's a logical explanation why companies opt for such measures. Departments allow employees and teams to focus on specific tasks based on their domain expertise. We might not want the head of human resources to build aeroplanes or the finance director to determine the budget for a dedicated community fund. There is value in craft and specialism. Working in departments can streamline the work, creating a standard way of working, increasing productivity and reducing duplicity of efforts. The process becomes more scalable, and employees have clear roles and responsibilities. But our world is more interconnected, and our problems and opportunities require a system thinking approach. Paradoxically, our world has become more interdependent, but our ways of working and how we approach challenges have become more siloed. Our response to complexity is more boxes to help us label objects and events. Such an approach focuses on the parts but misses out on the whole picture.

Comparisons could be made to individual vs team sports. Businesses and creating social impact are team sports, not individual endeavours. The traditional structures within most organizations produce a narrow worldview. Our understanding of business and social problems is fractured, fragmented and disjointed. Such structures can hinder the exchange of ideas and information across different parts of the organization. The same organizational departments and specialism created to maximize effectiveness become counterproductive once the world changes. They will no longer drive efficiency but increase waste. Breaking down silos is a necessity when navigating a complex and interconnected world. Future business and social challenges won't fit neatly with our clearly defined roles, responsibilities and departments. We don't have finance problems, HR problems, marketing problems or supply chain problems. We have interconnected business problems. We don't have education problems, employment problems or healthcare problems. We have interconnected social problems.

The £32 billion scandal

In winter 2013, four students from West Virginia University uncovered one of the biggest corporate scandals in history. They conducted an emissions test which has since cost Volkswagen £32 billion and counting.[10] The scientists discovered that the German car manufacturer was using software to reduce nitrogen emissions on diesel cars when they were being tested. The ingenious but illegal software, known as a defeat device, was installed on 482,000 cars in the US. The defeat device was designed to detect when a car was undergoing emissions testing – and would reduce nitrogen oxides emissions to meet regulatory standards. But, once away from testing conditions, the car would emit 40 times more pollutants on the road, failing to meet US emission standards.[11]

Why did Volkswagen decide to cheat on emissions tests? To understand, we need to look at the automaker's history. Volkswagen's leadership had set bold ambitions at the start of the 21st century to become the biggest car company in the world. It was lagging behind Toyota and General Motors. To knock competitors off their perch, Volkswagen needed to increase its miserly market share in the US market. The United States was the world's biggest car market, and, contrary to media stereotypes, it had stricter pollution regulations through the Environment Protection Agency. Volkswagen was already dominant in Europe and other international markets, so it decided to focus its strategy on diesel because of the fuel efficiency it delivered to consumers. It would appeal to American customers looking for better fuel economy. But there was a problem, Volkswagen engineers were unable to meet the US emissions standards. The company's business targets clashed with the engineering team's reality.[12] In a more open, collaborative and integrated culture, the engineering team would share this obstacle back to the business, creating space for constructive discussions on how to move forward. The teams would either need more time and resources, or the business would need to reconsider its aggressive sales targets. Unfortunately, the engine development and engineering teams didn't feel comfortable sharing the issue with the wider business and industry bodies. Rather than telling the truth, they created complicated software to obfuscate emissions. The company culture created an environment where it was safer to hide the problem. There was no financial incentive for teams to take such action. They most probably didn't want to lose their job or let the business down.

Meanwhile, the Volkswagen marketing team and agencies went on a major marketing spree to change American consumers' perception of diesel cars. This is probably the most brazen example to date of a brand misleading consumers about its product's benefits. The effective marketing campaigns positioned 'clean diesel' as the future. The funny and popular advertising spots dispelled common myths about 'dirty diesel'. Volkswagen promised people the best of both worlds: fuel efficiency and environmentally friendly machines. This was especially important given the popularity of the Toyota Prius. Climate change was rising higher in the public's consciousness. The multimillion-dollar adverts launched during the Super Bowl and other cultural events meant Volkswagen not only committed corporate fraud but also consumer fraud. It turned out Volkswagen's diesel wasn't that clean after all. According to *The New York Times* (2015), the company rigged more than 11 million cars globally.[13] What's striking about the Volkswagen scandal is how the business had multiple opportunities to address the problem and its mistakes, but every time it dug a deeper hole. Even when the manufacturer recalled some of its cars, they used it as an opportunity to update the software to improve recognition of when the vehicle was being tested. Volkswagen insists that the illegal software was the work of a small group of rogue engineers. Over time, it became obvious that the scandal was enabled and emboldened by groupwide company culture, aggressive sales targets and hierarchal structures which prevented dissent, sharing of information or pushback.

According to a study by MIT, excess emissions from Volkswagen vehicles could cause 1,200 premature deaths in Europe.[14] Following the scandal, the CEO of Volkswagen resigned. The fallout has caused irrevocable damage to the brand. In the first two months, Volkswagen lost 46 per cent of its value.[15] The share price in 2024 is less than half what it was before the scandal, whereas the German DAX index has increased by 87 per cent from 9,490 to 17,773 and the S&P500 has risen by 167 per cent in the same period. Volkswagen has paid £32 billion in penalties, recalls and legal costs. The legal battles are still ongoing. Following the scandal, more than 30,000 Volkswagen staff lost their jobs in a major organizational restructure.[16] Some might argue that the scandal has also damaged the reputation of Germany, a country which is considered the pinnacle of manufacturing, reliability and engineering. The state of Lower Saxony owns 11.8 per cent of the company and 20 per cent of votes.[17]

An abundance of silos, top-down management and smoky business activities meant that three graduates from West Virginia University working with a £50,000 research fund were able to uncover a scandal which a deeply siloed multinational was attempting to hide. The lack of dissenting voices within the company, communication across the business units and third-party independent adjudicators emboldened a considerable number of Volkswagen employees – pressured to deliver results – to mark their homework with no regard for the impact on society. According to Interbrand, the Volkswagen brand is considerably underperforming compared to competitors such as Mercedes-Benz, BMW and Tesla.[18] Investigative journalism suggests there were some easily preventable steps Volkswagen could have taken to prevent the loss of billions of dollars, thousands of lives and environmental pollution. The first would have been to create a culture where individuals can voice dissent and push back on unachievable top-down goals. Second, create more collaborative ways of working where problems can be flagged. Finally, invite independent board directors and public oversight to break down departmental silos.

Cultural exchange

There have been periods in history when we have managed to escape restrictive boxes and silos. The Islamic Golden Age was a period of economic, scientific, cultural and philosophical flourishing for the world. The Islamic

Empire's expansion coincided with the European Dark Ages and the decline in educational institutions and cultural exchange. At the time, Islam was mainly concentrated in the Arabian peninsula, but following the arrival of the Abbasid Caliphate, the city of Baghdad was founded as the new capital. Eventually, the Caliph of Baghdad, Harun al-Rashid, commissioned the House of Wisdom (*Bayt al-Hikmah*) which saw scholars from all over the Muslim world, from Andalusia to Bukhara, flock to Baghdad. An unquenchable thirst for knowledge took hold of the Muslim world between the 8th and 13th centuries. Islamic scholars were interested in the history of knowledge that had come before them. The Abbasids actively encouraged learning from different cultures, religions and disciplines. It spawned the translation movement: a large-scale, well-funded and long-term effort to translate Greek, Pahlavi, Sanskrit and Syriac texts into Arabic. The House of Wisdom was built on the traditions of the Zoroastrian Persian-Sasanian Empire. Islamic scholars took particularly great interest in the works of ancient Greeks like Aristotle, Plato, Socrates, Hippocrates and Galen.

Combining the foundational work of ancient Greece – which was largely forgotten in Europe – with the Quran and scientific experimentation created a new era of scientific discovery. During the Islamic Golden Age, scholars not only embraced other cultures, traditions and disciplines but proactively built on them. Scholars would combine Greek philosophy, Indian mathematics, Persian medicine and new thinking, creating the conditions for cross-cultural fertilization. The ground-breaking works of Islamic scholars were funded by the Abbasid Caliphate, which encouraged the pursuit of knowledge and exchange of ideas. A culture of intellectual tolerance and diversity was the foundation of the Islamic Golden Age. At the time, Muslims, Jews and Christians coexisted in cities like Baghdad. Ideas and contributions were encouraged from different people, nations and religions. Intellectuals would publicly debate and disagree on philosophical, theological and scientific matters. An open culture of scientific, social and ideological exchange promoted intellectual curiosity and different schools of thought.

The polymath

Unlike scientists today, Islamic scholars wouldn't fixate on a single theme. Most explored numerous fields of knowledge, with access to a wide range of ideas, cultures and knowledge from different traditions. People were encouraged to question established beliefs. The Persian polymath Ibn Sina – known as Avicenna – exemplifies this spirit of innovation and curiosity. Ibn Sina is arguably one of the greatest minds in history. He memorized the entire Quran aged 10 years old. He then learned arithmetic from an Indian greengrocer, before immersing himself in Islamic jurisprudence, geometry, physics and philosophy. By the time Ibn Sina was 18 years old, he was a physician and well versed in Greek science. Ibn Sina studied and built on the ideas of Greek philosopher Aristotle, developing a new branch of Aristotelian logic by viewing philosophy as a unified whole, culminating in *The Book of Healing*, a four-part encyclopaedia covering logic, physics, mathematics and philosophy. Contrary to the name, this was not a medical book. The canon aimed to cure the ignorance of the soul. It covered a wide range of topics including logical reasoning drawing upon philosophy from Aristotle, physics and the nature of the universe. It covered the essence of existence and the nature of reality and suggests a hierarchy of existence, more than 950 years before Maslow's hierarchy of needs. The book also explored psychology through observations on sensation, perception and memory, and described depression, anxiety and their impact on the human body. Ibn Sina broke all the rules of writing in the 21st century. He explored multiple disciplines and produced interrelationships between different fields of knowledge. Ibn Sina viewed the universe as a coherent whole where all parts are interconnected.

If that wasn't impressive enough, Ibn Sina furthered numerous other fields of knowledge. He is considered the father of early modern medicine thanks to his work *The Canon of Medicine (Al-Qanun fi al-Tibb)*, a medical encyclopaedia which combined knowledge from Greek, Chinese, Roman, Persian and Islamic sources into a comprehensive textbook of medical knowledge. It was used as a standard for medicine in Europe until the 18th century. He devised a holistic system for medicine with general principles, diagnosis, therapeutics and pharmacology, emphasizing the importance of the diagnosis process to identify different ailments. *The Canon of Medicine* provided a comprehensive account of medical drugs that could be used to prevent and treat illness. Ibn Sina encouraged prevention, maintaining a balanced diet and engaging in regular exercise. In the canon, Ibn Sina also advocated for the use of 40 days' quarantine to prevent the spread of infectious diseases, a policy that might have saved millions of lives if followed during the Covid-19 pandemic, especially at airports and main sources of migration.

In total, Ibn Sina wrote over 450 works, of which 240 still survive. If that wasn't enough, in the field of psychology, he is also credited with defining neuropsychiatric conditions like hallucination, insomnia, dementia, epilepsy and stroke. In physics, he was the first to use an air thermometer to measure temperature in his scientific experiments. In the field of optics, Ibn Sina discovered that light had a specific speed. He wrote poetry in both Persian and Arabic. This was a time when silos didn't exist. People had the creative freedom to explore different topics, cross-pollinate and stretch the boundaries of human knowledge. The Islamic Golden Age ended when the Mongols ransacked Baghdad in 1258.

The Renaissance

In the same way that the Islamic Golden Age was inspired by ancient Greece, the European Renaissance – a French word for rebirth – was inspired by the works of Islamic scholars who had preserved the works of Greek philosophers, scientists and mathematicians. European civilization greatly benefited from the discoveries of Islamic scholars in the fields of science, medicine, literature, art and philosophy. The works of Ibn Sina, Al Razi and Ibn Khaldun were being studied in Italy, Spain and France in the same way Islamic scholars would read Aristotle, Socrates and Ptolemy in Baghdad, Cairo and Samarkand. The cross-disciplinary intellectual curiosity of the Islamic Golden Age shone a bright light on Europe, sparking the beginnings of the Enlightenment period.

The Silk Road was an ancient network of trade routes stretching across 40 modern-day countries that provided travellers with the opportunity to share ideas, information and products. This coincided with the Islamic Golden Age and countless contributions in the fields of mathematics, sciences and philosophy. This also played a critical role in influencing the Renaissance in 14th century Europe. It opened access to Chinese inventions like paper, gunpowder and the compass. Like the Abbasid Caliphate, the European Renaissance was funded through patronage, in this case by the Medici family. Although definitions and the timeline of the Renaissance – whether it was a single period – are disputed by historians, the influence of the powerful Medici family in producing some of the greatest artists, thinkers and scientists in human history is undeniable. Florence, Italy is considered the birthplace of the European Renaissance. The Medici used their financial prosperity to sponsor a new wave of artists, architects and writers. The Medici were a banking family from the city-state of Florence. The family first consolidated power under Cosimo Medici, who used his wealth to make Florence the art capital of Europe. Cosimo's grandson Lorenzo Medici oversaw the peak of the Renaissance in Florence. He invited the best artists to Florence, sponsoring the likes of Sandro Botticelli, famed for paintings such as *The Birth of Venus* and *Primavera*, Leonardo da Vinci, who was attracted to Florence to further his creative ambitions, and Michelangelo, who was living with the Medici family in their palace.

Like Ibn Sina, many of the artists of the Renaissance period were polymaths, translated from Greek as one who knows many. Leonardo da Vinci had an extraordinary range of interests. As an artist, he is known for the *Mona Lisa* and *The Last Supper*. He was also fascinated by human anatomy, conducting extensive experiments on the human body, including the dissection of 30 human bodies. Da Vinci also invented a flying machine, robots, helicopters, parachutes and scuba diving suits. During the Renaissance – much like the Islamic Golden Age and most other periods of major progress in human history – silos didn't exist. There was no separation of art and science like there is today. Polymaths would work across different disciplines. Discoveries in one field would enlighten the body of knowledge in another. People would seek knowledge beyond the neatly defined confines of professions, departments or industries. The world was viewed as a whole, not as fragmented atoms.

The Industrial Disillusion

The Industrial Revolution transformed our economic, social and technological systems. Throughout much of history, humans viewed problems through a universal lens. Mass production required the division of labour and specialization to increase productivity. The most famous example is when Henry Ford invented the assembly line to produce the Ford Model T car. Until then, cars would be produced with teams working across the entire production process. Ford came up with the idea of a car assembly line after observing meat-packing lines in Chicago where each worker would be assigned to a single repetitive task. By breaking down the production process of cars into smaller tasks and optimising workflows, Ford could produce more cars and the economy could produce more products and services. His innovation reduced the time it took to build a car from more than 12 hours to 1 hour and 33 minutes.[19]

The problem is that we are now living in a post-industrial society, where division of labour, specialization and compartmentalization stifle us from seeing the big picture and tackling the interdependent challenges and opportunities facing business and society. As children, we don't split the world into binary choices; we are fascinated by different fields, regardless of whether art or science, maths or philosophy, engineering or physics. Our education system gradually forces us to specialize at school and university, and when we enter the world of work. It's much easier to land a job when you have specific qualifications and skills. We end up like typecast actors who struggle to escape their categorization. Jennifer Aniston might find it hard to move out of romantic comedies, Christopher Lee is known as the super-villain and Morgan Freeman is the wise old man. There are valid reasons to specialize. Exploring numerous interests might lead to becoming average at many but great at none. There's much to be said in honing a specific craft over a lifetime. However, research indicates that developing diverse interests can fuel creativity and productivity. Perusing multiple fields can boost success in your main area of expertise. According to the BBC, Nobel Prize-winning scientists are about 25 times more likely to sing, dance or act than the average scientist. They are also 17 times more likely to create visual art, 12 times more likely to write poetry and 4 times more likely to be a musician.[20]

Being interested in different disciplines promotes the cross-pollination of ideas, learning and experiences that can be taken from one domain and applied to another. Polymathy harnesses the power of collisions, divergent thinking and randomness. When we view the world as interconnected, we begin to make connections and think in systems.

The hero complex

Thinking in systems facilitates open collaboration with others. But a common barrier to progress is the hero complex. A hero complex is when a person, company or group of people feel they are single-handedly responsible for solving the problem. Whether in a business or social impact space, some actors want all the credit. This often comes from the need to feed the ego, when the desire for recognition becomes more important than the mission and outcome of the project. It can also stem from the need to exert power and maintain or establish control. The desire to solve problems and make a positive impact is admirable, but a hero complex can lead to the individualization of collective problems. Here the intention is not only to create social change but, more importantly, be recognized as the agent of change. Actions become the vehicle for the ultimate objective of being the hero.

Let's imagine there's an FMCG giant called Hero Complex Food Co and they have a new mission to improve access to water for local communities.

If the company was thinking in systems, it would identify existing grassroots organizations and community movements and work with them to improve existing solutions. Instead, the Hero Complex Food Co team want greater visibility for the funding and support they are delivering. So, they decided to start a brand-new programme with zero field experience or knowledge of local needs because they could call it the 'Hero Complex Food Co Programme' and personally take credit for all the impact it delivered. The CEO and management team might win some awards if things go well. Because of the lack of local knowledge and integration into the local ecosystem it takes 12 months to get the project off the ground, and more than $8 million is spent on a technological solution, but adoption is close to zero. If Hero Complex Food Co dropped its ego it would have been able to reach and change the lives of millions of people while also strengthening the wider ecosystem, delivering jobs to the local economy and learning from its strategic partners on the ground. Such is the difference between silos and systems.

The hero complex creates an urge to brush away the existing system and become the hero of the story. There is something strangely alluring about being celebrated for contributions to business or social impact, like a superhero who single-handedly transforms the company or society. Such a mentality can stifle new solutions, radical collaboration and collective progress. It overlooks the importance of shared missions and collective action. The ego can cloud judgement and prevent the establishment of bridges with other people, companies and groups operating in the same space. The same is true when charities compete for the same pool of funding. Let's say you want to donate to support people in Haiti. Should you donate to UNICEF, UNHCR, Red Cross, World Vision, Save the Children or some local charity? If you want to donate to environmental conservation, should you donate to WWF, Greenpeace, Friends of the Earth or Rainforest Alliance? Why can't organizations pool together to make an even bigger collective impact? After all, we're not going to remember which NGO had the most impact if we don't end up saving the planet. The mission should always be bigger than any individual.

Open collaboration

The blueprint for a new collaborative, open-source and beneficial model comes from an unlikely source: Wikipedia. The free online encyclopaedia operates on an open collaboration model where users can contribute and edit the world's knowledge without any approval required. Thanks to a large number of readers and contributors, Wikipedia is regularly reviewed to ensure accuracy and updated to include the latest discoveries in human knowledge. Rather than gatekeeping the editorial process to a handful of academics, Wikipedia decided to tap into the collective intelligence of the public. The platform is governed by a decentralized community of volunteer editors who determine the content, policies and guidelines. Wikipedia operates in 326 languages; each language edition is operated by a different community but shares the same principles of open collaboration. The founder of Wikipedia decided not to monetize the platform through a private membership model or ad-revenue model, a decision which has made the world's knowledge accessible to anyone with an internet connection. The website was visited by 4.3 billion unique visitors in 2023.[21] More than 47 million editors have contributed to its 60 million pages of knowledge,[22] although, interestingly, 77 per cent of Wikipedia content is written by 1 per cent of superfans.[23] The open-source model produces a more interesting and diverse range of content – breaking down silos and specialism, and inviting divergent global perspectives on the same topic. The collaborative nature makes contributors feel part of a community and agency over the project. Open collaboration also allows for the continuous improvement of articles based on the latest news, research and development.

Open source

Similar trends can be seen in the business world. Future-facing companies are realizing that we can't change the world in silos. The attention has shifted towards sharing platforms, knowledge and resources to accelerate impact and reach more people. We need to take a collectivist approach to social change. When Allbirds created the world's zero-carbon shoe design it did something previously unimaginable in the ultra-competitive, dog-eat-dog sports shoe category. It encouraged competitors to steal its approach to sustainability because it would make the industry more sustainable. Allbirds have some ambitious targets, like 75 per cent of all materials coming from sustainably sourced natural and recycled materials. The brand also introduced carbon labelling to the footwear industry. When the company released the Moonshot shoe, which has a carbon footprint of 0.0 kilograms CO_2e without relying on carbon offsets to reach that level, it also released a toolkit for other businesses to create their own versions. The toolkit was created to help other footwear manufacturers achieve net zero.[24] It is a detailed guide-book explaining the design process, materials used, packaging, manufacturing, transportation, end-of-life process and numerous calls to action for collaborating on new solutions. Within the traditional Industrial Revolution business model, companies would protect their intellectual property to create a competitive advantage. In the post-industrial economy, open collaboration creates a better ecosystem for all parties.

ACTIVITY

What happens if we don't view business as a binary choice between competition and collaboration? What if we could all contribute to a collective mission? How can we combine our collective resources and intelligence? What if we let go of the hero complex and embraced a collective mindset? Unlike the business models of the Industrial Revolution, progress doesn't have to come at the expense of others. Individuals, groups and companies can work collaboratively to solve industry-wide problems. Spend some time exploring the following questions.

1 **Are we applying categorical thinking that prevents us from thinking in systems?**
   Categories can create a fixed worldview, which is unhelpful when the outside world changes. Remember how the platypus was suspected to be a hoax because it didn't fit into any of the existing categories. Categorical thinking might include your assumed audience, strategic approach and collaborators.

2 **What are the silos in our organization or movement that need breaking?**
   Silos are a natural outcome of a group of people collaborating, but they can harm communication, collaboration and exchange of ideas. Remember how centralized management and departmental silos further exacerbated the Volkswagen emissions scandal.

3 **How can we avoid the hero complex? Who could we collaborate with to make an even bigger business and social impact?**
   The hero complex creates an urge to brush away the existing system and become the hero of the story. Such a mentality can stifle new solutions, radical collaboration and collective progress. It overlooks the importance of shared missions and collective action.

4   How can we champion open-source collaboration?

We can't change the world in silos. We should seek to create shared platforms, knowledge and resources to accelerate impact and reach more people. This requires taking a more collectivist approach to social change:

o   Crowdsourcing projects.

o   Producing useful toolkits for the wider ecosystem.

o   Signposting people to relevant resources.

o   Exchanging knowledge and resources with other players in the industry.

Examples include Wikipedia's crowdsourcing model and Allbirds' open-sourcing technology for other footwear manufacturers to implement.

Notes

1   R Garner. NASA satellite reveals how much Saharan dust feeds Amazon's plants, NASA, 22 February 2015. www.nasa.gov/centers-and-facilities/goddard/nasa-satellite-reveals-how-much-saharan-dust-feeds-amazons-plants (archived at https://perma.cc/B2M3-Z4J2)

2   I Koren et al. The Bodélé depression: A single spot in the Sahara that provides most of the mineral dust to the Amazon forest, *Environmental Research Letters*, 2006, 1 (1). doi.org/10.1088/1748-9326/1/1/014005 (archived at https://perma.cc/ET37-REA9)

3   F Richter. (Not) everybody loves chocolate, Statista, 7 July 2023. www.statista.com/chart/3668/the-worlds-biggest-chocolate-consumers (archived at https://perma.cc/8Z9H-TR5U)

4   A Craig. Discovery of 'thought worms' opens window to the mind, Queen's Gazette, Queen's University, 13 July 2020. www.queensu.ca/gazette/stories/discovery-thought-worms-opens-window-mind (archived at https://perma.cc/TJ5B-Y46M)

5   R Cazzolla Gatti et al. The number of tree species on Earth, *Proceedings of the National Academy of Sciences*, 2022, 119 (6). doi.org/10.1073/pnas.2115329119 (archived at https://perma.cc/MQN4-PGYD)

6   Z Adesina. Is it easier to get a job if you're Adam or Mohamed? BBC News, 6 February 2017. www.bbc.co.uk/news/uk-england-london-38751307 (archived at https://perma.cc/EM4K-KJKC)

7   R Dobson. British Muslims face worst job discrimination of any minority group, according to research, *Independent*, 30 November 2014. www.independent.co.uk/news/uk/home-news/british-muslims-face-worst-job-discrimination-of-any-minority-group-9893211.html (archived at https://perma.cc/HEH9-6Q35)

8 A Alrababa'h et al. Can exposure to celebrities reduce prejudice? The effect of Mohamed Salah on Islamophobic behaviors and attitudes, *American Political Science Review*, 2021, 115 (4), 1111–28. doi.org/10.1017/ s0003055421000423 (archived at https://perma.cc/7TTT-WAZG)

9 A Ohlheiser. The platypus is so weird that scientists thought the first specimen was a hoax, *Washington Post*, 1 April 2015. www.washingtonpost.com/news/ speaking-of-science/wp/2015/04/01/the-platypus-is-so-weird-that-scientists-thought-the-first-specimen-was-a-hoax (archived at https://perma.cc/ JC5F-ZVCN)

10 Reuters. Factbox: The state of legal cases in VW's diesel scandal, 27 June 2023. www.reuters.com/sustainability/state-legal-cases-vws-diesel-scandal-2023-06-27 (archived at https://perma.cc/M26Q-FNBD)

11 G Topham. The Volkswagen emissions scandal explained, *The Guardian*, 23 September 2015. www.theguardian.com/business/ng-interactive/2015/ sep/23/volkswagen-emissions-scandal-explained-diesel-cars (archived at https://perma.cc/8XMG-29FU)

12 J Ewing (2017) *Faster, Higher, Farther: The inside story of the Volkswagen scandal*, Corgi Books, London

13 J Ewing. Volkswagen says 11 million cars worldwide are affected in diesel deception, *New York Times*, 22 September 2015. www.nytimes.com/ 2015/09/23/business/international/volkswagen-diesel-car-scandal.html (archived at https://perma.cc/J3Z7-332V)

14 J Chew. Study: Volkswagen's excess emissions will lead to 1,200 premature deaths in Europe, MIT, 3 March 2017. news.mit.edu/2017/volkswagen-emissions-premature-deaths-europe-0303 (archived at https://perma.cc/ RG8W-8D3Z)

15 G Colvin. 5 years in, damages from the VW emissions cheating scandal are still rolling in, *Fortune*, 6 October 2020. fortune.com/2020/10/06/volkswagen-vw-emissions-scandal-damages (archived at https://perma.cc/54E8-9VP2)

16 P Campbell. VW to cut 30,000 jobs in wake of diesel emissions scandal, *Financial Times*, 18 November 2016. www.ft.com/content/78d194aa-ad72-11e6-9cb3-bb8207902122 (archived at https://perma.cc/Q4QZ-B932)

17 C Rauwald. Germany's Lower Saxony defends its role as VW anchor shareholder, Bloomberg, 23 June 2016. www.bloomberg.com/news/ articles/2016-06-23/germany-s-lower-saxony-defends-its-role-as-vw-anchor-shareholder (archived at https://perma.cc/62PF-S3XJ)

18 Interbrand. Best global brands 2023, 2023. interbrand.com/best-global-brands (archived at https://perma.cc/84GG-FU9S)

19 History. Ford's assembly line starts rolling, 2009/2020. www.history.com/ this-day-in-history/fords-assembly-line-starts-rolling (archived at https://perma.cc/KK5A-69DX)

20 D Robson. Why some people are impossibly talented, BBC, 18 November 2019. www.bbc.com/worklife/article/20191118-what-shapes-a-polymath---and-do-we-need-them-more-than-ever (archived at https://perma.cc/3WXH-Y2L5)

21 T Bianchi. Total global visitor traffic to Wikipedia.org 2023, Statista, 2024. www.statista.com/statistics/1259907/wikipedia-website-traffic (archived at https://perma.cc/7SZC-XUEY)

22 Wikipedia. Wikipedia: Wikipedians, Wikipedia, nd. en.wikipedia.org/wiki/Wikipedia:Wikipedians (archived at https://perma.cc/FQP3-F4ED)

23 D Oberhaus. Nearly all of Wikipedia is written by just 1 percent of its editors, *Vice*, 7 November 2017. www.vice.com/en/article/7x47bb/wikipedia-editors-elite-diversity-foundation (archived at https://perma.cc/DB4N-7Q6M)

24 Allbirds. *Recipe Book*, 2023. cdn.allbirds.com/image/upload/v1687810959/marketing-pages/23Q3-M0.0SHOT-RECIPE-B0.0K-Final.pdf (archived at https://perma.cc/EF32-9K2U)

9

The power of co-creation

Ancient Egyptian society was divided into six distinct social classes. Pharaohs were at the top of the pyramid and were considered God's representatives on Earth. Pharaohs had absolute authority on religious, political and economic matters. They were responsible for prosperity, calling upon Hapi, the Nile God, to flood the Nile and guarantee a good harvest. Pharaohs were the ancient equivalent of modern-day CEOs, responsible for the overall vision and direction of the company. The second class on the pyramid was the vizier, which was the most powerful position after the pharaoh. The vizier could be compared to a managing director or chief operating officer, who is more involved in the day-to-day activities and making sure that operations are running smoothly. The vizier was an advisor to the pharaoh on executive decisions like agricultural policy, legal matters and military expenditure. The third social class was priests, who were mainly responsible for conducting rituals and ceremonies to ensure the Gods were happy. Priests played an important role in creating a shared sense of identity and moral values within ancient Egyptian society, somewhat like a Chief People Officer.

The fourth social class were the scribes, who were an essential part of ancient Egyptian society. Most of our understanding of ancient Egypt comes from this group's record-keeping. Scribes maintained written accounts of ancient Egyptian life: contracts, tax records, wills, census data and religious texts. This was a crucial role in society, when under 1 per cent of people could read or write.[1] Scribes might be compared to modern managers, who are responsible for achieving the goals of the organization and reporting back to the managing director (vizier) and CEO (pharaoh). The fifth group comprised artisans and craftsmen, who specialized in producing jewellery, pottery, textiles, carpentry and sculptors. Artisans and craftsmen were professional specialists like modern-day data scientists, sustainability experts and finance leads. The sixth and bottom group in the ancient

Egyptian social structure were the labourers who constructed buildings, the farmers who produced food and the slaves who built the pyramids. Comparisons could be made to most of the workforce who are not in managerial positions or specialist roles (though, hopefully, working conditions have somewhat improved over the last 5,000 years). Much of the progress, wealth and civilization of ancient Egypt was built on the backs of 80 per cent of workers and peasants. It was a hierarchal system which benefited the few, not many.

Modern society has undergone profound change since the time of ancient Egypt. Advancements in technology mean we can practically connect with any human being on the planet using computers, the internet, mobile phones and video chat. We can travel from Cairo to Rome in three hours. Ancient Egypt was a monarchy; many countries are now democracies although there are still 43 nations with a head of state. Ancient Egypt and Mesopotamia were pioneers of the agricultural economy predicated on cultivating crops. We now operate within an industrial economy producing goods and services. There have also been major changes in social norms and values. Women are now active participants in the economy in most countries, and slaves are no longer an acceptable class within society. But a top-down hierarchy still seems to be the modus operandi of most governments, companies and societies.

Why hierarchy?

The main purpose of social hierarchies – like ancient Egypt and modern companies – is to organize individuals, groups and resources in a way that achieves a certain set of goals. But who gets to set the goals and who will the organizational structures serve? When reviewing hierarchal structures, we shouldn't ignore the inherent power relations that dictate how society is structured. The higher up on the pyramid, the more likely you are to benefit from the arrangement. Business publications, academic literature and public opinion generally oppose the idea of a top-down, command-and-control management model. Yet when we look at how modern business and society are structured, hierarchy seems to be the dominant operating system.

If social hierarchies are so bad, why have we continued to endure them throughout human history? There are multiple reasons why hierarchies have stuck around. First, humans need order and structure to navigate the complex and unpredictable world. Being aware of the so-called rules, our place within business or society and how things work helps us make sense of the world around us. Thanks to hierarchies, we can build consistent patterns and routines. Imagine turning up to work each day and not having any idea of our role and responsibilities. Hierarchy prevents us from having to think about the complexity of systems around us. We weren't responsible for the fertility of the river Nile. We simply had to produce four new leather shoes to sell at the local market or carry giant blocks of stone for the pyramids. That was our contribution to the overall equation.

Our role within the hierarchy can also instil a deep sense of identity and belonging. In business, identity formation is a crucial part of maintaining organizational hierarchies. It manifests itself dependent on the individual or group's position and perception within society. People who work in banking and finance have a unique set of visual and linguistic codes. The same could be said for techies and program developers. And creative people too. Some people within society refuse to play by the rules, like people who live off-grid, entrepreneurs, freelancers and some criminals. But even they adhere to certain structures and customs. Gangs, despite having a reputation for being unruly, have a strong social order. The Mafia has an organizational operation that would make multinational companies jealous. There is a boss (*Capo di tutti i capi*), the underboss who is second in command, the *consiglieri* who serves as an advisor and the captain (*capo*) in charge of overseeing the crews. Then you have the soldiers, who are known as 'made men'; they are initiated into the organization and have to take an oath. Finally, you have associates who work closely with the Mafia but are not part of the organization.

Hierarchies can deliver faster decision-making when compared to more decentralized organizations. China was able to grow tremendously over a relatively short period thanks to centralized economic planning and investment. Unlike Western economies, tied down to protracted discussions between the state, private sector and local communities, China was able to invest in large-scale infrastructure projects at breakneck speed. The Chinese central government was able to make decisions on how resources should be allocated and develop a long-term vision that transcended short-term economic and political cycles in most Western economies.

The final reason why hierarchies exist is self-explanatory. Social hierarchies create and uphold unequal power dynamics. The groups at the top can establish rules, norms and laws that benefit their interests at the expense of the groups at the bottom of the pyramid. The social order codifies and normalizes the exploitation of the groups at the bottom of the hierarchy. In business, hierarchy allows groups at the top to extract resources, labour and value from groups at the bottom. In society, hierarchy determines access to resources like education, healthcare, housing and employment. We are all part of the social hierarchy in our neighbourhood, within our families, at our workplace and even in the brands we buy.

Colonial roots

The pyramid-shaped corporate structure is rooted in colonialism. Colonialism is as old as history itself. It was practised by the ancient Greeks, Romans, Egyptians and Phoenicians. Contemporary colonialism, however, peaked in Europe during the Industrial Revolution. Advancements in technology increased production capacity and the appetite for raw materials like cotton, rubber, metals, spices and labour. The invention of steamships and the expansion of railways made it easier to create trade routes and maintain control over colonies. The most brutal form of colonialism is settler colonialism, a system of oppression where colonizers invade and displace the existing population with settlers who claim the land and establish a permanent society.

European exploration of the Americas began in the 15th century with Spanish, Portuguese, English, French and Dutch explorers making voyages to the New World. Christopher Columbus is widely credited for 'discovering' the Americas in 1492. Columbus Day is a federal holiday in the US. The narrative disregards that native people had lived in the Americas for at least 20,000 years, forming complex and sophisticated societies with unique art, culture, traditions and history.[2] The first successful English settlement was Jamestown, Virginia, which was established in 1607 – it was named after King James I. The initiative was financed by the Virginia Company in search of gold. When gold was in short supply settlers started to die from starvation and disease. The colony began to cultivate tobacco as a cash crop. Tobacco was discovered and cultivated for over 8,000 years by Native Americans for religious ceremonies and medicinal purposes. Tobacco became a highly profitable crop, producing lucrative returns for colonial settlers.

The demand for tobacco in Europe fuelled the transatlantic slave trade and the expansion of large-scale plantations in Virginia. Slaves were captured or kidnapped in Africa and loaded on a boat for the Americas. For European colonialists, slaves were viewed as property, not human beings.

Dehumanization and religious justification were essential for legitimizing the transatlantic slave trade. Between 1501 and 1867, an estimated 12.5 million African men, women and children were kidnapped, forced into European ships and trafficked across the Atlantic Ocean to be subjugated in a lifetime of captivity, oppression and misery,[3] and forever separated from their ancestral roots. Eventually, the trade triangle was formed. European colonialists would take manufactured goods like weapons, beer and textiles to Africa. They would then kidnap or buy slaves from the West Coast of Africa. The second leg of the journey was known as the Middle Passage across the Atlantic to the Americas. Two million Africans died during the voyages, which lasted 80 days. In the final leg, ships returned to Britain with valuable goods like tobacco, sugar, coffee and rice produced by enslaved labour.

The plantation became central to the colonial economy, shaping social and political structures in America. Slavery was a lucrative business. Slave-produced tobacco made Glasgow one of the richest cities in the world. Glasgow had direct access to the Atlantic Ocean, making it a strategic trade route. The journey from Glasgow to the colonies was faster than from other British ports. By the 1770s Glasgow controlled more than 50 per cent of the British tobacco trade.[4] It created the Tobacco Lords of Glasgow, who dominated the Tobacco trade. If you walk through the streets of Glasgow today you will still see remnants of the trade with statues and street names like Virginia Street, Jamaica Street and Tobago Street. The life expectancy of a slave at birth on plantations was 22 years old.[5] Meanwhile, wealthy merchants extracted resources and accrued vast generational wealth from slavery. Tobacco was eventually overtaken by cotton in economic importance, but the system of control and exploitation remained intact for more than a century. By 1860, the final census taken before the American Civil War, there were four million slaves in the South.[6]

As for Native Americans, between 80–95 per cent of the population died within the first century of European contact. European settlers killed 56 million indigenous people in the Americas.[7] Following the Declaration of Independence, westward expansion became a strategic priority for the newly formed United States of America. The document described Native Americans as 'merciless Indian savages'. The government authorized the Indian Removal Act of 1830, which effectively removed Native Americans from their ancestral homelands in the Eastern United States. This became known as the Trails of Tears, with 60,000 members of Cherokee, Muskogee, Seminole, Chickasaw and Choctaw forcefully removed.[8] It was a form of cultural genocide. The United States government then set its sights on western expansion. Many settlers were attracted to the promise of farmland, gold mines and a fresh new start. It was Manifest Destiny: the idea that white settlers had a divine right to settle the entire continent of North America, from the East Coast to the West Coast.

The 1862 Homestead Act further accelerated western expansion by granting settlers 160-acre plots of land. The federal government's investment in railroad infrastructure further facilitated westward expansion. Until then, Native Americans were seen as independent nations, but they were now viewed as an obstacle to expansion. This became known as the 'Indian Problem'. The Dawes Act of 1887 made the United States responsible for the sale of land in reservations. It allowed the federal government to break up tribal lands by partitioning them into individual plots. The policy was designed to destroy the social fabric and assimilate Native American tribes. The Dawes Act resulted in over 90 million acres of tribal land being stripped from Native Americans and sold to non-natives.[9] By the 1880s, most American Indians had been confined to reservations in the least desirable land for settlers. US military officials even ordered the killing of millions of buffalos to starve the Native American tribes who resisted the takeover of their lands. The bison population went from 30 million to 325 in 1884.[10] Native American children were forcefully removed from their families, names, language and culture and placed into American Indian boarding schools. Similar assimilation models occurred in other colonial settlements like Canada, Australia and New Zealand. Based on the data from the 2018 US census, Native Americans have the highest poverty rate among all minority groups. The US economy was built on vicious and murderous slave labour, and settlement of land and territories through the erasure of Native American culture. It's important to note that, throughout the history of colonialism, Native Americans and slaves resisted oppression.

Chartered companies

In the 17th century the Dutch East India Company (*Vereenigde Oostindische Compagnie*) became the world's first multinational corporation. The company was a legal entity owned by shareholders and granted exclusive rights to carry out trade activities in Asia. It was also the first corporation to issue stock. Dutch citizens could buy shares in the newly emerged Dutch East India Company to raise funds for expeditions and trade ventures with

Asia. This would later become the Amsterdam Stock Exchange. The company also had the first internationally recognized corporate logo. The Dutch East India Company had a complex corporate governance structure. The company was state-backed with a centralized board of directors known as *Heeren Zeventien* (The Lordship Seventeen) with the head office in Amsterdam. The board consisted of eight directors from Amsterdam, four from Zeeland, one each from Delft, Rotterdam, Hoorn and Enkhuizen and the seventeenth seat rotated among the smaller chambers. The new business structure allowed for a new form of economic development. It allowed companies to sell shares in return for investment to undertake business activities. The stock market is still the engine of our modern economy. The separation of ownership and management, and establishment of limited liability for investors, were breakthrough innovations from the Dutch East India Company.

Initially, the Dutch East India Company wanted to trade with Asia and gain a foothold in the lucrative spice trade, which was previously dominated by the Portuguese. Soon the Dutch East India Company realized the opportunity of monopolizing the spice trade to maximize profit. Spice was a highly valuable commodity and in relatively low supply in Europe. Before the invention of refrigerators, people would use spices like pepper, cloves and cinnamon to preserve their food and prevent decay. Spices enhanced the flavour and aroma of food. To make food more enjoyable, Europeans started using nutmeg, cardamom, ginger and cumin to spice up their food. The usage of spice was also a social status symbol. This was not just about survival. Affluent Europeans wanted to showcase their rare, exotic and high-cost spices.

The Dutch East India Company started to ship more fleets to the Indonesian Islands. The voyages into the Far East delivered tremendous returns on investment. The company eventually used military control to annex the Moluccas, known as the Spice Islands, which already had a thriving trade scene and numerous indigenous inhabitants. The company established monopoly control over the production of spices in the Moluccas: the world's primary source of cloves, nutmeg and mace. It shifted focus towards the production of spices, establishing colonies and spice plantations in Java, Sumatra and Moluccas using forced labour from indigenous people and indentured servants. Colonization made the Dutch East India Company the most valuable company of all time. It is estimated, based on present-day calculations, that the Dutch East India Company would be worth $7.9 trillion.[11]

When the company dissolved, following internal turmoil and shifting European tastes from spices to sugar and cotton, the British were better positioned for these new markets due to the transatlantic slave trade. However, the East India Company created the infrastructure for the Dutch occupation and colonization of Indonesia. The Netherlands took possession of all East India Company assets, building on the existing trade outposts, military forts and colonial administration. The Dutch continued to rule over Indonesia until 1949. It was known as the Dutch East Indies. They instigated a new social order with the Dutch and Europeans at the top, living separately from the native communities, followed by 'foreign Orientals' like Chinese, Arabs and Indians. The native population was at the bottom. The Dutch government forced the local population to plant crops for export. This cultivation system meant that 20 per cent of village land had to be used for government crops for export back to the Netherlands.[12] The policy made the Dutch enormously wealthy from the free labour, cash crops and surplus revenue. A conservative estimate is that the income amounted to 50 per cent of the Dutch government's income in 1850.[13] Many local farmers didn't have enough food to feed themselves, causing numerous famines and epidemics. The colony became a strategic producer of sugar cane, coffee, rubber, gold and oil, industries powered by free, forced and cheap labour. The emergence of the Indonesian independence movement proved a threat to Dutch interests. Following World War II, Indonesia declared independence – after being occupied by Japan – but the Dutch government sought to regain control. More than 100,000 Indonesians were killed in the battle for self-determination. Indonesia was even forced to pay 4.5 billion guilders for Dutch losses from the war by The Hague.[14]

The Dutch East India Company wasn't the only chartered company making fortunes from the exploitation and extraction of valuable resources. FMCG company Unilever has roots in the British Empire's extraction of palm oil and coconut oil from African land. The Royal Niger Company was a chartered company instrumental in the formation of colonial Nigeria, providing companies like Dutch margarine company Margarine Unie and British soap maker Lever Brothers access to raw materials like palm oil – which is a key ingredient for soap and margarine – from the West Coast of Africa. The Royal Niger Company eventually integrated into Unilever. British oil and gas company Shell, formerly known as Royal Dutch Shell plc, has roots in oil exploration, extraction and production in the Dutch East Indies. The oil fields discovered in Sumatra provided a significant portion of the company's early success. HSBC (Hong Kong and Shanghai Banking

Corporation) was established after the British made Hong Kong a colony to facilitate trade and finance in British colonies. Standard Chartered was the amalgamation of two chartered companies – Standard Bank operating in South Africa and Chartered Bank operating in Asia. Standard Bank offered financial services to colonial settlers, businesses and mining companies. BP (British Petroleum) started as the Anglo-Persian Oil Company. The British government had 51 per cent controlling shares in the company.[15] When Iran's Prime Minister Mohammed Mossadegh nationalized the resource MI6 and the CIA initiated a coup codenamed Operation Ajax to overthrow the democratically elected government.[16] Colonialism isn't confined to Western corporations. Japanese companies like Mitsubishi played an important role in Japanese expansion into Korea and China. The company operated mines, factories and enterprises. More than 150,000 Koreans were forced to work in factories and mines during World War II.[17] It can be easy to view colonialism as a relic of ancient history, but colonialism continues to shape the world we currently inhabit. These aren't stories from the history books but a modern reality.

Decolonization

Modern organizational structures are a legacy of colonialism. We might not always realize how colonialism shaped our current world. This is not only about events in history books but the foundations and formations of the 21st century. Between 1492 and 1914, Europeans conquered 84 per cent of the globe.[18] For countries, cultures and communities that have been colonized, the impact is undeniable. People with European ancestry might find the term decolonization to be frightening. Decolonization is the process of identifying colonial systems, structures and hierarchies and actively working to challenge them. If we are unaware of the history and impact of colonialism, we are less likely to question how business and society are organized. We end up viewing the current social and economic hierarchies as the norm.

In recent years, decolonization has made waves in the academic world. After World War I and World War II, decolonization was viewed as the disbanding of Empires and the liberation of independent states. Between 1945 and 1975, as struggles for independence were won in Africa and Asia, United Nations membership grew from 51 to 144 countries.[19] The concept of decolonization was mainly political and physical. Following independence, what remained was a form of cultural colonialism where the ideas, language, traditions and beliefs of the European colonialists superseded indigenous cultures and traditions. Many countries and communities have made concerted efforts to embrace their ancestral roots. It has been argued that Western nations have simply replaced political imperialism with cultural imperialism, a process where oppression and submission are no longer solely carried out through military intervention but through the successful fertilization of popular culture and American ideals like Hollywood, cheeseburgers and Coca Cola.

Frantz Fanon was born in the Caribbean Island of Martinique under French Colonial rule. He witnessed the Algerian resistance against French occupation which influenced his seminal work, *The Wretched of the Earth*.[20] Fanon's involvement in the Algerian revolutionary struggle shifted his perspective from focusing purely on the Black experience to a more global anti-colonial struggle of the Global Majority. Fanon was working as a psychiatrist on the outskirts of Algiers when France systematically massacred and tortured innocent Algerians. His background in philosophy combined with his practice in psychiatry helped Fanon arrive at a fundamental insight: colonialism was not just physical, but psychological. Fanon's work greatly inspired liberation movements from around the world. The aim was individual and collective freedom from the structures of oppression. Palestinian-American scholar Edward Said is another contributor to the decolonization movement. His book *Orientalism* argues that colonialism was not only a political system, but a worldview that simply believes the West is superior to the East.[21] Orientalism legitimizes and reinforces Western power over the East. It reduces the culture, religion and ethnicity of the 'other' into convenient stereotypes. These images intentionally strip people of their humanity. Said references his own experience growing up in Palestine and the difference between his lived experience and portrayals in Western media, academia and society at large. It showed how colonial power structures are reinforced through language and representation. We only have to look at movies like *Lawrence of Arabia*, *Indiana Jones*, *The Mummy* and many more which reinforce the idea of civilized European protagonists and primitive and uncivilized locals.

In more recent years, terms like decolonization have started to enter mainstream discourse. We live in a more global and self-aware society. Young people from countries and cultures with a colonial history are proactively reconnecting with their roots, traditions and history. And young people with European ancestry are more aware of the legacy of colonialism than their parents thanks to the availability of different stories and perspectives on the internet. Decolonization doesn't have to be violent. It doesn't have to be intimidating. It doesn't even have to be restrictive for individuals, groups and countries with a colonial past.

What often escapes the decolonization narrative is the sheer violence and trauma colonialism caused local populations in Europe. Colonialism didn't benefit all members of Empires equally. Most often a tiny minority would reap the fruits of oppression and extraction, while poor young men had to travel to faraway lands to subjugate groups whom they had nothing against. Colonialism oppressed European populations who were forced to go on dangerous expeditions where they would die from disease, war and starvation.

Decolonization is about shining a light on colonial power structures and imagining new forms of social structures which are more equitable, inclusive and collaborative for all. It represents a golden opportunity to imagine a better future. It does, however, require understanding and undoing the harmful colonial legacies of history. This is a process and journey that all members of society can undertake. Decolonization is also beginning to enter mainstream discourse in business. Young people no longer accept the hierarchal structures of the past.

Participatory action research

Unlike the hierarchal structures of ancient Egypt, European settler colonialism in North America or corporate extractivism of the Dutch East India Company new models of anti-colonial community engagement and participation are emerging. The process begins with research. In business and society, research is a valuable way of generating knowledge, identifying problems or opportunities and making better decisions. The term 'research' probably conjures up images of scientists in lab coats, psychologists conducting focus groups or clients sitting behind a mirror eating biscuits and watching 'ordinary' people.

Participatory action research involves community members as active contributors in the research process. It represents a more collaborative, inclusive and equitable way of conducting research, generating knowledge and taking action, smashing the traditional boundaries, power relations and social hierarchies between researcher and subject, and instead, viewing all participants as partners working towards a shared goal. Participatory action research places power in the hands of the individuals and communities experiencing or impacted by the problem, recognizing the lived experiences of people, communities and cultures. It doesn't remove people who experience the phenomena from the process, decisions and actions. Top-down research doesn't deliver the most powerful insights and won't create the most impactful social change. There's far more value in developing an inside understanding of the problem or experience. The difference can be seen in the following examples: being a mother versus studying motherhood; being from Tanzania versus studying the history of Tanzania; starting a business versus taking a course in business management. Theory and practice are not the same.

Under true participatory action research, partners undertake a shared decision across all phases of the research. Communities are involved in the design, engagement and production of insights. This includes identifying the theme that should be researched, a phase where many research projects go wrong. Because if the research isn't tackling the right question, then the answer is irrelevant. The members of the research project take part in a co-learning journey, building capacity along the way. A critical characteristic of participatory action research – as evident in the name – is the emphasis on action. Unlike traditional research, the practice acknowledges that the ultimate goal should be social change. We can learn as much from action as we can from research. Participatory action research is an iterative and adaptive process that appreciates the complexity of our interconnected world. Knowledge generation is not limited to the most powerful people or groups within a social hierarchy.

For example, in the world of business, expertise is viewed as tiered based on seniority. The CEO is expected to have all the answers, employees often act on the decisions made by leadership teams. Similar patterns can be seen in field academia with deans, professors, doctors and graduates being able to contribute according to their standing. In both business and academia, if you're not a stakeholder, then your voice seldom matters. Participatory research gives communities agency by democratizing research work that often feels distant, disconnected and exclusionary. The concept has roots in academia, but the same process can be applied in business and marketing to create social change. In the same way, scientists must shift from studying subjects to collaborating with partners on shared projects. Business needs to shift from marketing to consumers and hiring employees to collaborating with citizens.

Participatory action research recognizes the importance of power relations in creating social change. It actively works to include the voices, experiences and contributions of individuals and communities who are directly impacted, encouraging all parties involved to collaborate, co-create, co-learn and take collective action. Change isn't possible without community engagement.

Mental health and indigenous Australians

People have lived in Australia for over 60,000 years.[22] The indigenous Aboriginal and Torres Strait Islander people are the oldest known civilization with one of the richest surviving cultures in the world. Settler colonization has profoundly damaged the fabric of indigenous culture. indigenous Australians have lower life expectancies, they are nine times more likely to be homeless and 14 times more likely to be in prison. They are 3 per cent of the Australian population but 26 per cent of the prison population.[23] They are also more likely to suffer from long-term mental health and behavioural conditions. Australian government policies and mental health programmes have struggled to understand or address the unique cultural and historical traumas facing indigenous communities.

Colonization separated indigenous people from their ancestral land. Aboriginals and Torres Strait Islanders have always had a spiritual connection to the land, forming their self-identity, culture and community. The land is viewed as sacred; it can never be owned. Indigenous Australians were part of nature, not separate from nature. The loss and dispossession of ancestral land by British settlers led to a collective loss of identity, belonging and meaning. Many indigenous Australians lost their search for meaning. Until the 1970s indigenous children were systematically stolen from their families if they had white ancestry in them. The objective was to assimilate indigenous populations by uprooting children from their heritage and teaching them European customs. They would later become known as the Lost Generation. Some communities would paint their children using tree sap so they wouldn't be stolen. More than 50,000 indigenous children were stolen and placed into churches, fostered or adopted by non-indigenous families.[24] In 2008, Australian Prime Minister Kevin Rudd apologised for the Stolen Generation but stressed there would be no compensation. Federal government data shows the Stolen Generation is the poorest and most disadvantaged among indigenous communities, with worse health, employment, housing and family outcomes.[25]

When assessing the mental health challenges facing indigenous Australians, using a top-down approach would prevent mental health practitioners from understanding the history, culture and current realities of Aboriginal and Torres Strait Islander people in Australia. Indigenous communities are still experiencing the aftermath of settler colonialism. The trauma is passed down from generation to generation. There are a growing number of studies that suggest trauma like stress, famine and war can impact a person's DNA and potentially influence the health of future generations far removed from the traumatic event through epigenetics. When working in collaboration with indigenous Australians, with an understanding of institutional racism, structural inequality and lack of economic opportunities mental health practitioners would have a better idea of why indigenous communities suffer from disproportionate levels of mental health conditions.

Europeans changed the social fabric and locked indigenous people out of the new system. The conventional Western mental health system fails to understand indigenous cultures, values and beliefs. Without understanding the culture, medical interventions are ineffective at best and harmful at worst. Indigenous communities view mental health in a more holistic, spiritual and emotional way than European traditions. Indigenous communities call it spiritual wellbeing. In indigenous Australian cultures if the spirit isn't well, then the body and mind will suffer too. Spirit and connection to land are the foundation of indigenous cultures.

COMMUNITY ENGAGEMENT

When working with indigenous Australian communities, mental wellbeing initiatives need to exist outside of clinical settings and academic textbooks. The healing process should be a partnership designed to support indigenous-led community initiatives in search of spiritual wellbeing, a more participatory process creating safe spaces and looking at prevention, not just medical prescriptions. Mental wellbeing projects are more successful when indigenous leaders and communities are involved in the process from design and implementation to delivery. It requires governments, charities and organizations to take time and build trust and relationships with local communities. Community participation can also make the job of non-indigenous practitioners less stressful and more effective. Doctors and nurses don't have to worry as much about offending or misdiagnosing patients. Crucially, participation gives ownership and power to marginalized indigenous communities. Most indigenous Australian people didn't have full voting rights until 1965.[26] The participatory nature of new mental health programmes can make indigenous communities feel included in modern Australia while maintaining their cultural roots.

A grassroots example of participation in practice comes from the Wurrumiyanga (Nguiu) community on Bathurst Island in the Northern Territory. The local health centres' approach to mental health combines indigenous cultural practices with Western therapy and medicine. Unlike top-down practices, indigenous culture has been embedded into the treatment. Members of the community get to connect with the land by visiting the bush, gathering roots and walking near the sea, reconnecting community members with their ancestral land and cultural identity. Unlike Western psychotherapy, counselling sessions aren't done one-to-one in a formal room but collectively in the great outdoors through sharing circles where individuals and groups get to share what's on their minds.

The top-down Australian mental health system has failed to recognize the cultural identity, spiritual connection with land and kinship system of indigenous communities. Luckily a new generation of indigenous-led community initiatives supported by non-indigenous partners is finding ways to promote spiritual wellbeing by first understanding the culture. The ability and resilience of indigenous Australian communities to survive cultural erasure and tell their own stories is incredible. New participatory models to promote reconciliation, restorative justice and collaboration will hopefully be the start of a new chapter.

New Coke

A top-down approach can be equally damaging in the business world. It caused one of the biggest mistakes in marketing history. In the 1980s Coca-Cola was engaged in a fierce rivalry with Pepsi-Cola, who at the time was eating up market share. This would later become known as the Cola Wars. After World War II, Coca-Cola had a 60 per cent share of the US cola market but by 1983 the number had dwindled to 24 per cent.[27] Pepsi ran a successful marketing campaign called the Pepsi Challenge which invited people to blind taste two unlabelled drinks. One was Pepsi and the other Coca-Cola. It showed that consumers preferred Pepsi. The message was a simple but powerful one – Coca-Cola is more famous, but Pepsi tastes better.

The success of the Pepsi Challenge – combined with the brand's appeal to younger demographics – inspired Coca-Cola to change its formula. Coca-Cola was worried about the Pepsi Challenge. Internal research verified Pepsi's claim. On 23 April 1985, Coca-Cola announced it was changing its century-old secret formula. The decision was driven by top executives at The Coca-Cola Company, led by CEO Roberto Goizueta. It launched 'New

Coke' with a sweeter and smoother taste. After commissioning 200,000 taste tests, the company went all-in with the launch of 'New Coke'. Coca-Cola's CEO called it the boldest marketing move in the history of packaged goods. The new product was designed to win back market share from Pepsi, but it did the exact opposite. Coca-Cola superfans were not upset, they were furious. Long-time drinkers had developed an emotional connection to the original formulation and felt betrayed by the sudden change. The company's switchboards were soon drowning in nearly 10,000 calls a day from angry customers. Polls revealed that only 13 per cent of soda drinkers liked New Coke. A grassroots movement was built to overturn the decision from Coca-Cola HQ spearheaded by 'Old Cola Drinkers of America'. The people eventually overcame the corporation. President of the Coca-Cola company Donald Keough appeared on a TV advert to give consumers a choice between Original and New Coke. When interviewed a decade later Coca-Cola management shared a valuable lesson: the loyal consumers and not the company own the brand. In the 21st century, this statement is being further expanded to citizens and communities.

Timpson and upside-down management

On the flip side, we are witnessing a new wave of collaborative, inclusive and participatory business models. Unlike chartered companies or top-down multinational corporations, such companies involve employees and communities in their decision-making process. In the United Kingdom, the family-owned business Timpson, which has a portfolio of 2,100 stores and more than 5,000 employees, operates an 'upside-down management' culture.[28] Timpson proactively hires ex-offenders and offers them an opportunity to make a fresh new start. Since 2008, the company has hired more than 1,500 ex-prisoners, with only four employees returning to jail. The innovative recruitment model helps to rehabilitate offenders and addresses the root cause of criminal activity: feeling abandoned by society. The policy combines social impact with business impact by delivering a consistent pipeline of talent for the retailer. Unlike most companies which operate top-down, Timpson gives employees full autonomy and responsibility to make decisions. Frontline workers can do whatever they like if they follow two rules. The first rule: employees should put the money into the till. The second rule: always look presentable. Beyond these two conditions, Timpson's is a decentralized organization. The staff in each shoe repair, dry cleaner and photo shop can decide how they work, and when they work. Staff make decisions about the supply and sales of goods and services. They are encouraged to

THE POWER OF CO-CREATION 171

run the shop like a business. Employees can offer discounts, negotiate with suppliers and change the design of the shop. Most Timpson shops are run by a single person like a small business. This is a business decision to make sure employees are happy and customers have the best possible experience. Timpson CEO James Timpson noticed that the happier the team, the better the business result. Therefore, the company launched the Happiness Index Score which has become the most important business metric. The role of area managers at Timpson isn't to maximize profit or reduce costs, it's to make sure colleagues in local stores are happy. The business also allows employees access to 19 holiday homes. The upside-down management is also a source of innovation. Timpson employees can suggest new ideas and launch new products and service offerings. For example, Timpson didn't have watch repairs until a colleague started promoting the service at a local branch. Watch repairs have now become a considerable source of revenue for the business.

The People and Pentland Brands

In my own company, The People, we launched a collaboration with Pentland Brands, owner of sports, outdoor and lifestyle brands, including Speedo, Berghaus and ellesse, to build a global youth advisory board called The Pentland Collective. Pentland Brand's mission is to pioneer brands that make life better. The People's mission is to amplify the voices of young people and underserved communities. This was the beginning of a complementary and long-term partnership. Pentland Brands recognized the importance of having a global perspective and connecting with future employees, consumers and communities. We worked together to identify and onboard a youth advisory board with members from the UK, USA, India, China and Vietnam, to offer fresh outside perspectives on business priorities and future direction. Crucially, the Pentland Collective collaborated with internal employee groups to maximize the impact of insights, ideas and recommendations before being shared with the executive team on a quarterly basis.

The Pentland Collective is another example of participatory business and social change. It was born from the need to include youth voices in the boardroom. Today, 50 per cent of the global population is under the age of 30, but the average age of a director is almost 60. The success of the Pentland Collective came from the collaboration between a global business, mission-led start-up and local communities. The project was only made possible because the company was willing to listen, learn and support a new generation of global talent. Since its launch, the Pentland Collective has become a vehicle of positive social change for the business. Youth advisory board members have also gained leadership skills and contributed to the future direction of a global business. We are now in the process of creating an open-source playbook on how to set up a youth advisory board that other companies can adopt, further strengthening the wider youth engagement ecosystem and bridging the gap between business and young people.

Participatory budgeting in Brazil

In Porto Alegre, Brazil, citizens directly participate in the budgeting process and allocation of resources to community projects and priorities. Residents attend local assemblies to discuss and vote on spending priorities, allowing for greater citizen engagement in local governance and decision-making. The idea seems so simple and yet radical when compared with the top-down centralized management of most nations. Citizens rarely get an opportunity to shape policy and their community, apart from voting in local and general elections. The participatory process creates space for citizens to present their demands and priorities for municipal improvement and discussions. Since 1989, budget allocations for public welfare works in Porto Alegre have been made only after the recommendations of public delegates and approval by the city council. The success of people's participation in determining the use of public welfare funds in the city of Porto Alegre has inspired many other municipalities to follow suit. This is an important case study for citizen participation and engagement. The co-creation model, whether in business, civil society or government, demonstrates the opportunity to scale up participatory projects.

ACTIVITY

1 Decolonization

It can be easy to view colonialism as a relic of ancient history, but colonialism continues to shape the world we currently inhabit. These aren't stories from the history books but a modern reality. From ancient Egyptian social classes to European settler colonialism in North America or the corporate extractivism of the Dutch East India Company, the legacy of colonialism persists.

Take a moment to reflect on the following questions:

o   Which social structures and practices have a legacy in colonialism? This could be ways of working, historical connections and even language.

o   Which people or groups continue to be affected by colonialism? Explore ways to reflect this reality into all future business and social actions.

o   How can we rethink our sources of knowledge? We have an opportunity to overcome historical inequities by exploring different canons of knowledge.

2   Decentralization

In the world of business, expertise is viewed to be tiered based on seniority. The CEO is expected to have all the answers, and employees often act on the decisions made by leadership teams. Remember the lessons from the New Coke debacle? Centralized structures are equally common in government, academia and the charity sector.

We have an opportunity to explore new engagement and participation models. Ask yourself:

o   How could your movement become more decentralized?

This might be exploring ways of working, organizational structure and governance.

British retailer Timpson operates an 'upside-down management' culture to give employees the freedom to make decisions. Frontline workers can do whatever they like if they follow two rules. The first rule: employees should put the money into the till. The second rule: always look presentable. The People collaborated with Pentland Brands, owner of sports, outdoor and lifestyle brands, including Speedo, Berghaus and ellese, to build a global youth advisory board, challenging the outdated concept that ideas can only come from from the top, delivering fresh outside-in perspectives, and making sure young people, employees and communities are stakeholders in future plans and decision-making.

3   Participation

Participatory action research recognizes the importance of power relations in creating social change. It actively works to include the voices, experiences and contributions of individuals and communities who are directly impacted, encouraging all parties involved to collaborate, co-create, co-learn and take collective action. Change isn't possible without community engagement.

You can make your mission more participatory by exploring the following questions or, even better, working with relevant communities to establish new questions:

- o How can we promote a more participatory model?
- o What people, groups and communities need to be invited?
- o How can we decentralize the research and decision-making process?

In Porto Alegre, Brazil, citizens directly participate in the budgeting process and allocation of resources to community projects and priorities. Residents attend local assemblies to discuss and vote on spending priorities, allowing for greater citizen engagement in local governance and decision-making. The success of people's participation in determining the use of public welfare funds in the city of Porto Alegre has inspired hundreds of other municipalities to follow suit.

Notes

1 A G McDowell. Daily life in ancient Egypt, *Scientific American*, 1996, 275 (6), 100–05. www.jstor.org/stable/24993496 (archived at https://perma.cc/6YYH-QNZB)

2 A Rutherford. A new history of the first peoples in the Americas, The Atlantic, 3 October 2017. www.theatlantic.com/science/archive/2017/10/a-brief-history-of-everyone-who-ever-lived/537942 (archived at https://perma.cc/N4QX-QJAH)

3 A O'Neill. Number of slaves taken from Africa by region 1501–1866, Statista, 2 February 2020. www.statista.com/statistics/1150475/number-slaves-taken-from-africa-by-region-century (archived at https://perma.cc/Z3LN-MW8T)

4 D Olusoga. How tobacco farming made Glasgow so wealthy, BBC, YouTube, 2023. www.youtube.com/watch?v=cHohEaiHyj0 (archived at https://perma.cc/HQ5A-DTXC)

5 R W Fogel and S L Engerman (1995) *Time on the Cross: The economics of American Negro slavery*, Norton, New York

6 A O'Neill. United States: Black and slave population 1790–1880, Statista, 2 February 2019. www.statista.com/statistics/1010169/black-and-slave-population-us-1790-1880 (archived at https://perma.cc/ASU5-BNYW)

7 A Koch et al. Earth system impacts of the European arrival and Great Dying in the Americas after 1492, *Quaternary Science Reviews*, 2019, 207, 13–36. doi.org/10.1016/j.quascirev.2018.12.004 (archived at https://perma.cc/9K3M-7A3Y)

8 History. Andrew Jackson signs the Indian Removal Act into law, 2021. www.history.com/this-day-in-history/indian-removal-act-signed-andrew-jackson (archived at https://perma.cc/CHU3-8CZ3)

9 US National Park Service. The Dawes Act, 2021. www.nps.gov/articles/000/dawes-act.htm (archived at https://perma.cc/JE38-3Y5A)

10 US National Park Service. Bison, buffalo, tatanka: Bovids of the Badlands, 2020. www.nps.gov/articles/bison_badl.htm (archived at https://perma.cc/ZT54-9MU9)

11 J Desjardins. The most valuable companies of all-time, Visual Capitalist, 8 December 2017. www.visualcapitalist.com/most-valuable-companies-all-time (archived at https://perma.cc/C3JJ-3D3X)

12 M Dell and B A Olken. The development effects of the extractive colonial economy: The Dutch cultivation system in Java, *The Review of Economic Studies*, 2020, 87 (1), 164–203

13 D Albarrán, A Rijpma and P de Zwart. Demographic effects of colonialism: Forced labour and mortality in nineteenth-century Java, CEPR, 4 April 2022. cepr.org/voxeu/columns/demographic-effects-colonialism-forced-labour-and-mortality-nineteenth-century-java (archived at https://perma.cc/3GS8-QEZQ)

14 Y Tanamal. Dutch PM recognizes 1945 as Indonesia's independence, *Jakarta Post*, 16 June 2023. www.thejakartapost.com/paper/2023/06/16/dutch-pm-recognizes-1945-as-indonesias-independence.html (archived at https://perma.cc/48BH-R2CS)

15 R Cavendish. The Iranian oil fields are nationalised, History Today, 2021. www.historytoday.com/archive/iranian-oil-fields-are-nationalised (archived at https://perma.cc/WL7D-T5VR)

16 B Allen-Ebrahimian. 64 years later, CIA finally releases details of Iranian coup, Foreign Policy, 20 June 2017. foreignpolicy.com/2017/06/20/64-years-later-cia-finally-releases-details-of-iranian-coup-iran-tehran-oil (archived at https://perma.cc/J6UY-34UM)

17 G Choy. Forced labour a sore topic between South Korea and Japan as court verdict looms, *South China Morning Post*, 22 November 2018. www.scmp.com/week-asia/politics/article/2174385/forced-labour-sore-topic-between-south-korea-and-japan-court (archived at https://perma.cc/5HQH-9Z2P)

18 P T Hoffman (2015) *Why Did Europe Conquer the World?*, Princeton University Press, Princeton

19 United Nations. Growth in United Nations membership, 2023. www.un.org/en/about-us/growth-in-un-membership (archived at https://perma.cc/PSV5-642A)

20 F Fanon (1961) *The Wretched of the Earth*, Kwela Books, Cape Town

21 E W Said (2003) *Orientalism*, Penguin, London

22 AIATSIS. Australia's First Peoples, 2021. aiatsis.gov.au/explore/australias-first-peoples (archived at https://perma.cc/JC8R-FUV8)

23 Australian Human Rights Commission. *Human Rights and Aboriginal and Torres Strait Islander Peoples*, 2008. humanrights.gov.au/sites/default/files/content/letstalkaboutrights/downloads/HRA_ATSI.pdf (archived at https://perma.cc/5HWT-N7G3)

24 J Pilger. Another stolen generation: How Australia still wrecks Aboriginal families, *The Guardian*, 21 March 2014. www.theguardian.com/

commentisfree/2014/mar/21/john-pilger-indigenous-australian-families (archived at https://perma.cc/BKD7-SA8N)

25 Australian Institute of Health and Welfare. Aboriginal and Torres Strait Islander stolen generations aged 50 and over: Updated analyses for 2018–19, 2 June 2021. www.aihw.gov.au/reports/indigenous-australians/indigenous-stolen-generations-50-and-over/contents/summary (archived at https://perma.cc/P39M-F55Q)

26 National Museum of Australia. Indigenous Australians granted the right to vote, nd. digital-classroom.nma.gov.au/defining-moments/indigenous-australians-granted-right-vote (archived at https://perma.cc/EU9K-M4Y7)

27 B Mikkelson. Was the 'New Coke' fiasco just a clever marketing ploy?, Snopes, 1 May 1999. www.snopes.com/fact-check/new-coke-fiasco (archived at https://perma.cc/KNE2-8W29)

28 Timpson Group. Upside down management, nd. www.timpson-group.co.uk/about-timpson/upside-down-management (archived at https://perma.cc/HU8M-QTM7)

10

Managing backlash

Sir Isaac Newton's third law states that for every action in nature, there is an equal and opposite reaction. When you bounce a ball on the ground it jumps back up. What happens when your mission begins to create change? How can we maintain momentum, avoid relapse and manage backlash? Until now, we have focused on how to turn purpose into business and social impact. There comes a point where you will gain traction, build a community and create meaningful change. However, it would be unwise to treat social change as a one-way road, as things can go backwards as well as forwards. The road ahead is jam-packed with hurdles, milestones and setbacks. The journey to creating social change shouldn't be viewed as a one-person computer game where everything goes according to plan. When we are reading books and making business plans, we have total control of our conditions, like playing a computer game at our own pace. The outside world is radically different; there are countless variables outside our circle of influence. Thus, we should view our mission as a multi-player online game which is fast-paced, dynamic and unpredictable. What we can control is our ability to adapt to the game.

Somewhere in your mission, you are likely to receive criticism, pushback or backlash. Social change doesn't make everyone happy. Individuals, groups and organizations might have different reasons for not agreeing with your mission, movement and actions. Some might be perfectly valid, like suggestions on how to become more effective, innovative and inclusive. This won't make the critique more palatable, but if taken on board it can improve your chances of making a business and social impact. Other forms of criticism might be more subjective, such as not agreeing with your project's mission, future direction and intended change. Some people like pizza, others prefer pasta. Some people love Marmite, others hate Marmite. Some people love heavy metal rock and others prefer the opera. There are as many opinions as there are people on the planet. However, social change movements also experience another form of criticism which is more destructive: rejection of the intended change. Some actors don't want things to change. Certain people, groups and organizations will actively seek to destroy your mission. The following chapter is a playbook on how you can navigate, understand, respond to and manage the backlash.

Before we get into how to do this, it's worth stating that social change isn't independent of ideology. More nations are experiencing extreme political polarization, a cultural struggle between social groups that is further inflamed by identity politics.

Regardless of where we sit on the political spectrum we have something in common. Much of our identity, worldview and self-worth stems from being part of a group (us) and being against other groups (them). In 2020, the match-making website OkCupid asked five million hopeful daters around the world: 'Could you date someone who has strong political opinions that are the opposite of yours?' 60 per cent answered 'No'.[1] Political polarization is further exacerbated by social media and carefully constructed algorithms which feed us what we believe and omit what we don't. The content we see merely confirms our existing worldview, further entrenching our sense of political identity without exposing us to other views. The outcome is deep divisions within democratic societies and no room for collective memory because, unlike traditional media, we are not all experiencing the same thing at the same time. We have to find ways to build bridges and burst bubbles.

Start with the basics

When thinking about how to manage backlash, the best place to start is with the factors that are within our control. As mentioned previously, there will be people and groups who you will never be able to convince to create change. But, at the same time, we must ensure our house is in order before we ask others to embark on a journey of business and social impact. This begins with getting the basics right. The journey towards social change starts with making sure that your movement is not causing harm. For more established companies, it begins with remembering that business is a part of society. Companies can and should make a positive contribution to people's lives. This begins with paying tax: an agreed fee for doing business and making a profit. Yet, many businesses view tax as a cost to be minimized, rather than an investment back into society. Corporation tax helps to fund essential healthcare, education and social services for the very customers and employees who buy and work for a business. In truth, there's not much point in having a lofty brand mission if you're not even holding up your end of the bargain. According to the Institute on Taxation and Economic Policy, 55 per cent of the largest corporations in America paid no federal corporate income taxes on their 2020 profits.[2] The companies include names like Whirlpool, FedEx, Nike, HP and Salesforce. Other companies shift money to subsidiaries in low-tax countries or transfer money to tax havens like Bermuda, the Cayman Islands and Ireland.

The second basic responsibility is making sure employees, suppliers and partners are paid fairly. Making sure workers have the best possible conditions for work and actively addressing the CEO–worker pay gap, which has been rising exponentially. Making sure that fair payment and treatment are not only standard in the company HQ but throughout the business across different locations and throughout the entire supply chain. Historically, multinational corporations have been found to exploit cheap labour in developing countries. Fulfilling your responsibility as a business provides a foundation for social impact. It begins with paying your taxes, looking after your employees and not destroying the environment. Not meeting the above criteria will leave you susceptible to purpose washing. Consumers are more informed and empowered than ever before. They can check whether your words are backed by action via a quick Google search.

Yet most business sustainability reports or marketing campaigns focus on marginal topics like plastic straws, reusable bags and recycling. If companies want to be seen as credible, dependable and responsible, they need to reshape all future brand communications and commitments to focus on their own responsibilities. Any attempt to shift responsibility to consumers will be called out and met with instant backlash, especially if contradictory to internal practices. Companies should accept their social and environmental footprint. Once this has been established, they can work with communities to co-create projects, gain external feedback and scale impact through partnerships.

Education and capacity building

What should you do when you encounter rejectors? The best place to start is with the assumption that people have good intentions. It might be circumstances, upbringing or unfamiliarity which make them combative to social change. Instead of engaging in conflict, why not initiate open dialogue with your counterparts? The journey towards social change begins with education. We have talked plentifully about the importance of decentralized organizations. It should, however, be noted that in traditional organizational structures, change is often inspired, instigated and enabled from the top. If senior leadership is unwilling or uninterested in changing things it will be more challenging to get traction. Employees and outsiders often get frustrated when they have bright new ideas to make a positive business and social impact, but the initiative is not supported, or even worse is repelled, by leadership teams. Again, in more established, legacy organizations, more groundwork needs to be done to bring leadership on a journey from education to empowerment. If the CEO and board of directors don't have lived experience, detailed understanding or expertise about your mission, it will be much harder for them to become champions of change. The key is to make sure knowledge is shared in a non-judgemental and friendly manner. This is not about telling people why they are wrong. When we are blamed, our automatic response is to defend ourselves and our actions, and redirect the blame to someone else. Greater emphasis should be placed on the opportunity to explore new ideas and opportunities. We should create the conditions for education before making the business or social case for change.

Education equips people with new tools, knowledge and skills to navigate change. People will no longer view change as a threat to their existing interests but as an opportunity to expand their capabilities. More importantly, knowledge sharing makes change a collective effort. More work should be done to embrace learning, build capacity and challenge the status quo. We can't achieve social change by only interacting and exchanging views with people who share our beliefs. Change comes from creating space to have an open dialogue with people who have different ideas and experiences. Facilitating conversations – while investing in education – helps to align your mission with the rest of the organization. Future interactions come from a shared understanding of values and expectations. All parties might not agree on the best possible course of action, but topics will be discussed through a shared understanding. Most importantly, education makes the mission bigger than you. It gives others the tools to become agents of change. You will have the opportunity to share what you know with more people. People will no longer be reliant on you to deliver business and social impact. The mission becomes scalable, and you will learn more by imparting your learning, failures and experiences to others.

Microsoft accessibility awareness training

Tech giant Microsoft provides accessibility awareness training for its employees to ensure products and services are inclusive and accessible to people of all abilities. The course covers topics like inclusive design, assistive technologies and accessibility standards. Employees can apply the learning from the training – including accessibility principles – to make Microsoft products more inclusive, user-friendly and innovative. After successfully launching the training internally Microsoft has now made the course available to technology partners and the public to improve education and awareness when it comes to inclusive design. The work Microsoft is doing is good for business as it allows more people to access (buy) its products and services. But it's equally beneficial for society, as more than 1.3 billion people live with some form of disability. This represents 15 per cent of the world's population.[3] More recently, Microsoft has set its sights on tackling the 'disability divide'. In developing countries, 80–90 per cent of people with disabilities of working age are unemployed, whereas in developed countries the figure is 50–70 per cent.[4] Over the past two years, more than 1.5 million people have undertaken the Microsoft accessibility fundamentals training.[5] The course is also promoted by more than 26,000 employment coaches in the UK alone. The company has expanded access to the tool even further through a strategic partnership with LinkedIn (owned by Microsoft) to make the workplace more accessible for everyone. The courses are available for people with disabilities, managers and allies.

What began as an internal initiative to educate employees has developed into a larger social movement to improve the accessibility and employment chances of more than a billion people globally. Education provides the foundations for capacity building. Capacity building is the engine for creating long-term business and social impact. This is a two-way road which requires participants – especially those in senior positions of power – to put aside their egos and be willing to learn new skills. Education, when facilitated properly, can lead to better decisions.

Progress not perfection

The pursuit of perfection can be counterproductive. Perfection might raise standards, but it can prevent us from getting started and making steady progress. In our personal life, perfectionism can be a self-sabotaging endeavour. Let's say you want to start going to the gym and exercising.

If you start with little to no expectations and simply head to the gym for a 10-minute session you are more likely to make your first session. This can provide the evidence and motivation for your next session. Before you know it, you are spending 10 minutes on bench press, 10 minutes on the treadmill and 10 minutes rowing. Soon enough, you have a personalized gym routine built on six months of experience. You are doing cardio on Monday, legs on Tuesday, arms on Wednesday, chest on Thursday and abs on Friday. Above all, you feel good about the progress you are making. Regular exercise makes you feel in better physical and mental shape. You are sharper at work and more present around your family.

Now let's reimagine the same scenario, but this time instead of beginning with a 10-minute trip to the gym you begin by watching 10 hours of YouTube content with multiple personal trainers sharing their best fitness advice. You then search for the perfect gym wear for when you finally grace the gym, before spending a couple of days researching the best facilities in your local area. Three months have passed, and the unattainable physique of YouTube trainers and uncountable number of gym routines available have deterred you from getting started. Your brand-spanking-new gym wear taunts you when you open the wardrobe every morning. This is the curse of perfection. Setting unattainable standards makes us less likely to begin the journey of change. Lowering our expectations, no matter how blasphemous it sounds, will allow us to achieve more. The same is true when it comes to business and social change.

Something is better than nothing

Often, companies look for the perfect opportunity to make a positive business and social impact. They set high expectations from the outset with the project scope, expected deliverables and key performance indicators. The business or social mission is grand in ambition – which is great – but so are the steps needed to realize it. In the search for the perfect outcome, companies fail to create the conditions to make the first step on the journey. As a result, the mission feels intimidating for colleagues, partners and investors. People feel lost, unsure of where to begin and fearful that they will never meet the high expectations set at the beginning of the project. What would a 10-minute gym visit version of your mission look like? How can you help people get started straight away? And build evidence and confidence? Could they volunteer 30 minutes of their time? Could they nominate more people to get involved? Are they able to contribute tools and resources towards the project? At the beginning of the change journey, we want people, companies and partners to get started. Dipping their toes in the swimming pool could jumpstart a swim across the Atlantic Ocean. But if we tell people that they need to swim the Atlantic Ocean, we will get blank stares and complete silence.

When thinking about perfection in the context of managing backlash the sad reality is that some people and companies never get started because they fear the negative backlash that might come their way. The fear of being criticized prevents business leaders from engaging in the process of creating social change. The implications of getting things wrong or being called out may seem to outweigh the benefits of making positive changes to business practices. The truth is that no human, group or company is perfect. We all make mistakes; we are not infallible. Citizens have an inalienable right to call out governments, companies and NGOs – keeping them accountable – to make sure they meet their responsibilities. Nevertheless, the call for perfection shouldn't become a barrier to making strides in the right direction. Imagine if a company has been working hard to learn and build capacity. The team works hard to convince leadership to invest in the project, which would reduce the company's carbon emissions. Despite the good intentions, a small number of online activists rightly criticize the company for its contribution to climate change in the past. The criticism worries the legal and corporate affairs teams, and the project is scrapped before it builds traction or changes the narrative within the business. It makes the company more cautious about sharing information publicly for fear of receiving backlash or damaging the brand's reputation.

There are instances when the pursuit of perfection by internal teams or external stakeholders can have the opposite effect. It can become a barrier to entry for creating social change. From personal experience of speaking to professionals in different industries, people are afraid to act on sustainability and diversity, equity and inclusion because getting it wrong is more harmful than not trying in the first place. We should all, therefore, create open and non-judgemental spaces for individuals, groups and allies to make progress, not just criticize them for not achieving perfection. For people on the receiving end of the criticism, there is no shame in showing vulnerability and asking for help. There is great power in admitting that you don't know the answers but you're doing your best to learn. Social change is a journey, not a destination. Expecting people and companies to be perfect from day one can cause more harm than good. We should view people, governments and companies in the same way teachers view students – based on the progress they are making on a weekly, monthly and annual basis, not just where they started in the first place. The same framework should be applied when assessing organizations. The world will not change if we only preach to the converted. We must make a concerted effort to include and engage the less perfect players in the market.

Be clear about your mission

Your mission is a powerful shield, protecting you from receiving backlash. If you are clear on your mission, can mobilize people and make decisions accordingly then your likelihood of receiving criticism is greatly reduced. Your personal, company or community mission creates a shared vision for the future. This is not a fancy statement; it should manifest itself in your daily actions. Backlash often occurs when your mission is not aligned with your actions. The public is tired of organizations whose actions don't match their words. Any indication of double standards, inconsistent values or performative actions will naturally be called out. In the past, companies would produce a product, service or message and consumers had no choice but to receive it. Under this arrangement, companies had complete control of every aspect of the experience. And citizens had no way of sharing their feelings towards the organization. In this new era of people-powered change, a company is no longer what companies tell people, but instead what people tell their friends.

Avoiding backlash requires clarity of mission, unyielding principles and radical transparency, not viewing social change as a seasonal trend to win consumer trust. A short-sighted approach to business and social impact is inherently flawed and liable to backlash. Citizens and communities can tell the difference between performative gesturing and genuine conviction. In a politically charged environment, organizations can't afford to be meandering to the most popular flavour of the day. Unless you stand for something, you will fail to build a meaningful connection with either side. Brands can no longer afford to remain neutral because neutral is viewed as complicit. That said, empty statements of solidarity no longer suffice either. The consumers of today are more informed and empowered than ever before. They expect you to turn your words into action. And if brands don't stick to their promises, consumers possess the knowledge, determination and platform to call them out. In short, there's nowhere to hide.

Target Pride backlash

In 2023, US retail giant Target decided to celebrate Pride Month by creating LGBTQ+ Pride merchandise. Target became the recipient of conservative backlash. Right-wing activists online were furious with the company's LGBTQ+ support. The retailer was selling a range of 2,000 products including T-shirts with rainbows, greeting cards to celebrate people coming out and books for children. The backlash from conservatives dented Target's sales by 5.4 per cent within the first three months.[6] The retailer decreased its profit outlook. The CEO acknowledged that the Pride Month collection hurt sales. The company viewed it as a signal to review activities. Despite selling Pride merchandise for over a decade, Target announced that it would remove some of the Pride merchandise following 'volatile circumstances' and move other displays to the back of stores to draw less attention. Target did not state declining sales as the primary motivation for the change in direction. The main reason the company provided was that an increasing number of customers were threatening employees. Target's response then triggered a counter-backlash from the LGBTQ+ community and allies who felt that Target was selling out the community. Advocacy groups demanded that Target return all the merchandise removed from its stores and websites and reaffirm its commitment to the LGBTQ+ community.

Not being clear on its mission and what Target was fighting for and against produced the worst possible outcome. This was a lose–lose scenario for the retailer. Aligning itself with the LGBTQ+ community upset conservative consumers. Not maintaining such support in the face of growing backlash and declining sales lost the trust built with the LGBTQ+ community. Ultimately, Target's decision was viewed to be performative, drawing backlash without making a stand or connecting with either community. The company didn't win favour from either camp. It was viewed as a vacuous attempt to win consumer appeal without making a stand.

Black Lives Matter

Following the murder of George Floyd in 2020, companies made bold statements about allocating funds to tackle racial inequality. According to a McKinsey report, more than 1,100 organizations committed a total of $340 billion to racial justice initiatives.[7] There were two sides to the funding pledges. The first was to invest in making their internal practices more inclusive. This included commitments to increase diversity within the organization and supplier diversity. The second was to spend resources to address structural inequalities within society. This was during a time of heightened awareness about racism, structural inequality and corporate responsibility. Early evidence indicates that certain companies have made progress and built internal capabilities to talk about these topics in ways that have never happened before. But, at the same time, companies are finding it challenging to follow through with the pledges that they made during a time of racial reckoning where they needed to appear progressive. A LinkedIn study found that Chief Diversity Officer positions grew by 168.9 per cent from 2019 to 2022. But, soon enough, the honeymoon period was over with declining levels of investment and advocacy. An estimated one in three diversity, equity and inclusion (DEI) professionals lost their jobs in 2023.[8] Following the economic slowdown, many companies have backtracked on their commitments to racial justice, further highlighting the difference between organizations that were serious about tackling racial inequality and others that simply wanted to follow the trend.

The change in tone is perhaps most evident with tech giants, who made some of the biggest pledges. Google, Meta and others slashed their DEI programmes. This includes investments in employee resource groups (ERGs) and overall budgets[9] as they rowed back on the promises that they had made employers and wider society. The message this sends to diverse talent, communities and investors is that racial justice is only a priority during economic upturns or when there's heightened public pressure. The story also demonstrates the dangers of making bold public commitments without having the appetite to follow through on them. More companies will be scrutinized as time passes and people will compare commitments with actions.

If you are championing a more inclusive world, choosing to invest in more equitable business practices isn't a 'nice to have'. It is an integral part of the business, especially in organizations where diversity of experiences and backgrounds is critical in creating more inclusive products and services.

Community participation

The best way to increase your probability of making a positive impact, while at the same time avoiding, or at least mitigating, backlash is by collaborating with communities. Many examples of public backlash – less so institutional backlash from activist investors – stem from organizations making decisions on behalf of communities without including members of the community in the process. The problem has origins in top-down company cultures that prevent the involvement or inclusion of diverse voices. Using more collaborative ways of working enables companies to include the voices of citizens, communities and people with lived experience in the design stage before plans are finalized. Simply talking with the intended audience – and in certain scenarios also including rejectors – is the best possible way to mitigate risks. The simplicity of the solution makes it less attractive to global organizations. Because the process doesn't feel high-tech, companies are more reluctant to champion participatory business models.

Organizations are willing to spend millions on the latest tech stack, product innovation and marketing campaigns. But, somehow, they are unwilling to engage with community members to make the solution resonate. What often prevents us from truly collaborating with communities is the ego. As professionals with decades of experience, there is an unwritten expectation that we should have all the answers. Community participation takes a slightly different approach to the challenge. It assumes that we don't know everything, but by working in partnership with experts in different fields we can arrive at a better outcome, forgoing the hero complex of needing to solve everything individually and instead tapping into a collective intelligence.

Perhaps the most spectacular example of community non-participation is Pepsi's famous Kendall Jenner advert. The story has been shared millions of times since the fiasco, but understanding how the campaign was created is critical to preventing, mitigating and managing backlash. When it comes to backlash, we can learn more from what not to do than we can from getting things right. Following the economic recession of 2007–09, companies decided to refocus their budgets and create in-house agencies. This is when a company invests in internal resources to market its products and services rather than hiring an external marketing agency. The concept has been around since the 19th century, but the trend has radically accelerated. More global companies are adopting this way of working to save on external costs, increase transparency and gain ownership of projects including first-party data, and intellectual property. According to a survey conducted by WFA and The Observatory International, 66 per cent of brands now have in-house agencies.[10]

The Kendall Jenner Pepsi advert is a cautionary tale of what could go wrong as a company becomes more insular. Not gaining outside-in perspectives from agencies, consumers and communities could come at the cost of the brand's reputation. The advert was produced in-house. It highlights the dangers of groupthink, monotony and lack of involvement from different stakeholders. The campaign positioned Pepsi as the solution to racism. The brand was trying to project a global message of unity, peace and understanding. But it completely missed the mark. A simple conversation with people not working at Pepsi would have exposed how preposterous the advert's narrative was. It can be easy to get stuck in our bubble of familiarity. Collaborating with communities injects a much-needed dose of honesty and accountability which would stamp out any inauthenticity before it gets picked up in mainstream culture.

Communication and honesty

No matter how hard you attempt to get things right there are bound to be moments when you get things wrong. We are all human, nobody is perfect. How you respond to backlash is arguably more important than the event itself. The first step is a simple one: acknowledging the issue and apologising. Showing humility and remorse is an underrated action when de-escalating the situation. Acknowledgement only works when individuals, companies and governments are sincere. Using the setback as an opportunity to learn from your mistakes, engage with the communities affected and set up processes to do better in the future. There's a long history of organizations opting for the opposite approach – being defensive about what's happened, deflecting responsibility or releasing a corporate statement lacking in substance or humanity. The speed of response is equally important – don't wait for the criticism to pile up before you act. You might think that things will probably cool down, but that's beyond your circle of influence. Showing your concern speedily limits the damage caused. It can also prevent the build-up of rumours and speculation – allowing you to demonstrate leadership – and showcase that you care. Many organizations end up ghosting, which only makes matters worse.

Experiencing problems can lead to new business and social opportunities. Depending on the scale of the nature and backlash, you have an opportunity to take full responsibility and work with communities to develop solutions that would prevent the problem from happening in the future. This is the main difference between apologising because of the harm it can cause your reputation, and truly being sorry about the situation. It is important to make sure your message is consistent and regular. Lastly, create space to listen to citizen, consumer and community concerns. Make sure you have a forum to listen to their experiences, gather insights and address the feedback. Learning from the experience is the best way to value communities and turn purpose into business and social impact.

KFC chicken shortage

In 2018 KFC in the UK ran out of chicken because its delivery partner DHL encountered problems with its warehouses. For a quick-service restaurant that exclusively serves chicken, things can't get much worse than running out of chicken. More than 75 per cent of stores had to close nationwide due to the chicken shortage.[11] The crisis was front-page news in most UK media outlets. Only 266 of the 870 restaurants in the UK and Ireland were open and the company was in a pickle. Disruptions are a common occurrence in supply chains, but usually they are less noticeable. Your favourite restaurant might run out of ketchup or ice cream. But the problem was at a much larger scale. KFC aficionados were calling the police complaining about the limited menu and a movement was building in south-west England to nationalize KFC to prevent future shortages. Hashtags like #ChickenCrisis and #KFCCrisis were trending on social media.

It was clear that the management had to do something about the situation before frustration turned into backlash. Rather than downplaying or hiding the problem – it was difficult to sweep the news under the rug – KFC was transparent about the supply chain problem and communicated openly. The company offered a public apology explaining why it was experiencing chicken shortages. But that wasn't all. KFC harnessed the power of creativity and humour to turn things around and win the affection of the UK public. Instead of blaming its delivery partner DHL or launching a corporate statement that no one would read, KFC launched a print advert with three letters 'FCK' with an empty bucket with a message under: 'We're sorry.' The copy read: 'A chicken shop without any chicken. It's not ideal.' Somehow by admitting its mistake, KFC managed to make itself more likable in the hearts and minds of the British public. In social psychology, this is known as the pratfall effect: when people or companies who are highly competent become more likeable when they make a mistake.

Notice how the KFC crisis management playbook was the opposite of Volkswagen's handling of diesel emissions. Of course, the crisis is not of the same magnitude, but KFC used every opportunity to learn from the mistake and communicate with the public, whereas Volkswagen refused every opportunity to admit its mistakes, escalate to the appropriate authorities and take immediate action.

ACTIVITY

1 The basics

When thinking about how to manage backlash, the best place to start is with the factors in our control. The journey towards social change starts with making sure that your mission is not causing harm.

o   Are we covering the basics before communicating externally?

This begins with paying your taxes for making a profit, paying employees and suppliers fairly and creating a responsible product or service.

2 Education and capacity building

Education equips people with new tools, knowledge and skills to navigate change. People will no longer view change as a threat to their existing interests but as an opportunity to expand their capabilities.

o   How can we promote education and capacity building?

People will no longer be reliant on you to deliver business and social impact. The mission becomes scalable, and you will learn more by imparting your learning, failures and experiences to others.

3 Progress not perfection

The pursuit of perfection can be counterproductive. Perfection might raise standards, but it can prevent us from getting started and making progress.

o   How can we encourage people to get started?

The fear of being criticized prevents business leaders from engaging in the process of creating social change. Nevertheless, the call for perfection shouldn't become a barrier towards making strides in the right direction.

4 Community participation

The best way to increase your probability of making a positive impact while at the same time avoiding, or at least mitigating, backlash is by collaborating with communities. The problem has origins in top-down company cultures that prevent the involvement or inclusion of diverse voices.

Using more collaborative ways of working, enables companies to include the voices of citizens, communities and people with lived experience in the design stage before plans are finalized, therefore avoiding consumer backlash like the Kendall Jenner Pepsi fiasco.

5 Honest communication

No matter how hard you attempt to get things right there are bound to be moments when you get things wrong. We are all human, nobody is perfect. How you respond to backlash is arguably more important than the event itself.

o How can we create a culture of honest and transparent communication in ways that help us learn from the experience?

Communication doesn't have to be overly boring or corporate. Remember how KFC managed to turn around a supply chain crisis by quickly apologising and showing humility and remorse, which de-escalated the situation, before using creative communication to strengthen its relationship with KFC fans.

Notes

1 D Packer and J van Bavel. The big idea: Are we really so polarised? *The Guardian*, 15 November 2021. www.theguardian.com/books/2021/nov/15/the-big-idea-are-we-really-so-polarised (archived at https://perma.cc/ED3C-X3YC)

2 M Gardner and S Wamhoff. 55 corporations paid $0 in federal taxes on 2020 profits, ITEP, 2 April 2021. itep.org/55-profitable-corporations-zero-corporate-tax (archived at https://perma.cc/85VW-6LBX)

3 World Health Organization. Disability, 7 March 2023. www.who.int/news-room/fact-sheets/detail/disability-and-health (archived at https://perma.cc/54TX-MMP9)

4 United Nations, Department of Economic and Social Affairs. Disability and employment, nd. www.un.org/development/desa/disabilities/resources/factsheet-on-persons-with-disabilities/disability-and-employment.html (archived at https://perma.cc/6VA3-2UX2)

5 Microsoft. Accessibility resources, nd. www.microsoft.com/en-gb/accessibility/resources (archived at https://perma.cc/L2UB-E7XK)

6 J Holman. Target's sales hit by Pride Month merchandise backlash, *New York Times*, 16 August 2023. www.nytimes.com/2023/08/16/business/target-sales-pride-backlash.html (archived at https://perma.cc/B7MN-PXNH)

7 McKinsey. Corporate commitments to racial justice: An update, 2023. www.mckinsey.com/bem/our-insights/corporate-commitments-to-racial-justice-an-update (archived at https://perma.cc/5URN-LTRK)

8 K Alfonseca and M Zahn. How corporate America is slashing DEI workers amid backlash to diversity programs, ABC News, 7 July 2023. abcnews. go.com/US/corporate-america-slashing-dei-workers-amid-backlash-diversity/ story?id=100477952 (archived at https://perma.cc/5FRU-E4D5)

9 J Elias. Tech companies like Google and Meta made cuts to DEI programs in 2023 after big promises in prior years, CNBC, 22 December 2023. www.cnbc. com/2023/12/22/google-meta-other-tech-giants-cut-dei-programs-in-2023.html (archived at https://perma.cc/JD36-ELM3)

10 World Federation of Advertisers. In-housing set for rapid and continued growth at major multinationals, World Federation of Advertisers, 20 December 2023. wfanet.org/knowledge/item/2023/12/20/In-housing-set-for-rapid-and-continued-growth-at-major-multinationals (archived at https://perma.cc/L4QD-9U5R)

11 R Priday. The inside story of the great KFC chicken shortage of 2018, *Wired*, 21 February 2018. www.wired.com/story/kfc-chicken-crisis-shortage-supply-chain-logistics-experts (archived at https://perma.cc/QZ8Z-CVL5)

A SOCIAL CHANGE PLAYBOOK

To paraphrase Aristotle: the purpose of this book is action, not knowledge. The book should equip you with questions, stories, tools and resources to create social change. This section is a playbook for social change. A summary of learnings from the book and questions which you can explore on your personal and collective journey.

If you played or watched sports, you're probably familiar with the concept of a playbook. Every player gets one – it's basically a manual on how to play the game. But, ultimately, it's the players who go on the field and play the game. The same is true with this book. You are the one who is best placed to take action and create change.

There is no right or wrong way to explore this playbook. The sequence of chapters provides step-by-step guidance on how to create social change. But you can jump between sections based on your interests, needs and progress.

TOP TIP

The playbook is a live resource, you can update it regularly, as you test and learn. Please make sure you feed the playbook so that it becomes a trusted compass and not just another forgotten artefact.

Chapter 1: Can I really create change?

Summary

When I mention social change, you probably think of Mahatma Gandhi, Nelson Mandela or Greta Thunberg. But all of us have the power to create change – in big and small ways. Whether you're a global brand, scrappy start up or independent freelancer, this book will give you the tools to accelerate social change. The primary ingredient for creating change is imagination. If we can't imagine a more desirable future, we certainly won't be able to create it. Imagination is the foundation of creation.

Creating social change feels like a Herculean challenge. You're probably thinking: I'm only one person, what can I do? I have good news for you – there are another eight billion people who are thinking the exact same thing. This book is about starting small and encouraging collective action. Change doesn't have to be stressful or scary, it can even be fun. It can be as simple as smiling at a stranger, leaving a positive review for a small business and letting your friends know how much you appreciate them. Small acts of kindness can create a virtuous ripple effect.

The work of Professor Erica Chenoweth reaffirms the power of a small number of committed people. After studying 323 violent and non-violent protests that occurred between 1900 and 2006 worldwide, Chenoweth posited the 3.5 per cent rule. It takes 3.5 per cent of the population to actively participate in protests to create political change. What seems improbable can become unstoppable.

Activity

1 **Select one thing that you can change**
   This should be something within your circle of influence. Here are some examples to spark your imagination:

   o Buy from an independent business.

   o Join an interest group.

   o Smile at strangers.

2 **Do one thing differently from how you've always done it**
   The purpose of this exercise is to form new neural pathways. Here are some examples to spark your imagination:

o   Brush your teeth with your non-dominant hand.

o   Take a different route to work.

o   Read a book outside your comfort zone.

3   **Launch a social change experiment**

We know what the status quo looks like, but change requires experimentation and new ways of working. There's no such thing as failure, only lessons. Here are some examples to spark your imagination:

o   A/B test between your default action (A) and something radically different (B).

o   Kickstart a new project or crowdsource new ideas.

o   Allocate 10 per cent of your time/budget to an experimental project with no expectations.

o   Explore a new consumer segment or untested hypothesis.

The intention is to uncover an MVC: the smallest possible action that creates social change. This process is designed to overcome the greatest internal barriers to social action: not getting started and overcomplicating things.

Chapter 2: Challenge the status quo

Summary

The status quo is a comfortable place with embedded systems and structures. It can take considerable energy to uproot the existing way of seeing and doing things. Facilitating change can feel like an overwhelming undertaking. When there is so much to do where do you even start? How can you challenge the dominant narrative? How can you show people that the status quo is outdated, unjust and defunct?

On 11 April 1992 three young men in jumpsuits performed at a music competition. The leader of the band was Seo Taiji, who was previously in a heavy metal band before starting a new band called Seo Taiji and Boys, combining Korean lyrics with African American hip-hop, Europop and R&B. This was a completely new sound, blurring genres and, with it, shattering the status quo within Korean music. The group received heavy criticism from the judges and the country's music establishment. Even though the group didn't win the competition, the next day young people couldn't stop talking about the performance. Seo Taiji and Boys challenged the existing paradigm and introduced K-pop to the world.

Actions can also cause unintended negative consequences. When Chairman Mao, the founding father of the People's Republic of China, decided to kill hundreds of millions of sparrows, he didn't expect it would lead to the greatest starvation in history with as many as 45 million people dying. It turns out that locust populations ballooned without sparrows to predate them, destroying all the crops. Networks like nature are far more dynamic than individual behaviour. We can't afford to ignore complexity and connectivity when enacting social change. Our world is interconnected.

Social change can come from a vision for a better future. In 1976 Anita Roddick started a little green shop in Brighton called The Body Shop. The products were never tested on animals. It might sound normal today but in the 1970s this broke all the standard protocols of the beauty industry. Not testing on animals wasn't enough – Anita wanted to change the industry. In 1989 The Body Shop started campaigning to end animal testing in cosmetics. An unusual move at a time when most companies were only preoccupied with economic activity. The company continued its advocacy work in collaboration with animal rights group Cruelty-Free International. In 1996 The Body Shop delivered a petition signed by four million people to the

European Commission and in 1998 Britain introduced a ban on animal test-ing on cosmetic products and ingredients. Animal testing was the status quo and Anita made it her mission to challenge the cruel practices of the cosmet-ics industry. Today, 44 countries have banned cosmetic animal testing. This all started with a single demand.

Activity

1 **What is the status quo you are trying to change?**
   o What's the problem with the status quo?
   o What are you looking to change? Why?
   o What are you hoping to achieve?
   o What are the barriers to change?

2 **Map out the key players and the power relations between them**
   o Who are the key players?
   o Who are the main individuals?
   o Who are the main groups?
   o What are the main institutions?
   o Who else is involved?

   Write down all the agents you can think of. It's important not to discount any groups at this point, even if you think they are oppositional or lack influence. The process works best when you map out the entire process and allow room for unknown unknowns. Remember the disproportionate impact of Black Swans? We can't afford to discount any players at this stage of the process. Once you've listed all the individuals, groups and institutions, it's time to visualize the map.

3 **Identify relationships**
   o Identify the connections between all actors.
   o Map out the flow of interaction in a visual way.
   o Analyse the power relationships, including positive and negative.

4 **What's the one action you can take today?**
   What's the first action you can take within your circle of influence? Think of no more than one action that would influence decision-makers and involve more players in the process.

5 Action plan

You should now have an action plan with the following ingredients:

o   A clear definition of the status quo.

o   A map of key players and relational power-lines.

o   First-mover action for social change.

Your action plan doesn't need to be perfect. We are talking about a work-in-progress outline which you can refine through action, feedback and exploring the upcoming chapters. The main purpose is to articulate your thoughts and ideas into words that can eventually be shared with others.

Chapter 3: Craft your mission

Summary

A mission is something we might associate with Jesuits evangelizing about religion, James Bond defeating evil villains or the USS Enterprise exploring new worlds in *Star Trek*. But we don't have to discover a new planet to be on a mission. Missions can offer individuals and companies direction, inspiration and meaning.

Ingvar Kamprad grew up in poverty on a small farm in rural Sweden. In the mid-20th century, furniture was an expensive commodity, the pursuit of a privileged few. Ingvar started IKEA on his family farm and started selling affordable furniture in the 1940s. During IKEA's international expansion in the 1970s, Ingvar Kamprad published his vision and ideology in *The Testament of a Furniture Dealer*. The manifesto begins with a clear mission statement: 'To create a better everyday life for the many people'. Kamprad embodied the IKEA mission. He lived a frugal existence, re-using his teabags, driving an old Volvo car and opting to fly economy class despite being worth $58.7 billion. This isn't an endorsement, but simply an example of living and breathing the company's mission. IKEA has become the largest furniture retailer in the world.

In the 1960s Swedish scientists discovered that most people suffer from lactose intolerance. A student at the University of Lund, Rickard Öste, was fascinated by this topic and started to experiment with removing lactose from milk. After testing barley and rye, Öste invented oat milk. Oat milk was mainly for people with allergies and lactose intolerance. Initially, the company supplied oat milk to bigger food companies but there wasn't enough interest or demand. In the 2000s it created its own brand called Oatly. Until 2012, Oatly was a small Swedish brand with 50 employees operating in a highly technical, uninteresting and niche category. But then, the board hired a young CEO who prioritized defining and articulating the company mission. Oatly positioned itself as an activist brand on a mission to challenge big dairy. If you want to turn your mission into a movement you need a common enemy to rally against. For Oatly this was the Swedish dairy lobby and big food companies. The simplicity of the Oatly mission has produced an entirely new category and made plant-based milk mainstream.

The Fridays for Future movement started in the summer of 2018 when a 15-year-old Greta Thunberg decided to skip school and protest outside the

Swedish Riksdag (parliament) holding a placard reading *Skolstrejk för klimatet* [School strike for climate]. In the beginning, Greta was a solo protester holding a cardboard sign outside the giant stones of the Swedish parliament. Eventually, she was joined by friends, family and fellow school strikers. People started to notice and started talking to her and showing support. Media outlets started to interview her to understand why she was doing this. Greta was able to share her mission around the world. Momentum gathered, and soon enough 20 young people were protesting, and then 100. After the Swedish elections, Greta and her fellow students went back to school. However, they continued to miss class on Fridays to protest. The Fridays for Future movement has mobilized more than 3.8 million people globally across 3,800 cities.

Activity

1 **What's your vision for the future?**
   o IKEA wanted to make furniture more accessible.
   o Oatly had a vision for a more sustainable milk alternative.
   o Fridays For Future demanded better climate leadership.

2 **Who are you fighting against?**
   o IKEA is against expensive furniture.
   o Oatly challenged the dairy industry.
   o Fridays For Futures is fighting against climate change.

3 **What is your unique gift to the world**
   o IKEA championed democratic design for the many, not the few.
   o Oatly is more human (less corporate) than other food companies.
   o Fridays for Future is about youth participation and global solidarity.

Combining your vision for the future with who you are fighting against and your secret sauce will generate your mission statement, a monumental step in turning your purpose into business and social impact.

Chapter 4: Find your community

Summary

Humans are inherently social beings. We are wired to connect with other people; natural selection prefers humans with a stronger propensity to look after family members and collaborate in groups. From an evolutionary perspective, we have relied on cooperation to survive and thrive. There's safety in numbers, whether you are a human, a herring or a hyena. The human brain is designed to form and maintain relationships with others. Many of our conscious and subconscious decisions are driven by the primary need to belong. We have designed human civilization around the need to belong. In most cultures, the family is the main unit where early socialization happens. Afterwards, schools encourage children to make friends and learn in groups. Many of us end up working for a company, which is an association of people working towards a shared mission. Along the journey, we might find a partner, marry and form our own family. The desire to belong is universal across all human cultures. It is a fundamental human motivation which can explain much of our actions and hidden preferences.

Finding your community is critical to social change. Visionary leaders can see beyond the status quo, but such ideas can only be actualized through collective effort. How do ideas spread? The diffusion of innovation theory attempts to answer this question. The theory was first invented by E M Rogers after observing how farmers in rural communities were adopting hybrid corn seeds, new tools and farming techniques. At first glance, the model seems irrelevant. But the theory helps to explain how innovation goes from niche interest to mass appeal. Every norm, idea and technology we take for granted today started life on the periphery, not the mainstream.

The diffusion of innovation theory has five main stages of adoption. The first group are the innovators, who love taking risks and experimenting. Innovators are not afraid of getting things wrong. While only 2.5 per cent of the population, they have a disproportionate impact on the emergence and collapse of new ideas since they are the first group to experience them. The second group are the early adopters, who are opinion leaders and trendsetters. They feel comfortable with change and adopting new ideas but need to understand how to get started. Early adopters are 13.5 per cent of the population. Then we have the early majority (34 per cent), late majority (34 per cent) and the laggards (16 per cent). New ideas follow a similar pattern of adoption. It would be a waste of time if you allocated the same level of resources to communicating your mission with all groups concurrently. Begin with innovators and early adopters. These groups are more receptive to new ideas, even if the mission is still a work in progress and you haven't figured everything out yet.

Your mission needs 100 true champions to build a movement. A major barrier to social change is the belief that actions need to be enormous in scale, global in reach and leave an everlasting legacy. The size of the challenge is the first and often most intimidating obstacle that prevents people from getting started in the first place. Alternatively, if we start with the premise that our message is not meant for everyone – and that's okay – we can then begin to focus efforts on the people most passionate about the mission. Change happens when a small group of committed people believe they can upend the status quo. You don't need a million people to build a movement. All you need is 100 champions who are equally passionate about the challenge and share the same vision for a better future. If you were to add one champion every day starting today it would take just over three months to have a powerful movement of 100 champions aligned towards a common goal.

Activity

1 **Early adopters**

 o Who are your early adopters?

 o Who is most open to your ideas and mission? Why?
 Beginning with people who share your worldview creates early momentum before reaching more mainstream audiences.

2 **Road to 100**

 o How can you connect with 100 true champions?

 o What are the key activities that will help you connect with 100 true champions?

 o Where can you connect with people who are equally passionate about the challenge and share the same vision for a better future?

Remember this is about creating a relatively small number of deep connections, not meaningless scale. If you connect with one champion every day, within three months you will have a powerful movement of 100 champions aligned towards a common goal.

3 Emotional connection

What is the emotional benefit of joining your mission? The most powerful way to create social change is by building an emotional connection, not delivering cold, hard facts.

o Apple make people feel more creative.

o De Beers connected diamonds with love and commitment.

o Coca-Cola has associated itself with happiness.

We tend to think of ourselves as logical creatures. But humans are not as logical as we might imagine. We are primarily driven by emotion, not reason. We use logic to justify and make sense of our decisions. It is estimated that 95 per cent of human decisions are made unconsciously by the emotional brain system. Brands and marketing agencies have long realized that stories are a more powerful way to build an emotional connection than cold, hard facts. To paraphrase Maya Angelou, people will forget what you said to them, but they won't forget how you made them feel. It is emotions, not statistics, that build social movements.

Chapter 5: Rise to the challenge

Summary

Nothing in life works according to plan. Your mission needs to interact with the randomness of the outside world. Ask any military general, business owner or wedding planner. No plan survives first contact with the enemy. Nonetheless, the planning process gives you the best possible chance to prepare and respond. We can't address challenges if we are unaware of their existence. In business, transformation projects fail because leadership is unable to bring the rest of the organization on the journey. In society, movements fail when they are unable to build a critical mass. The inability to build a coalition can be one of the biggest barriers to achieving business and social impact.

If you wait for everyone to get on board with the mission you will be waiting forever and things will never change. At some point, you will need to commit and go for it. You'll need to set a direction of travel and see who joins your ship for the journey. There's no point waiting for permission. People are never going to agree on a particular course of action. Nothing meaningful has come from consensus decision-making. Loss aversion, status quo bias and vested interests are too-powerful forces. Early on, you are looking for commitment, not consensus. Who is really with you? And who can be persuaded? Making everyone happy creates a culture of mediocrity. Leaders should proceed with a single vision for the future. Not everyone will agree with the vision. You should listen to others, understand their concerns and see things through their lens. The problem is if you build in everyone's feedback at this early stage – before you've acted and received real-world feedback – it will dilute the original vision. Everyone might be mildly satisfied, but no one will be excited about your mission.

In the 1950s, Britain was experiencing a fuel shortage because of the Suez Crisis. Petrol was scarce so the President of the British Motor Company briefed automotive designer Alec Issigonis to create a fuel-efficient vehicle. Issiggonis invented the world's first Mini. The magic of the Mini was its surprisingly spacious interior relative to the vehicle's size. It was one of the first cars to be front-wheel drive, which opened 80 per cent of the floor space for passengers. The team that designed the Mini was small, consisting of 10 people. Three engineers, Issigonis, two engineering students and four draftsmen. Proof that a small number of committed people can punch above their weight. The Mini was born from crisis, imagined by a visionary leader and brought into reality by a small but mighty team of experts and fresh minds.

In 2016, 49ers quarterback Colin Kaepernick refused to stand during the US national anthem. Kaepernick made the conscious decision to take the knee in protest against racial injustice and police brutality. Kaepernick's action sparked a movement within the NFL. At one point in 2017, more than 200 NFL players took the knee, sat or raised their fist during the anthem. It can be difficult to grasp, in retrospect, how controversial taking the knee was in 2016. Kaepernick was booed on the pitch. The 49ers planned to release him so he opted out of his contract and every single team in the NFL refused to give him a contract. The move would mean the end of his playing career. Despite the backlash, Nike decided to make Colin Kaepernick the hero of its 'Just do it' campaign titled 'Dream crazy'. Nike received heavy criticism from politicians, the media and consumers. News channels showed clips of people burning their Nike trainers. Shares in Nike dropped by 3.2 per cent by the next day, but Nike held their nerve. The gamble paid off in the long term – it increased Nike's share price by 5 per cent and earned Nike a cool $6 billion.

Activity

1 **Communicate the mission**
   Communicate a vision for the future that is more attractive than the current reality. You might personally feel that the need for change is clear, but not everyone is as close to the mission as you. Keep communicating the message through words and actions at every opportunity. Remember, people need to hear your message at least seven times before they take action.

   Your mission needs to answer the following questions:

   o Why is change needed?

   o How will the change be better for people?

   o How will the change be better for business?

   o How will the change be better for society?

2 **Active listening**
   Once you've got your point across, now is the time to hold space and listen to people's thoughts, ideas and resistance. Change can be scary for people for numerous reasons. The first step in turning sceptics into

believers is to understand their concerns. Unless you know why people are resisting change, there's nothing you can do to support them or change your approach. Remove your ego, put yourself in the audience's shoes and ask open, clarifying and non-judgemental questions. Becoming defensive will put people's barriers up and prevent dialogue. Active listening improves our chances of meeting people's personal, professional and social needs. Sometimes, it will require flexibility to adapt our initial approach based on feedback. You need to identify the reason for resistance and create a plan to overcome the challenge.

Holding space and active listening will help you understand where people are at on the social change journey. You can use the following questions to spark conversations:

o How do you feel about the change?

o What are you concerned about?

o How can I support you on the journey?

3 **Bring people on the journey**
Change can be exciting for some, but overwhelming for others. Your mission should invite and involve people, not tell them what they should do. Human beings value autonomy and making personal decisions. Studies show we feel less inclined to change our behaviour if we don't feel like we have a choice over the decision. Once you've understood people's worries and incentives, you need to bring them on the journey. This is not the same as death by committee. By now, you should have created a vision for a better future and assigned roles and responsibilities. However, there should be enough room in the process to include ideas, thoughts and involvement from new people. The mission should be 80 per cent complete but leave enough room for people to create their own stories and actions. No one wants to be dictated to. Why not involve your audience in key milestones in the process? And I'm not talking about fake participation, where people pretend they are open to new ideas but steamroll in with their existing plans. In contrast, develop genuine forums for people to share ideas, feedback and stories. Change is not only about the 'why' and 'what' but also the 'how'. The best change initiatives make people feel like they are creating the change, rather than the change is happening to them. Projects don't fail because of technical reasons but because we fail to factor in social interaction and adoption.

Here are some ways you can get people involved and invested in the mission:

o   Ask for people's ideas and thoughts.

o   Share early ideas and get feedback (sharing is better than presenting).

o   Create a mechanism to crowdsource ideas and share progress on collective goals.

4   **Start small**

Most change agents are remarkably ambitious. They always overestimate the amount of time and effort required to achieve collective goals. That's not a bad thing. We just need to combine big thinking with small bitesize actions to build trust, engagement and buy-in from people and groups. We should help people build confidence and new stories. People will be unsure about their place when things change. How will the change impact my life? Do I have the skills? Where do I stand? Starting small builds confidence, capacity and social proof. If my goal is to go to the gym, lifting 10kg weights gives me the confidence that I might be able to lift 15kg weights and eventually 20kg. Conversely, beginning with 100kg weights, failing to lift them while everyone stares at me at the gym may discourage me from going to the gym again.

Here are some questions that might make it easier for people to get started:

o   What's the smallest change people can get started with today?

o   How can we help people build confidence and proof around this new story?

o   How can we break down long-term ambitions into smaller actionable goals? For example, turning five-year plans into a 12-week cycle.

5   **Keep going**

When you look at business transformation or social change, it seems to happen suddenly. Most change initiatives gain traction over time. They can feel small, slow and insignificant. Small ripples can turn into enormous tsunamis. The trick is to keep believing, listening and adapting your approach based on real-world feedback. How do you maintain interest after the honeymoon period? This is the true task of the leader. It takes patience, urgency and consistency.

Here are some questions to explore as you begin to engage with different people and groups:

o   How can we maintain momentum after the launch?

o How can we improve our approach using the feedback we've received?

o How can we celebrate small wins?

6 **Make a stand**

There comes a point where you need to draw a line in the sand. It's important to understand people's resistance to change. It's equally important to actively listen and bring people on the journey with us. The truth is, however, there will be people who will never join our mission. And that's okay. We must be comfortable with this reality. There comes a point where we must make a stand for what we believe and what we are fighting against. We have to show through actions and not words what we stand for.

There are many examples of brands standing for something. These brands are more memorable, famous and engaging. Even those who don't like the brand have feelings towards them. The same cannot be said about 98 per cent of brands in the market that are dull, boring and unremarkable.

Your mission should be the ultimate decision-making framework. It should make it easier to answer the following questions:

o What are our non-negotiables?

o How should we respond to this situation?

o How should we communicate our mission with the world?

Chapter 6: Lead a revolution

Summary

Movements face a perennial dilemma. How to best respond to defunct economic, social and political systems? Should we reform them or spark a revolution? These kinds of questions emerge when existing institutions and systems fail to serve us. We seldom ponder reform or revolution if things are working smoothly. If your marriage is going well, you are less likely to think about marriage counselling (reform) or divorce (revolution). If you're happy with your car, you are unlikely to take it to the mechanic (reform) or consider buying a new car (revolution). And if you are thriving at work, you are less likely to change roles (reform) or switch industries (revolution). The desire for change stems from the dissatisfaction with the old way of doing things.

The general belief is that revolution and reform are in direct conflict. Reforms seek to improve the existing system, whereas revolutions seek to uproot it. The truth is that reform and revolutions work in tandem to create change. If you are a revolutionary, you are a reformist and if you are a reformist, you are a revolutionary. Change happens when we press existing systems as far as possible with the tools and resources at our disposal. Radical change can emerge from small reforms. When Mikhail Gorbachev became the new leader of the USSR he set his sights on improving the system. The intention wasn't to overthrow the system but simply make sure it worked better. Gorbachev implemented two main reforms to modernize the Soviet Union. The first was known as *Perestroika* (Restructuring), which enabled private enterprise, and the second was known as *Glasnost* (openness) to encourage transparency. What seemed like gradual reforms culminated in the collapse of the world's second-biggest superpower.

Occupy Wall Street looked destined to change America. The movement was born from dissatisfaction with economic inequality and corporate greed. The early 2010s was a time of renewed collective awakening. We were witnessing the Arab Spring, in North Africa and the Middle East, mass student protests against the government in the UK and anti-austerity protests throughout Europe. The Occupy Wall Street movement was the continuation of the dissatisfaction with the status quo on US soil, in the world's biggest economy and the epitome of 'free market' capitalism. It was so successful that the movement spread worldwide. People from all around the world shared the same frustration against a ruling elite. Occupy Wall Street spread across 900 cities in 82 countries. What happened to the Occupy Wall Street movement? Occupy Wall Street was incredibly effective at bringing people together to fight against the status quo. The Occupy movement, however, lacked leadership. There was no set of established demands or goals. There was no defined strategy. The movement created an important narrative, but it wasn't able to embed this energy into concrete actions. Occupy Wall Street knew what it was against, but it failed to outline an alternative.

For much of the 20th century, business has existed to maximize shareholder value. This is known as shareholder primacy – the belief that companies should primarily, or only, focus on maximizing profits for shareholders. Shareholder capitalism fails to account for the negative externalities caused by the business. In economics, a negative externality occurs when the production or consumption of a product doesn't include the true costs. Most companies aren't incentivized to carry out activities that don't increase shareholder profits. Perhaps the greatest example of a negative externality is climate change. Damage from the global climate crisis is costing the planet $391 million per day. That's $16 million per hour. And still, in 2022–23 fossil fuel companies logged record profits for shareholders. A prime example of how the true costs of products and services are not built into our current economic system.

In 2022, the founder of outdoor apparel company Patagonia, Yvon Chouinard, announced a new ownership model. He was giving the company (valued at $3 billion) away to the planet. Unlike other successful companies, Patagonia wasn't going public, being acquired by another conglomerate or being sold to a private equity firm. All profits from the company, at the time of the new governance model ($100 million per year), would go towards combatting climate change. In many ways, Patagonia has flipped shareholder capitalism on its head. The company is using profits from product sales to pay dividends to its only shareholder, planet Earth. Critics have argued that Patagonia is still operating within the paradigm of consumerism. But there's no doubt that the move sets a precedent when it comes to reimagining the role of business.

Activity

1 **Reform and revolution**

   o What's a small reform you can instigate today that might lead to a bigger change in the future?

Something that builds confidence and belief around the new story. Remember the Soviet Union collapsed following a series of reforms, not a revolution.

2 Establish your demand

- o What are your demands?
- o What are you hoping to achieve from the change?
- o How will you get there? What are the current barriers to change?

Remember the Occupy Wall Street movement and the dangers of not having a coherent vision and strategy.

3 Build a governance model

- o What is your governance structure?
- o Who is leading what?
- o How are decisions made?

Without a governance structure, your movement is less likely to be aligned and working towards a shared mission. A robust governance model would also improve decision-making, mitigate internal and external risks and increase accountability and trust in the movement. Governance is the boring but important part of activism.

4 What's your metric?
In the old world, companies existed to maximize profits for shareholders. This was the only lens through which leadership viewed progress, irrespective of the negative externalities.

- o How will you be measuring progress?
- o How will this be different to shareholder primacy?
- o What are your annual and quarterly metrics? Do they include people and planet?

5 Proposition
If you are a business, the product or service you are producing is the most direct, tangible and conclusive reflection of what the company stands for.

- o How can we make sure the product/service is more beneficial?
- o What could be improved? How?
- o How can we reduce the harmful impacts of the product?

Without designing a product or service that enriches business and society, everything else becomes irrelevant.

Chapter 7: Start collaborating

Summary

Competition can be good for business and society. There are many benefits to healthy competition. According to classical economics, perfect competition between many sellers produces better products, lower prices and more innovative solutions for consumers. The idea is competition for buyers means no party can risk having higher prices, a substandard product or poorer customer service. For example, if you had the choice to pick from three identical internet providers. Company A is $30 per month. Company B is $50 a month. Company C is $100 per month. Most buyers would opt for Company A and eventually, Company C will go out of business unless it lowers its prices or differentiates from the other two companies. Perfect competition creates an equilibrium between the price and the demand for the product and service.

The problem is that economic models don't always reflect reality. Perfect competition is a figment of the human imagination; it doesn't exist in the real world. Can you think of an example of perfect competition? Perfect competition is an economic unreality. The business reality looks somewhat different. Companies are always engaged in a type of warfare – fighting to control a bigger chunk of the market. After years of collaboration, Rudolf and Adolf Dassler separated and started two shoe companies. Adidas and Puma were born from this brotherly rivalry. Adolf (Adi) Dassler started Adidas and Rudolf Dassler started Puma. The brothers sued each other numerous times over the years over design and trademark issues, costing each other a fortune in lawsuits. The two factories were built in the same Bavarian town of Herzogenaurach – situated on opposite sides of the Arach river – forcing people to choose a side. If you worked for one company, you wouldn't be found dead going to the other side of the river. The two brothers remained rivals until the very end. Before their deaths, both brothers demanded not to be buried next to each other. Both companies are still headquartered in Herzogenaurach, and still trying to steal market share from each other.

Before the Covid-19 global pandemic was announced in 2020, vaccines would take several years to develop. The quickest vaccine to be invented before this was the mumps vaccine, which took four years. But the coronavirus vaccine shattered this record, taking only nine months to develop. The reason is a mixture of urgency – people were dying around the globe – and radical international collaboration. Governments, companies, non-governmental organizations (NGOs) and communities began collaborating. Scientists used past research from SARS and MERS viruses to get started. The science community around the world shared information about the novel pathogen to help increase understanding of the virus and develop tools to test for the coronavirus. The approach was collaborative, using pre-print and open-access journals. This helped to build a collective scientific understanding, share knowledge and receive feedback in ways not seen in other outbreaks. A staggering 19,389 articles about Covid-19 were shared in the first four months of the pandemic.

Run-DMC was one of the hottest rap acts of the 1980s, but they still struggled to break through into mainstream audiences. It was impossible to break out beyond the group's existing young, urban and multi-ethnic audiences and reach the suburbs. The group weren't getting any play time on pop radio stations. Run-DMC's record producer and co-founder of Def Jam Rick Rubin had an idea how to bridge the gap between the two worlds. He asked Aerosmith if they would be up for collaborating with Run-DMC. The group said yes. The collaboration ended up being transformative for both parties. For Run-DMC, it helped them break into mainstream audiences. The crossover made rap music palatable and enjoyable for white, middle-class and rural listeners. The collaboration was arguably even more fruitful for Aerosmith, as it opened a new generation of fans.

Activity

The shift from competition to collaboration is an intentional move. It represents a transition away from a scarcity mindset towards practising an abundance mindset. There are enough opportunities and resources for everyone to thrive. We can go further to make a business and social impact if we can collaborate with others. Here are some questions which might spark an intentional approach to collaboration:

1 Who can you collaborate with to make an even bigger impact?
2 What are the strengths that you can bring to a strategic partnership?
3 What complementary skills are you looking for from partners?
4 What is the cost of collaborating? Eg time, resources, creative freedom, etc.
5 What is the cost of not collaborating?

6 What would be the best way to structure the partnership? Eg equity, informal, joint venture, etc.

7 How can we agree on the scope and parameters of the partnership? Establishing a shared mission, values and expectations is critical to building a long-term and impactful partnership.

Chapter 8: From silos to systems

Summary

The term 'systems thinking' can be misleading. When we think about systems, we usually think about a computer system or a business process. Systems thinking is not about thinking systematically, but it is based in the realization that everything is interconnected. Take a minute to think about your personal life. You are probably part of a family. Your family is a system with interrelated members. Simply understanding one member won't produce a complete picture of the entire family. Your family is probably part of a wider neighbourhood or community. Once again, simply focusing on a single family won't provide a comprehensive understanding of the whole community. Your community is likely to be part of a town or city and country. At each level, there are multiple webs of interdependence and layers of complexity. But the whole is greater than the sum of its parts. If we were to analyse the parts in isolation, we would miss out on the big picture. A comparison could be made to staring at a single piece of a jigsaw puzzle from 2,000 pieces and attempting to understand the whole picture.

We live in a complex and interconnected world where rock particles from the Sahara desert travel across a body of saltwater covering one-fifth of Earth's surface to deliver nutrients to a tropical rainforest. It is estimated that 50 per cent of the dust comes from a single spot known as the Bodélé Depression, a prehistoric lake which used to be filled with algae and other microorganisms. More than 7,000 years ago the lake dried out and receded, leaving tonnes of nutrient-rich dust behind. The Bodélé Depression is covered with crushed skeletons of diatoms which are a form of plankton. This sand is lighter than other sand found in the Sahara desert, making it easier to pick up and carry in the air for weeks. The location of the depression, within a large mountain-rimmed valley, makes it more exposed to surface wind. Thanks to the dust particles, the Amazon rainforest acts as the natural air conditioner of the world by releasing 20 trillion litres of water into the atmosphere daily.

Why don't we always think in systems? There is a perfectly reasonable explanation. The average person has 6,000 thoughts a day. Without the ability to place objects and events into categories, our brains would be overloaded with information. We are hardwired to sort information into boxes. This is a valuable faculty which helps us process large volumes of data in a relatively short amount of time. Categorization allows humans to understand objects, ideas and events by grouping them based on similar features. Like most other human cognitive abilities, categorization was born from the need to minimize the risks when living in social groups and enhance chances of survival. Early humans gained immense value from being able to differentiate tigers from harmless giant sloths, poisonous red-capped mushrooms from nutritious edible mushrooms, and whether the community next door was friendly, collaborative and peaceful or hostile, competitive and homicidal.

But categorical thinking creates silos within an organization. We begin to attribute group features to individuals. Categories can create a fixed worldview, which is unhelpful when the outside world changes. It means the company is unable to escape from existing patterns of thoughts and actions. Innovation requires the ability to find new patterns, break boundaries and create new connections. Future solutions don't fit neatly within existing categories. Cognitive entrenchment can prevent us from exploring new ideas and discoveries.

The traditional structures within most organizations produce a narrow worldview. Our understanding of business and social problems is fractured, fragmented and disjointed. Such structures can hinder the exchange of ideas and information across different parts of the organization. The same organizational departments and specialism created to maximize effectiveness become counterproductive once the world changes. They will no longer drive efficiency, but increase waste. Breaking down silos is a necessity when navigating a complex and interconnected world. Future business and social challenges won't fit neatly with our clearly defined roles, responsibilities and departments. We don't have finance problems, HR problems, marketing problems or supply chain problems. We have interconnected business problems. We don't have education problems, employment problems or healthcare problems. We have interconnected social problems.

Activity

What happens if we don't view business as a binary choice between competition and collaboration? What if we could all contribute to a collective mission? How can we combine our collective resources and intelligence? What if we let go of the hero complex and embraced a collective mindset? Unlike the business models of the Industrial Revolution, progress doesn't have to come at the expense of others. Individuals, groups and companies can work collaboratively to solve industry-wide problems. Spend some time exploring the following questions.

1 **Are we applying categorical thinking, which could prevent us from thinking in systems?**
   Categories can create a fixed worldview, which is unhelpful when the outside world changes. Remember how the platypus was suspected to be a hoax because it didn't fit into any of the existing categories. Categorical thinking might include your assumed audience, strategic approach and collaborators.

2 **What are the silos in our organization or movement that need breaking?**
   Silos are a natural outcome of a group of people collaborating, but they can harm communication, collaboration and exchange of ideas. Remember how centralized management and departmental silos further exacerbated the Volkswagen emissions scandal.

3 **How can we avoid the hero complex? Who could we collaborate with to make an even bigger business and social impact?**
   The hero complex creates an urge to brush away the existing system and become the hero of the story. Such a mentality can stifle new solutions, radical collaboration and collective progress. It overlooks the importance of shared missions and collective action.

4 **How can we champion open-source collaboration?**
   We can't change the world in silos. We should seek to create shared platforms, knowledge and resources to accelerate impact and reach more people. This requires taking a more collectivist approach to social change:

   o Crowdsourcing projects.

   o Producing useful toolkits for the wider ecosystem.

   o Signposting people to relevant resources.

   o Exchanging knowledge and resources with other players in the industry.

   Examples include Wikipedia's crowdsourcing model and Allbirds' open-sourcing technology for other footwear manufacturers to implement.

Chapter 9: The power of co-creation

Summary

The main purpose of social hierarchies – like ancient Egypt and modern companies – is to organize individuals, groups and resources in a way that achieves a certain set of goals. But who gets to set the goals and who will the organizational structures serve? When reviewing hierarchal structures, we shouldn't ignore the inherent power relations that dictate how society is structured. The higher up on the pyramid, the more likely you are to benefit from the arrangement.

The pyramid-shaped corporate structure is rooted in colonialism. Colonialism is as old as history itself. It was practised by the ancient Greeks, Romans, Egyptians and Phoenicians. Contemporary colonialism, however, peaked in Europe during the Industrial Revolution. Advancements in technology increased production capacity and the appetite for raw materials like cotton, rubber, metals, spices and labour. The invention of steamships and the expansion of railways made it easier to create trade routes and maintain control over colonies. The most brutal form of colonialism is settler colonialism, a system of oppression where colonizers invade and displace the existing population with settlers who claim the land and establish a permanent society.

Modern organizational structures are a legacy of colonialism. We might not always realize how colonialism shaped our current world. This is not only about events in history books but the foundations and formations of the 21st century. Between 1492 and 1914, Europeans conquered 84 per cent of the globe. For countries, cultures and communities that have been colonized, the impact is undeniable. People with European ancestry might find the term decolonization to be frightening. Decolonization is the process of identifying colonial systems, structures and hierarchies and actively working to challenge them. If we are unaware of the history and impact of colonialism, we are less likely to question how business and society are organized. We end up viewing the current social and economic hierarchies as the norm.

On the flip side, we are witnessing a new wave of collaborative, inclusive and participatory business models. In the United Kingdom, the family-owned business Timpson, which has a portfolio of 2,100 stores and more than 5,000 employees, operates an 'upside-down management' culture. Timpson gives employees full autonomy and responsibility to make decisions. Frontline workers can do whatever they like if they follow two rules. The first rule: employees should put the money into the till. The second rule: always look presentable. Beyond these two conditions, Timpson's is a decentralized organization. The staff in each shoe repair, dry cleaner and photo shop can decide how they work, and when they work. Staff make decisions about the supply and sales of goods and services. They are encouraged to run the shop like a business. Employees can offer discounts, negotiate with suppliers and change the design of the shop. They can also suggest new ideas and launch new products and service offerings.

In Porto Alegre, Brazil, citizens directly participate in the budgeting process and allocation of resources to community projects and priorities. Residents attend local assemblies to discuss and vote on spending priorities, allowing for greater citizen engagement in local governance and decision-making. The idea seems so simple and yet radical when compared with the top-down centralized management of most nations. Citizens rarely get an opportunity to shape policy and their community, apart from voting in local and general elections. The participatory process creates space for citizens to present their demands and priorities for municipal improvement and discussions. The success of people's participation in determining the use of public welfare funds in the city of Porto Alegre has inspired many other municipalities to follow suit.

Activity

1 **Decolonization**

It can be easy to view colonialism as a relic of ancient history, but colonialism continues to shape the world we currently inhabit. These aren't stories from the history books but a modern reality. From ancient Egyptian social classes to European settler colonialism in North America or the corporate extractivism of the Dutch East India Company, the legacy of colonialism persists.

Take a moment to reflect on the following questions:

o Which social structures and practices have a legacy in colonialism? This could be ways of working, historical connections and even language.

o Which people or groups continue to be affected by colonialism? Explore ways to reflect this reality into all future business and social actions.

o How can we rethink our sources of knowledge? We have an opportunity to overcome historical inequities by exploring different canons of knowledge.

2 Decentralization

In the world of business, expertise is viewed to be tiered based on seniority. The CEO is expected to have all the answers, and employees often act on the decisions made by leadership teams. Remember the lessons from the New Coke debacle? Centralized structures are equally common in government, academia and the charity sector.

We have an opportunity to explore new engagement and participation models. Ask yourself:

o How could your movement become more decentralized?

This might be exploring ways of working, organizational structure and governance.

British retailer Timpson operates an 'upside-down management' culture to give employees the freedom to make decisions. Frontline workers can do whatever they like if they follow two rules. The first rule: employees should put the money into the till. The second rule: always look presentable. The People collaborated with Pentland Brands, owner of sports, outdoor and lifestyle brands, including Speedo, Berghaus and ellese, to build a global youth advisory board, challenging the outdated concept that ideas can only come from the top, delivering fresh outside-in perspectives and making sure young people, employees and communities are stakeholders in future plans and decision-making.

3 Participation

Participatory action research recognizes the importance of power relations in creating social change. It actively works to include the voices, experiences and contributions of individuals and communities who are directly impacted, encouraging all parties involved to collaborate, co-create, co-learn and take collective action. Change isn't possible without community engagement.

You can make your mission more participatory by exploring the following questions or, even better, working with relevant communities to establish new questions:

o How can we promote a more participatory model?

o What people, groups and communities need to be invited?

o How can we decentralize the research and decision-making process?

In Porto Alegre, Brazil, citizens directly participate in the budgeting process and allocation of resources to community projects and priorities. Residents attend local assemblies to discuss and vote on spending priorities, allowing for greater citizen engagement in local governance and decision-making. The success of people's participation in determining the use of public welfare funds in the city of Porto Alegre has inspired hundreds of other municipalities to follow suit.

Chapter 10: Managing backlash

Summary

Sir Isaac Newton's third law states that for every action in nature, there is an equal and opposite reaction. When you bounce a ball on the ground it jumps back up. What happens when your mission begins to create change? How can we maintain momentum, avoid relapse and manage backlash?

The journey towards social change starts with making sure that your mission is not causing harm. This begins with paying tax: an agreed fee for doing business and making a profit. The second basic responsibility is making sure employees, suppliers and partners are paid fairly. Finally, make sure your product or service isn't causing any harm.

What should you do when you encounter rejectors? The best place to start is with the assumption that people have good intentions. It might be circumstances, upbringing or unfamiliarity which make them combative to social change. Instead of engaging in conflict, why not initiate open dialogue with your counterparts? The journey towards social change begins with education. Education equips people with new tools, knowledge and skills to navigate change. People will no longer view change as a threat to their existing interests but as an opportunity to expand their capabilities. More importantly, knowledge sharing makes change a collective effort. More work should be done to embrace learning, build capacity and challenge the status quo. We can't achieve social change by only interacting and exchanging views with people who share our beliefs. Most importantly, education makes the mission bigger than you. It gives others the tools to become agents of change. You will have the opportunity to share what you know with more people. People will no longer be reliant on you to deliver business and social impact. The mission becomes scalable, and you will learn more by imparting your learning, failures and experiences to others.

Avoiding backlash requires clarity of mission, unyielding principles and radical transparency, not viewing social change as a seasonal trend to win consumer trust. A short-sighted approach to business and social impact is inherently flawed and liable to backlash. Citizens and communities can tell the difference between performative gesturing and genuine conviction. In a politically charged environment, organizations can't afford to be meandering to the most popular flavour of the day. Unless you stand for something, you will fail to build a meaningful connection with either side. Brands can no longer afford to remain neutral because neutral is viewed as complicit. That said, empty statements of solidarity no longer suffice either. The consumers of today are more informed and empowered than ever before. They expect you to turn your words into action. And if brands don't stick to their promises, consumers possess the knowledge, determination and platform to call them out. In short, there's nowhere to hide.

In 2023, US retail giant Target decided to celebrate Pride Month by creating LGBTQ+ pride merchandise. Target became the recipient of conservative backlash. Right-wing activists online were furious with the company's LGBTQ+ support. The backlash from conservatives dented Target's sales by 5.4 per cent within the first three months. The retailer decreased its profit outlook. The CEO acknowledged that the Pride Month collection hurt sales. The company viewed it as a signal to pause activities. Despite selling Pride merchandise for over a decade, Target announced that it would remove some of the Pride merchandise following 'volatile circumstances' and move other displays to the back of stores to draw less attention. This was a lose–lose scenario for the retailer. Aligning itself with the LGBTQ+ community upset conservative consumers. Not maintaining such support in the face of growing backlash and declining sales lost the trust built with the LGBTQ+ community. Ultimately, Target's decision was viewed to be performative, drawing backlash without making a stand or connecting with either community. The company didn't win favour from either camp. It was viewed as a vacuous attempt to win consumer appeal without making a stand.

The best way to increase your probability of making a positive impact, while at the same time avoiding, or at least mitigating, backlash is by collaborating with communities. Many examples of public backlash – less so institutional backlash from activist investors – stem from organizations making decisions on behalf of communities without including members of the community in the process. The Kendall Jenner Pepsi advert is a cautionary tale of what could go wrong as a company becomes more insular. A simple conversation with people not working at Pepsi would have exposed how preposterous the advert's narrative was. It can be easy to get stuck in our bubble of familiarity. Collaborating with communities injects a much-needed dose of honesty and accountability which would stamp out any inauthenticity before it gets picked up in mainstream culture.

Activity

1 **The basics**

When thinking about how to manage backlash, the best place to start is with the factors in our control. The journey towards social change starts with making sure that your mission is not causing harm.

   o Are we covering the basics before communicating externally?

This begins with paying your taxes for making a profit, paying employees and suppliers fairly and creating a responsible product or service.

2 **Education and capacity building**

Education equips people with new tools, knowledge and skills to navigate change. People will no longer view change as a threat to their existing interests but as an opportunity to expand their capabilities.

   o How can we promote education and capacity building?

People will no longer be reliant on you to deliver business and social impact. The mission becomes scalable, and you will learn more by imparting your learning, failures and experiences to others.

3 **Progress not perfection**

The pursuit of perfection can be counterproductive. Perfection might raise standards, but it can prevent us from getting started and making progress.

   o How can we encourage people to get started?

The fear of being criticized prevents business leaders from engaging in the process of creating social change. Nevertheless, the call for perfection shouldn't become a barrier towards making strides in the right direction.

4 **Community participation**

The best way to increase your probability of making a positive impact while at the same time avoiding, or at least mitigating, backlash is by collaborating with communities. The problem has origins in top-down company cultures that prevent the involvement or inclusion of diverse voices.

   Using more collaborative ways of working, enables companies to include the voices of citizens, communities and people with lived experience in the design stage before plans are finalized, therefore avoiding consumer backlash like the Kendall Jenner Pepsi fiasco.

5 Honest communication

No matter how hard you attempt to get things right there are bound to be moments when you get things wrong. We are all human, nobody is perfect. How you respond to backlash is arguably more important than the event itself.

o How can we create a culture of honest and transparent communication in ways that help us learn from the experience?

Communication doesn't have to be overly boring or corporate. Remember how KFC managed to turn around a supply chain crisis by quickly apologising and showing humility and remorse, which de-escalated the situation, before using creative communication to strengthen its relationship with KFC fans.

INDEX

The index is filed in alphabetical, word-by-word order. Acronyms are filed as presented; Arabic names are filed ignoring the 'al' prefix; numbers are filed as spelt out.

Looking for another book?

Explore our award-winning
books from global business
experts in Marketing and Sales

Scan the code to browse

www.koganpage.com/marketing

More from Kogan Page

ISBN: 9781398609839

ISBN: 9781789668247

ISBN: 9781398607316

ISBN: 9781398610392

www.koganpage.com